DATE DUE

OC2? 9?			

Demco, Inc. 38-293

Iran and the International Community

Iran and the International Community

Edited by
Anoushiravan Ehteshami
and
Manshour Varasteh

London and New York

First published 1991 by Routledge
11 New Fetter Lane, London EC4P 4EE

Simultaneously published in the USA and Canada
by Routledge
a division of Routledge, Chapman and Hall, Inc.
29 West 35th Street, New York, NY 10001

© 1991 Anoushiravan Ehteshami

Typeset in Times by LaserScript Limited, Mitcham, Surrey
Printed and bound in Great Britain by
Mackays of Chatham PLC, Chatham, Kent

British Library Cataloguing in Publication Data
Iran and the international community.
  1. Iran. Foreign relations
  I. Ehteshami, Anoushiravan II. Varasteh, Manshour
  327.55
  ISBN 0-415-04184-8

Library of Congress Cataloging-in-Publication Data
Iran and the international community / edited by Anoushiravan Ehteshami
and Manshour Varasteh

  p. cm.
  Includes bibliographical references and index.
  ISBN 0-415-04184-8
  1. Iran–Foreign relations. 2. United Nations–Iran.
I. Ehteshami, Anoushiravan. II. Varasteh, Manshour.
JX1581.I68173 1991
341.23'55–dc20

90–23182
CIP

Contents

Notes on contributors

ANOUSHIRAVAN EHTESHAMI is Lecturer in Middle East Politics and Research Fellow in International Relations and Strategic Studies at the University of Exeter. He is founder and editor of *Middle East Strategic Studies Quarterly* (published by Brassey's Defence Publishers) and Administrative Editor of *BRISMES Newsletter*. He is author of *Nuclearisation of the Middle East* (Brassey's, 1989) and co-author of *War and Peace in the Gulf: Domestic Politics and Regional Relations into the 1990s* (Ithaca Press, 1991).

FRED HALLIDAY is Professor of International Relations at the London School of Economics. He is author of *Iran: Dictatorship and Development* (Penguin, 1979), *Revolution and Foreign Policy: The case of South Yemen, 1967–1987* (Cambridge University Press, 1989) and *Cold War, Third World: An Essay on Soviet–US Relations* (Hutchinson Radius, 1989).

IAIN HAMPSHER-MONK is Senior Lecturer in Political Theory at the University of Exeter. He is the founder and editor of *History of Political Thought* and author of *The Political Philosophy of Edmund Burke* (Longman, 1987). He is currently involved in a European Science Foundation project on the origins of the European State.

ERIC HOOGLUND is Visiting Associate Professor of Political Science at the University of California, Berkeley. He is author of *Land and Revolution in Iran, 1960–1980* (University of Texas Press, 1982) and *Crossing the Waters: The Arab Immigration to the United States before 1940* (Smithsonian Institution Press, 1987). He is also on the editorial board of *MERIP*.

GEORGE JOFFE is a Research Associate of the Near and Middle East Centre at SOAS, London and has written extensively for the Economist

Intelligence Unit. He is also a political commentator and analyst, with particular knowledge of Near Eastern and North African affairs. He is co-author of *Iran and Iraq: The Next Five Years* (EIU 1987), and *Iran and Iraq: Building on the Stalemate* (EIU, 1988).

KAMRAN MOFID is Senior Lecturer in Economics at Coventry Polytechnic. He is author of *Development Planning in Iran: From Monarchy to Islamic Republic* (Menas Press, 1987) and *The Economic Consequences of the Gulf War* (Routledge, 1990).

GERD NONNEMAN is currently undertaking research on Oman and the Yemen at the University of Exeter. He is the author of *Iraq, the Gulf States and the War: A Changing Relationship 1980–1986 and Beyond* (Ithaca Press, 1986) and *Development, Administration and Aid in the Middle East* (Routledge, 1988). He is co-author of *War and Peace in the Gulf: Domestic Politics and Regional Relations into the 1990s* (Ithaca, 1991). He also contributes to the Economist Intelligence Unit.

COLONEL EDGAR O'BALLANCE is a defence consultant and commentator. He is the author of over twenty books, many of which have focused on the Middle East, including *The Gulf War* (Brassey's, 1988).

SIR ANTHONY PARSONS was British Ambassador to Iran from 1974 to 1979 and Ambassador to the United Nations from 1979 to 1982. He is the author of *The Pride and the Fall: Iran 1974–1979* (Jonathan Cape, 1984). He is now a member of the Centre for Arab Gulf Studies at the University of Exeter.

JAMES PISCATORI is Senior Lecturer in the Department of International Politics, University College of Wales, Aberystwyth. He is an editor of new *Oxford Encyclopedia of the Modern Islamic World*; editor of *Islam in the Political Process* (Cambridge University Press, 1983); co-editor of *Muslim Travellers: Pilgrimage, Migration, and the Religious Imagination* (Routledge/University of California Press, 1990) and author of *Islam in a World of Nation-States* (Cambridge University Press, 1986). He is also convenor of Islam group of Fundamentalism Project of the American Academy of Arts and Sciences.

MANSHOUR VARASTEH is a freelance researcher on the Persian Gulf generally and Iran in particular. He is currently undertaking research at the Department of International Politics, University College of Wales, Aberystwyth.

Foreword

James Piscatori

Rarely has there been a day in the past decade when Iran has escaped the attention of the world's foreign offices, press, and academic experts on the Middle East and Islam. Turbulent shifts of power within the revolutionary regime; the headstrong anathematizing of the great powers; the presence of Revolutionary Guards in Lebanon and, in general, the export of the revolution; seemingly interminable war with Iraq; secret arms deals with Israel and the United States; shadowy relations with Middle Eastern groups that hold Westerners hostage; and unambiguous threats of death against a British novelist – these have been the issues which have kept Iran at the centre of international attention and concern.

There is no doubt that the events set in motion in the period 1978–9 will always have an assured place in the history of modern times. Iran gave the modern world its first successful political revolution self-consciously framed in the language of Islam. For decades to come, scholars will debate whether the Khomeinist regime represented a fulfilment or distortion of Islamic – and, indeed, of Shia – notions of governance. Yet it is certain that, at least in the revolution's first stages, a great many of its own citizens and millions abroad – Sunni as well as Shia – identified with several of its avowed principles. This appeal and Iran's self-defined role of exemplar to the Islamic and developing worlds, to say nothing of its conventionally important strategic location, guarantee that it will remain one of the pivotal actors of the international order.

Assembling a first-class team of experts, Anoushiravan Ehteshami and Manshour Varasteh efficaciously present revolutionary Iran's international record in all its complexity. Whether it is Iran's interaction with the superpowers, the United Nations, the European Community, or the Arab states of the Gulf, we are given insight into how policy results, not from an unvarying post-Pahlavi consensus on national interest or even revolutionary mission, but from the unremitting competition amongst several elites for political, and ideological, primacy. When we keep in mind this intricate context in which tactical shifts of alliance are common, it is not hard to see how inappropriate the Western search for a categorically defined 'Islamic foreign policy' or, indeed, for 'moderates' within the regime has been.

The editors of and contributors to *Iran and the International Community* make an important contribution by casting a critical eye on such conventional wisdom. Their judgements will not be universally accepted, of course. But the careful review of the data at hand and the lively analysis of their significance, which are apparent in each chapter, are likely to secure this volume's place in the serious literature on the Islamic Republic.

James Piscatori

Editors' preface

The revolutionary Imam Hussein in Iran, who is fighting imperialism, is not alone now. In addition to [Iranians]... there are billions of Muslims and non-Muslims everywhere in Syria, Libya, Algeria, Lebanon, Palestine, Pakistan, Africa, the Omani Liberation Front, Eritrea, the Chilean resistance, the Chadian liberation movement, the Canary Islands' liberation movement, the Futami liberation movement, Spain, Korea and many other places as well as the entire Islamic world, and the oppressed all over the world, who all support Iran, the revolution and Imam Hussein, represented in leader Imam Ayatollah Khomeini.

(Radio Tehran, November 1979)

With his revolution, Ayatollah Khomeini thought, Iran, Islam and the whole world would change. The building of the Islamic state would not be easy, he conceded, but at the end it would certainly be worth it. Salvation, after all, followed liberation. He consoled his followers that patience was the essence. Yet, still he lashed out: 'where are the ears to listen to me, where is the perception to understand me?'. This as early as 1941! He would complain that, 'we have nothing to say to those whose powers of perception are so limited that they regard the wearing of European hats, the cast-offs of the wild beasts of Europe, as a sign of national progress!'.

Fortune favoured Khomeini and he got his chance in 1979. The Islamic Republic of Iran was born and with it the hopes and aspirations of millions inside and outside of Iran, thirsty for a new order. Ayatollah Khomeini became Imam Khomeini, the Supreme Guide of Islamic nations, the smasher of Idols, the One who humbles Satan, the Glorious Upholder of the Faith, the Vicar of Islam and of Muslims, the Regent of the Hidden Imam.... His new republic, unique in style and certainly extraordinary in religious zeal, promised the downtrodden, Islam, true and pure Islam. But what else? By modern-day standards the revolution was unique in its religious and Islamic make-up, its message novel. Contrary to the clerics' expectations, however, the people chose the Islamic route to liberation not purely for salvation, but for a better life on earth. The legacy of a successful revolution is surely not in its ability to overthrow the old and, by definition, unwanted order, but in its commitment to replace it with something better. If this could be said to be the acid test of any revolution, let alone one made in the name of God, there still remains the question of its international impact.

Partly because all revolutions generate outward energies, partly due to their inevitable universalizing tendencies and the inner urge to export their experience, and more importantly, partly because the nascent Islamic Republic was unable to meet the challenge of Islamic development it had promised the Iranian people, the international arena presented itself as an attractive bazaar to enter.

The effects of the Iranian revolution did indeed reach many corners of the globe. New Islamic organizations were born at Tehran's behest, and representatives of Islamic movements from Lebanon to the Philippines, the People's Republic of China and sub-Saharan Africa became regular visitors to Tehran. On the economic level also Western countries and companies scrambled to salvage their cherished share in the lucrative Iranian market. The displacement impact of the Iranian revolution on the many facets of the international economy ought not to be underestimated. But, above all the ruling mullahs, this ancient land's new political elite, reached for the skies and aimed to affect international relations directly. Why?

The past decade has shown that the Islamic Republic has thrived particularly well on the uncertainties of crises and regional tensions; it showed a real tendency to externalize its inner structural contradictions and revolutionary turmoil. The taking of American hostages in 1979 and its political implications within the country; the eight-year-old Iran–Iraq War; Tehran's support for some of the Afghan Mujahedin groups; its direct involvement in Lebanese politics and in determining the fate of Westerners held hostage; efforts to export the 'Islamic' revolution to other Muslim countries; and finally the edict passed on the British author, Salman Rushdie, all point to the reality that, at least in its first ten years (under direct control of Ayatollah Khomeini), the Islamic Republic chose to re-interpret international law and alter in an 'Islamic' way the sets of behaviour commonly known as international norms and conventions. Thus the clash of these two plates, Iran's unique interpretation of Islamic government and international order and the existing Western-formulated and Western-dominated system, on the world stage has produced explosive effects.

But, just as the Islamic Republic entered adolescence yet another politico-military crisis in the Persian Gulf, caused by the actions of its erstwhile enemy in the 1980s, introduced further uncertainties for its new leadership. We said earlier that throughout its young life the Islamic Republic had thrived on externalizing the new regime's inner structural contradictions. In 1990, however, the violent rupture beyond its control of regional tensions proved to be a source of anxiety and not of opportunity for Tehran. The pragmatists in charge of the executive and high leadership of the country trod with uncharacteristic caution apparently failing, at least in the early days of the crisis, to capitalize on it as a fountain of opportunity for further confrontations. Strictly speaking of course this is not exactly true, for Tehran did respond to the crisis soon after the Iraqi invasion of Kuwait, but not in a manner wholly in tune with its posture during the rule of Ayatollah Khomeini himself.

Initial silence brought criticism from many Islamic and secular national-ists that Iran was now a minor player in regional terms, and one not worth bothering with as far as the external powers were concerned. These critics pointed to the rapid foreign military build-up in Saudi Arabia and the Persian Gulf region generally and Tehran's inability to influence the diplomatic and military course of events either directly, in international forums (the UN and the Islamic Conference Organization, for instance) or indirectly, in such regional bodies as the GCC and the Arab League.

The passage of time in 1990, from Summer through to Autumn and Winter of the Gulf crisis showed, however, that even though Tehran's initial silence may have in part been a result of indecisiveness, the shrewd game of patience played by Tehran might indeed have been the underlying strategy of Ayatollah Khomeini's more pragmatic successors. Their strategy was aimed at maximizing the benefits of this crisis to the Republic. President Hussein's actions had made it unnecessary for the Iranian leader-ship to seek active participation in the crisis while still avoiding total isolation: Iran would emerge more powerful and influential almost by default! Shedding the Republic's wolf's clothing, the Rafsanjani leadership demonstrated its ability to turn away from violent interactions within the international system without necessarily jeopardizing its position at home. (This of course was partly because the radical forces within the state machinery were much weakened since the lection of the Majlis Speaker to the presidency and Ayatollah Khamenei as the Spiritual Leader of the Republic.) President Rafsanjani and his team were then able to concentrate on diplomatic initiatives to advance the regime's regional interests, but whether this marked a complete break with the past remained unclear.

The Iraqi invasion of Kuwait also enabled Tehran to rev up its engine of diplomacy in that part of the Middle East traditionally (and geostrate-gically) closest to the heart of the country; the Persian Gulf region. Much of Tehran's diplomatic efforts since the cease-fire in the Iran–Iraq War had concentrated on rebuilding bridges with, firstly, Gulf and, secondly, other

Arab states who had supported the Iraqi war effort in the 1980s. The gaining of influence here however was conditional upon the republic's successful re-entry into the system as a 'responsible' member of the international community. Fulfilment of such a task demanded a thorough overhaul of its (often contradictory) foreign policies. Iraq's invasion of Kuwait accelerated this process and, additionally, vindicated Tehran's strategy of concentrating its efforts on re-establishing the country's traditional role as the dominant power in the Persian Gulf, precisely as the attention of the whole world was again turning towards the Gulf region. From its vantage point of neutrality in the war between the Iraqi armed forces and the US-led, UN-sanctioned, military alliance the Republic aimed to gain further political and diplomatic credibility as well as dollars and technology for its economic reconstruction. By adhering to the rule of international law and the letter and spirit of the United Nations the regime derived much legitimacy too as the new peace-maker in the Persian Gulf region. Having exhausted its war-making capacity for a time, it can be argued that the regime had very little choice but to go on the diplomatic offensive. Bearing in mind the fact that geopolitical realities never really gave Tehran the option of insulationism, it should nevertheless have been none too surprising to find the Republic's pragmatist leaders busy in projecting their country as the source of stability in the region. It cannot be overemphasized that President Rafsanjani's brazen endorsement of the old Pahlavi Doctrine (the promotion of Iran to the role of regional 'policeman' and power-broker) in the course of the 1990–1 Gulf crisis required a complete reappraisal of the Republic's role in the international system and its expectations from it. The reappraisal process had indeed begun well before the start of the 1990–1 crisis in the Gulf, but it could not come to fruition without a crisis. So, paradoxically, the new leadership in Iran needed another crisis in the region, preferably one not instigated by them, not to push through their radical fundamentalism, but in order to display their revisionist strategies without incurring the wrath of the pro-Khomeini radicals in the system. Renewed respect for international law and the rediscovery of the UN body were the two high-profile manifestations of Tehran's policy of global accommodation. The re-establishment of diplomatic relations with 'little Satan' Britain in the West, and with a number of other moderate and pro-Western Arab regional actors like Kuwait, Jordan and Tunisia was the more concrete dimension of this strategy in that it involved implementation of new policies in the day-to-day functioning of this state among the community of nation-states.

This book presents an attempt at exploring the clash discussed earlier, between the Islamic Republic's interpretation of and interaction with the prevailing international order. The conclusions of the authors have a direct bearing on understanding the behaviour of the Islamic Republic in the years to come, even at times of such acute crisis as that which plagued the region at the turn of the 1990s. It has brought together the thoughts of many distinguished Western and Iranian experts and scholars on the subject. Fred Halliday's succinct introduction opens the debate on the Iranian revolution and the Islamic Republic. His historical overview serves as an important backdrop for the following chapters which deal with the Islamic Republic's foreign policy. Sir Anthony Parsons begins the case studies with an in-depth look at revolutionary Iran's relations with the United Nations. The next three chapters deal with the Republic's relations with the great and major powers. The objective was to focus on Iran's attitude towards the dominant powers and the emerging European power and also develop a feel for the great global actors' perceptions of the theocratic state. George Joffe has dealt with the extra-territorial reach of the Republic. It is clear from his chapter that the new rulers in Iran, perhaps as a way of compensating for their other weaknesses, developed the extra-territorial string to their foreign policy formulation bow – and, as Joffe shows, with some effect.

Nonneman and O'Ballance address the regional impact and repercussions of the advent of the Islamic Republic in the aftermath of the revolution and the overthrow of the Pahlavi dynasty. Their focus is primarily on the Persian Gulf region as the arena closest to home for Tehran and one in which the revolutionary clerics could demonstrate their influence most potently.

The revolution, it was proposed earlier, was made by the people for a better way of life. Besides the spiritual fulfilment promised by the dominant mullahs, the revolutionary masses had also demanded 'bread, housing and liberty'. Kamran Mofid assesses the economy of the new order through its foreign economic relations. National economic independence was another prerequisite to a successful revolution. Mofid provides tangible yardsticks by which to measure the validity of economic transformation in the revolutionary Islamic Republic.

It would be impossible to analyse the Islamic Republic's international presence without some reference to the inter-state cultural confrontation of what has become known as the Rushdie affair. Iain Hampsher-Monk provides a thought-provoking examination of the philosophical and ideological agitations which arose from the publication of *The Satanic Verses*.

Sir Anthony Parsons once commented that Iran's revolution, like other great modern revolutions, will need time to settle down. Time is needed for the dust to settle, as it were, and for a comprehensible picture to emerge. 'They've got their own music to march to', he said. One has to wait, and wait for a long time and with a great deal of patience. This book was compiled with the patience factor very much in mind. If Ayatollah Khomeini could be patient in making his 'Islamic' revolution, surely the observers could do likewise in assessing his 'offspring'. Ten years, we propose, gives a reasonable time frame within which to work – albeit only a drop in the ocean of Iranian history – and with this in mind the contributors to our collection have examined, extracted and evaluated to provide the reader with an appreciable illustration of a decade of the Islamic Republic in the international community.

The editors would like to thank the contributors for their hard work and for having produced excellent chapters for this collection despite their busy schedules. We thank all those who assisted us in the production of this book and gave us their unwavering support at various points in the course of this endeavour. The completion of this book, through all its arduous steps, of course, would not have been possible without the encouragement, hard work and enthusiasm of Emma C. Murphy. If this book were to be dedicated to any one individual we feel that she would certainly be a prime candidate!

Anoushiravan Ehteshami and Manshour Varasteh

Introduction

Iran and the world: reassertion and its costs

Fred Halliday

The international relations of Iran in this century have been marked by major ruptures. These have been the consequence both of external intervention and shifts in international alignment and of internal changes which, while often influenced by external factors, have also had roots within Iranian society and politics themselves. One point of rupture, when internal upheaval intersected external influence, came with the period of the Constitutional Revolution and the 1907 Anglo–Soviet delimitation of spheres of influence. Another break, equally a product of the internal and the external, was the First World War and the subsequent emergence of Reza Khan as ruler in 1921. Twenty years later, in 1941, Russia and Britain removed Reza Khan and turmoil followed until the coup which put his son, Mohammed Reza Pahlavi, back into power in 1953. Twenty-six years later, the apparently secure regime re-established in 1953 was swept away in the Iranian revolution out of which emerged the Islamic Republic. In short-term perspective, the revolution of 1979 appeared to interrupt a hitherto stable society: in the longer perspective, it was but the latest of the upheavals that have punctuated modern Iranian history and international relations, and may well not be the last.[1]

Within this record of abrupt changes, three elements of continuity can none the less be discerned. The first is the importance for Iran of the prevailing relationship between the great powers – Russia and Britain before 1914, Britain and Germany up to 1941, the USSR and the USA after the Second World War. Placed as it is on the southern frontiers of Russia, Iran has been especially vulnerable to international pressures and to changes within the strategic sphere. Secondly, for all these external pressures, domestic Iranian forces have played an important role, in frustrating the policies of indigenous governments and external powers alike – be this in 1906, 1919, 1951 or 1979. Successive political movements based in Iranian cities have risen against foreign influence, real or inferred, and have, in so doing, altered the politics of their country and the relationship of great powers to it. Thirdly, while Iran has been preoccupied with the influence of the great powers, it has gradually come to develop relationships with other states in the region and to play a role where previously it was absent – in the Persian Gulf, in Afghanistan, in the Arab–Israeli context. In playing the great powers against each other, or at least in trying to do so, Iran has also become a regional actor. What was begun in a low-key way under Reza Khan, with the Saadabad Pact with Turkey and Afghanistan, expanded greatly after the Second World War: the Shah's involvement in the Baghdad Pact and then as an active force *vis-à-vis* Iraq, the Peninsula, Pakistan, Afghanistan was followed by the substantial Islamic activism of the post-1979 regime. Historical perspective indicates that this is not something Iran is doing for the first time: far from being a novelty, it is rather a reassertion of something evident before the collapse of Iran into weakness in the early nineteenth century. In the Caucasus, Afghanistan, Central Asia, the northern parts of the Indian subcontinent, the Arabian Peninsula, and much of the eastern Arab world Iran has been a significant, if intermittent, force for much of recorded history.

All three of these trends have been strikingly evident in the period of the revolution itself: as the contributors to this book make clear, Iran now has a complex foreign policy, one in which domestic factors play an important role, and involving not just the USA and the USSR, but also the EEC, the Middle East and the broader Islamic world. The main sources of this reassertion lie within Iran. The post-1979 impact of Iran, and its distinctive place in the international system, arise less from anything in the international arena as such and more from the distinctive political and ideological character of this revolution itself. Speaking on the first anniversary of Khomeini's death, his successor as spiritual leader, Khamenei, spelt out the three main components of what Khomeini's political message were: the slogan 'Neither East Nor West'; the belief in the importance of spirituality and religious belief; and the stress on the role of the masses in shaping history.[2] It is easy to show how these three principles have not always been fulfilled, and indeed how each is less specific to Islamic thinking and more akin to a generic Third World radicalism than Khomeini and his successors might have us think. But there is equally little doubt that the Iranian revolution did strike a distinctive note in the international arena, and, for all its failures and exaggeration, made a substantial mark on the world scene.

Faced with this distinctive message, both the great powers have been concerned about the Islamic revolution and both, while drawing some benefit from it, have had reason to regret the passage of the Shah. One of the greatest achievements of the Iranian revolution has been not just to confound the great powers, but also to make Iran a factor in the domestic politics of both states: for the USA, whose politics have long been insulated from external factors, Iran provoked the greatest crises of the Carter and Reagan administrations and left a legacy of animosity towards Iran that was later to bedevil relations between the two countries; within the USSR Iran was not only an issue of dispute within the foreign policy making apparatus but also contributed to exaggerated Soviet leadership perceptions of an Islamic challenge in a number of the southern republics of the country. To this impact within Russia and the USA of the Iranian revolution can be added the strategic processes that it occasioned.

Throughout the early part of the 1980s the USSR and the USA saw Iran through the lens of East–West conflict: the consequence was that, apart from any threat which Iran posed directly to them, it continued to matter. A competition to 'win' Iran continued, with each side taking initiatives towards Iran at the expense of the other: this great power rivalry accounts for Soviet characterizations of the Iranian revolution as 'anti-imperialist' and Moscow's equivocations on the taking of US diplomatic hostages, but was also, on the US side, part of the intention behind the Irangate policy. But as, after 1985, relations between the USSR and the USA improved, Iran began to pay the price of this shifting international situation and lost the ability to play the two powers off against each other: at the end of the Iran–Iraq War, Moscow and Washington supported the same side, Iraq, at Iran's expense.

It is, perhaps, the third trend, that of Iran's growing role in the region, that is the most striking feature of Iran's new place in international affairs, and of the reassertion that has accompanied it. From having been, at the beginning of the century, a wholly passive factor in international affairs, Iran has now become a significant actor, whom other states, larger and smaller, must take into account. As far as the Middle East is concerned, Iran is a major military and ideological power that Arab states, however much they may dislike it, have to deal with. Iraq's attempt in 1980 to break the Islamic Republic by a sudden attack failed and, a decade later, that Republic remains. Iraq, which first hoped to overthrow the Islamic Republic and then hoped, after the 1988 cease-fire, to freeze it out of any stable peace, was frustrated by the regime's durability and was compelled instead to vent its fury on its far weaker Arab neighbour, Kuwait. Iran failed in its turn to overthrow the Ba'thist regime in Baghdad, but it retains considerable influence in some Arab states – Lebanon and Sudan amongst them. On its eastern flank, Iran has built up influence in Afghanistan, in previous eras a zone of Iranian influence, and its local allies there have insisted on a say in any settlement in that country.

This regional influence and that within the domestic affairs of both the

USA and the USSR is, as much as anything, a result of the actions of the Iranian state. To this state influence can, however, be added another dimension of the Iranian revolution's influence, namely that of repute and example. All revolutions project an image beyond their frontiers which, while it may be fostered and channelled by the state in question, is something beyond the influence of states and rests above all on what people in other countries *believe* to be taking place in the revolutionary society in question. This was true of Russia, China, Cuba, Vietnam and other revolutions of this century and applies equally to Iran. The impact of the Iranian revolution on the Islamic world, an influence that remains considerably more than a decade after the defeat of the Shah, owes much to this, to the belief that in Iran an oppressed Muslim people rose up and defied the great powers to create and sustain an Islamic state. In looking at Iran's new importance in the Middle East, and beyond, this exemplary influence may be as important as any more strictly identifiable state policies pursued by Tehran.

This combination of influences, official and unofficial, underlies the new influence that Iran has in the Middle East and west Asian regions as a whole at a time of major change in the international situation. In four respects above all the context in which Iran operates is markedly different from that which prevailed up to the late 1980s. In the first place, the end of the Cold War means that Iran's ability to manoeuvre profitably between East and West is reduced: it matters less to Moscow or Washington that Iran may fall under the influence of the other. Second, the related crisis of the USSR itself means that for the first time in nearly two centuries the regions of the Caucasus and Central Asia, Turkic in language but to a considerable degree Persian in culture, are now open to influence by Iran again. Iran may not have the inclination or resources to be drawn into these areas, but it will find it difficult not to be, especially as other states – Turkey, Afghanistan, China, Saudi Arabia – may seek to do so. Third, for all the containment of the Islamic revolution in its Iranian state form, Islamist movements remain strong and in some cases stronger in the Middle East, North Africa and beyond: the tenth anniversary of the emergence of the Iranian revolution in late 1978, coincided with the outbreak of mass Islamist revolt in the cities of another populous, authoritarian, modernizing, oil-producing state, Algeria. The prestige of the Iranian Islamic revolution will continue to inspire these forces as, in the 1990s, they continue to do battle with secular states. Finally, Iran faces, in the Arab world, a markedly new situation, with the emergence of Iraq as the dominant power in the Gulf. Iran held off Iraq but did not defeat it or force a change of its government. In the aftermath of the war, Saddam Hussein was therefore able to claim that he had in fact won it, and to pursue his domination of the Arab world and the Persian Gulf. The choice Iran therefore faced, of accommodation or conflict with its regional adversary, was an acutely difficult one and was unlikely to be resolved as long as either the Ba'thist or Islamic revolutionary regimes remained in power: the underlying cause of the 1980–8 war had been the attempt by each state to alter the political system in the other, and, since both failed, the source of their rivalry remained unaltered.

That the Iranian revolution has made a major impact is indisputable, as is the fact that this impact has continued despite the many setbacks the revolution has faced, most notably in its war with Iraq. Yet, for all the successes of the revolution, its foreign policy and international impact have been marked by weaknesses that, as much as its strength, arise from the specific character of this revolution. In the first place, as already noted, Iran has overestimated its ability to play off the great powers against each other and to defy them as it has done. Particularly with the end of the Cold War, Iran is a country of less interest to the USA, and the deep legacy of hostility to Iran, born of the hostages crisis and Irangate, makes it very difficult for a US administration to re-open relations with Tehran. After 1987, Iran had better relations with the USSR and the two countries moved closer together on Afghanistan: but the USSR was not prepared to supply military equipment at the level and in the quantity Iran needed, and the USSR could not provide the financial and technical support Iran needed to revitalize its economy.

Second, the internal bases of Iranian foreign policy, one of the sources of strength in one respect, have repeatedly harmed Iran on the international scene and limited its sphere of action. An early example was the crisis over the US embassy hostages, from November 1979 to January 1981: this arose out of a domestic crisis, between liberals and radicals, and its extension over many months owed much to factional disagreement within the regime. In the end, this did Iran no good at all: the final agreement reached with the USA was overwhelmingly favourable to the latter, making Iran the first revolution in history to promise repayment of debts. The failure to resolve the crisis meant that when Iraq invaded in September 1980, in clear violation of the UN Charter, the Security Council refused to take the prompt action that it should have. A later example was the Salman Rushdie issue: Iran got involved in this, in February 1989, only after its hand was forced by developments in Pakistan and India, but, once engaged, Tehran was unable to find any way out of a demagogic commitment that did it a great deal of harm in the Western world. Again, the force of radical opinion within the country and the inability to disentangle itself from militant and mistaken international positions did much to damage Iran.[3]

To these two forms of miscalculation can be added a third, that of timing. Driven as they often are by internal forces, and relying on a perspective on international relations born out of that domestic situation. Iranian leaders have in this century repeatedly miscalculated about the actions of external forces and underestimated Iran's vulnerability to their intervention. Thus Reza Khan, failing to understand the force of Russian and British intentions, refused to bend to their demands and allowed them to carry out the invasion of 1941. Mossadeq, seeking to alter the terms on which Iranian oil was produced, squandered his domestic and international support: he overplayed his hand, missed opportunities for beneficial compromise, and opened the way for the August 1953 coup. The Shah too misinterpreted the international situation, believing that he could count on Western support to remain in power and, in the aftermath of his overthrow, blaming his fall on the West. Khomeini, in some ways the most successful modern Iranian leader, was in this respect also one of the most inept: by allowing the hostages crisis to drag on in 1980, he left Iran, as we have seen, isolated when Iraq invaded; even more seriously, he failed to see when it would have been advantageous to settle the war with Iraq, in 1982, and continued it for six more years, obtaining, in the end, a less favourable peace than was possible in 1982 and at far higher cost to Iran.

The impact of Iran's foreign policy since the revolution has been singular and substantial. More than at any time in this century, Iran is an autonomous actor on the international scene. In sum, an assessment of Iran's foreign policy in this period has to take two broad considerations into account. On the one hand, Iran has pursued a militant foreign policy that has not only cost the country dearly, in loss of life, and economic and political isolation, but which has erected a set of obstacles, within Iran and in other countries, that will make any substantial improvement in its foreign relations and normalization of them all the more difficult. On the other, Iran's reputation as a beacon of defiance within the Islamic world remains strong and will continue to be so as long as the objective reasons for the radical Islamic appeal in the Muslim world persist. There is no reason to believe that the latter will not be the case for many years to come, given the social, economic and political tensions prevailing in many Islamic countries. At great cost to itself, and amidst a welter of miscalculation and bombast, the Islamic revolution has made Iran a significant force in the international arena.

1 Iran and the United Nations, with particular reference to the Iran–Iraq War

Sir Anthony Parsons

There is an interesting study to be written about the reasons why certain delegations have exercised continuing major influence in the United Nations whereas others, often representing states of greater size, power and geo-political significance, have had less impact on the scene in New York. I exclude from this analysis the Five Permanent Members of the Security Council (China, France, the USSR, the United Kingdom and the United States) whose prominence is *sui generis*.

There are many factors to be considered. First, in numerical terms, by far the largest political grouping in the UN is the Non-Aligned Movement (NAM) comprising nearly two thirds of the total membership of 160 states. With the exception of Yugoslavia, Cyprus and Malta, all the non-aligned states are from Africa, Asia and Latin America. In economic terms the Group of 77 (the less-developed states) now numbers about 120, including all those in the NAM. The priorities of the General Assembly and Security Council agendas understandably reflect the preoccupations of the majority, principally the Arab–Israeli dispute (the Arab Group = 23 states divided between Africa and Asia), the problems of Central and Southern Africa (the African Group = 51 states) and the disparity between the wealth of the North (about 35 states) and the poverty of the South (as already mentioned about 120 states).

It is therefore scarcely surprising that the most influential delegations are to be found amongst the NAM, and especially those which play a leading part in the consideration of the most prominent items on the United Nations agenda. Examples are Egypt (until its ostracism from the Arab League following the peace treaty with Israel in 1979) and Syria in the Arab–Israeli context; Tanzania, Nigeria and Zambia in regard to African problems; India, Yugoslavia and Algeria across the board of non-aligned preoccupations, both political and economic.

Second, outside the NAM, there are states which have concentrated on the United Nations as a main element in their foreign policy priorities.

Sweden and Finland are good examples, notably in the field of United Nations peacekeeping operations. Third, certain delegations – Spain, Malta and Singapore come to mind – have made a lasting impression on the UN through the skill and energy of individual Permanent Representatives, and others, for example the Federal Republic of Germany and latterly Japan, through the projection of their growing world economic power into the New York arena.

In all these instances, and I could of course quote many more, governments have made sure that the quality of their delegations reflects the priority which they give to the United Nations as a forum for negotiation, for mobilizing support for their causes, and for the formation of regional policies.

From the creation of the United Nations in 1945 up to the fall of the monarchy in 1979, Iran fell into none of these main categories. An Iranian (Nasrollah Entezam) was President of the 5th Regular Session of the General Assembly (1950–1) and Iran served on the Security Council in 1955–6; but, after decolonization of the European empires led to the major expansion of the membership and to the creation of the contemporary pattern of functional and geographical groupings and preoccupations, Iran did not command the prominence which might have been expected of a state of her size and regional, indeed global, importance. This phenomenon in no way reflected adversely on the quality of Iranian representation in New York: this was always high. It was a consequence of a kind of isolation. Because of Iranian membership of a Defence Pact which included extra-regional powers (the Baghdad Pact, converted after the Iraqi revolution of 1958 to the Central Treaty Organization (CENTO) the membership of which was Britain, Turkey, Iran and Pakistan with the United States a member of all the Committees without being an adherent to the Treaty itself), Iran was debarred from membership of the NAM until the dissolution of CENTO in 1979, thus separating herself from otherwise natural partners. Iran's close relationship with Israel and South Africa alienated her from the Arab and African groups respectively, while geography made it impossible for the late Shah to achieve what might have been his ambition, Iranian association with the Western Europeans. It is of course true that Iran was a member in good standing of the Asian Group, but this body, for obvious reasons, has always been the most amorphous and least coherent of the geographical groupings. There is no single 'Asian' issue which binds it together as, for instance, the evil of apartheid in South Africa binds the Africans, the Arab–Israeli dispute the Arabs and a common culture the majority of the Latin Americans. Furthermore, the diversity of states in Asia in terms of size, power, interests and economic and social development is far greater than in the other regions. What is there in common, except for an extreme interpretation of geography, between, say, Japan and the Peoples' Democratic Republic of the Yemen or Mongolia and the Solomon Islands? In this heterogenous galère, Iran was, in United Nations terms, a somewhat lonely player. Even the strenuous exertions of the Shah's twin sister, Princess Ashraf, in the fields of human and women's rights did not make a deep impression! In the economic deliberations of the Group of 77, Iran was never a lead figure, perhaps because of the general consciousness that the Shah's ambitions pointed towards Iran formally quitting this company in favour of membership of Group B (the developed states). To sum up, monarchical Iran's prominence in the United Nations was greater when the parliamentary configuration was dominated by the West (viz. the holding by Iran of important offices in the 1950s), and declined when the numerical majority came to be dominated by the newly emergent states of Africa and parts of Asia, as represented in the Non-Aligned Movement.

Iran's moments of conspicuousness in the United Nations marked the crises through which the country passed. Indeed, the first overt manifestation of the Cold War, also the first substantive item on the agenda of the Security Council, was the question of Iran, namely the reluctance of the Soviet Union to withdraw its forces in 1946 after the close of hostilities. Instead of the Permanent Members uniting to deter or punish a breaker of the peace, as envisaged in the Charter, one of them was the first to be in the dock and Iran was the plaintiff. Three resolutions were adopted, SCR 2 (1946), SCR 3 (1946) and SCR 5 (1946), the Soviet Union absenting itself on the last two occasions: history records that their forces withdrew from Iranian territory.

The next occasion came six years later, this time following the rejection by the Iranian government of a ruling by the International Court on Dr Mossadeq's nationalization of the Anglo–Iranian Oil Company in 1951. Britain requested the inscription of an item on the Security Council agenda but, lacking support for the draft resolution she put forward, agreed to the adjournment of the debate. It was not resumed.

In 1970, after agreeing to the good offices of the then Secretary-General, U Thant, to mediate a settlement of the Iranian claim to Bahrain, and following an ascertainment by the Secretary-General's representative of the views of the Bahraini population, Iran acquiesced in a Security Council resolution (SCR 278 (1970)) endorsing the report which concluded that 'the overwhelming majority of the people of Bahrain wish to gain recognition of their identity in a fully independent and sovereign state free to decide for itself its relations with other states'. The ancient claim had been put to rest with Security Council endorsement following confidential diplomacy by the Secretary-General with the consent of the parties: a classic case of successful UN action under Chapter VI (Peaceful Settlement) of the Charter.

Four years later there was a portent of things to come. A rebellion in Iraqi Kurdistan had for some time been supported by the Iranian government. In 1974 tension rose dangerously between the two governments and there were armed clashes in the border area. I was in Tehran at the time and it looked to outside observers as if full-scale war between Iran and Iraq was a distinct possibility. In May the Security Council debated the crisis and adopted SCR 348 (1974) welcoming the agreement of the two sides to observe a cease-fire, withdraw armed forces along the border and resume talks to settle bilateral issues. In the event the fighting flared up again and peace was ultimately achieved in the Algiers Agreement of 1975 under which the division of the Shatt al-Arab and the delineation of the land frontier were agreed: the Shah undertook to desist from supporting the Iraqi Kurdish rebels and President Saddam Hussein of Iraq agreed to abandon the campaign of irredentist subversion in Iran Khuzestan ('Arabistan') and Baluchestan.

In October 1979, the then Foreign Minister of Iran, Mr Ibrahim Yazdi, chose the United Nations as the forum at which to explain to the world for the first time the nature of the Iranian revolution and the internal and external changes which would come about as a result of the creation of the Islamic Republic. In his statement to the General Assembly, Mr Yazdi first made the point that, on several occasions, he had 'screamed the outrage' of the Iranian people at the delegates from the pavements outside the building. Now, for the first time since the 'coup engineered in Iran by the CIA in 1953' the Iranian delegation inside the building represented the true choice of the Iranian people. During the previous twenty-five years the Shah had been a 'puppet of imperialism and Zionism'. While the people of Iran felt solidarity with liberation movements, the delegation to the UN had sided with imperialism, exploitation, racism and Zionism.

At a later stage in his statement Mr Yazdi referred to the foreign policies of the Islamic Republic. He mentioned the speed with which Iran had acted against Israel and South Africa and Iran's commitment to the view that bloc military alliances served only imperialism and tyranny. Dismantling military bases and disassociating itself from military alliances was one of the first policy decisions of the Islamic Republic. It was logical for Iran to join the NAM and she hoped to be an active member. The late Dr Mossadeq had been one of the original advocates of non-alignment at a time (1952) when Stalinism and American imperialism did not even accept the legitimacy of non-alignment.

Mr Yazdi also expressed strong support for the Palestinian people and characterized Zionism as one of the most vicious forms of racism in recorded history. He criticized the hypocrisy of a system of oppression which had enabled the rich to distort the reality of their actions. When Israeli bombers killed impoverished Palestinians and Lebanese, their Western media apologists described this 'genocidal aggression' as 'defensive aerial attacks on Palestinian military bases'. When the Palestinians blew up a bus in occupied Jerusalem or assassinated an Israeli secret agent, they were described as 'terrorists'. Mr Yazdi also strongly criticized apartheid in South Africa stating that there had been a total cut off of the supply of Iranian oil to that country. Iran found the situations in South Africa, Namibia and Zimbabwe–Rhodesia deplorable. Existing sanctions against Rhodesia should be strengthened and the provisions of Chapter VII of the UN Charter should be applied to South Africa both because of her policies in Namibia and because of apartheid.

In a broader foreign policy context, Mr Yazdi spoke of the Iranian conviction that the struggle for justice, independence and freedom should in part be 'directed against our own habits and perceptions'. Racists and exploiters would not treat the nations and peoples of the Third World any better than they (the Third World governments) treated their own people and related to one another across national boundaries. Until recent decades, rulers in the 'official or unofficial colonies of Africa, Asia and Latin America' had not needed the aid of imperial powers to maintain their privileged positions. The cultural and ideological orientation of the traditional ruling class in the underdeveloped world was not too different from that of its own population.

Today this had changed. The peasants were still living under the same conditions or in urban ghettos, but the controllers of the means of production and the bureaucratic or military ruling classes had adopted alien cultural and ideological orientations and had little socio-cultural contact with the masses. They identified with the West and were alienated from their own roots. The enclaves of wealth and power were enclaves of imported cultures. There was a global standardization of values amongst the beneficiaries of international finance, the movement of goods and services, travel and communications. This standardization had added a fresh dimension of Western cultural domination to the character of imperialism.

Imperialism had produced unprecedented resentment in subordinated societies. This resentment, a reaction to exploitation, coercion and consumer manipulation, had stimulated an expanded revolutionary challenge from below. The responses to this challenge on the part of the ruling classes, namely manipulation, repression and militarism, were 'the organic commodities of imperialism in search of global markets'.

Sadly too many people in the Third World were eager customers for commodities of imperialism. Too much was being spent on arms and luxury goods at the expense of the needs of the masses. Too many people were the unconscious victims of imperialism. Cultural imperialism had penetrated deep. Too many resources were being spent on coercion. In this context, why did China have to 'teach Vietnam a lesson'? What justification was there for Pol Pot's massacres? Why did Vietnam invade Cambodia? In Afghanistan, thousands of people had died and tens of thousands had become refugees as a result of actions in defence of an imported 'ism'.

In earlier passages in his statement, Mr Yazdi explained the nature of the Iranian revolution and dilated upon the difference in the relationship between the religious and the secular in Christianity and Islam respectively. The Iranian revolution was committed to a transformation of society on the basis of the Koranic principles of justice, equality and participation. In the Islamic world view, one could only recognize God after freeing oneself from the conditions of one's alienation. This meant the destruction of the sources of human alienation be they found in capitalism, totalitarianism or exploitation. The moral explosion of the Iranian masses was inspired by the Koran and the efforts of the Prophet to transform the class-dominated society of his time into egalitarian and democratic communities of the Faithful.

In the West religion was defined as a relationship between man and the supernatural, leaving no room for political, economic and social considerations. Islam comprised a set of doctrines based on a world view with its own political, economic, social and cultural perspectives. It was the imposition of the Western definition of religion onto Islam which had prevented Western observers from understanding the revolution.

Second, the development of secular, scientific culture in the West had been opposed by the organized Church. In pre-Renaissance Europe, the papal system had transformed religion into an institution closely connected with the ruling classes, one of its principal functions being to comfort the oppressed masses with the promise of a heaven. With the Renaissance, scientific and secular thinkers regarded their activities as separate from religious doctrines. Western intellectuals chose freedom over the power of organized religion. They were against superstition, not against ethics and morality. This antagonism to the Church made a significant contribution to social and scientific advancement. However, when Western secularism was transmitted to Islamic societies (where no distinction between religious and secular existed) the result was the alienation of the intellectuals from themselves and from the masses.

The Western experience also contributed to the development of Marxism. When Marx described religion as the opium of the people he had in mind the history of Western Europe: he knew little of Islam. When the intellectuals in Islamic societies echoed either Marxism or Western Liberalism, they destroyed or weakened the moral force capable of confronting colonial aggression and imperialism, particularly in its cultural form.

Mr Yazdi then accused Western liberal and Marxist writers of judging Third World societies according to their own tools of analysis, and so-called Western Orientalists of being intrinsically antipathetic to Islam.

For all these reasons many outside observers, both the apologists for imperialism and those of socialist or liberal persuasion, had difficulties in appreciating the radical and progressive nature of the Iranian revolution. All societies had their own organic development. As a consequence of this reality the Iranian people had been enabled to force their illegitimate monarch into exile and to welcome home their most popular leader, Ayatollah Khomeini. The dominant slogans of the revolution had been 'Death to the Shah', 'Independence, Freedom and Islamic Republic' and 'Neither East, nor West, only Islamic Republic'.

I well recall the impact which this powerful exposition exercised on the delegates to the General Assembly. However, an event was shortly to happen which was to influence the international perception of Iran to a far greater extent than Mr Yazdi's presentation.

On 4 November 1979, the American Embassy in Tehran was invaded and the staff held hostage. This crisis, which lasted until the release of the last fifty-one Americans, unharmed, in January 1981, the day on which President Reagan took office, had a profound effect in the United Nations and formed a crucial part of the background to the attitude of the Security Council towards Iran at the beginning of the Iran–Iraq War a year later. It is necessary therefore to examine the elements which helped to shape opinion in New York in some detail. First, Iran, for reasons already suggested, although now a member of the NAM, had yet to acquire that privileged status which has helped to secure for leading NAM members something approximating to an automatic benefit of the doubt when they have departed from the straight and narrow path of international law and custom; as was the case over the Indian occupation of Goa and the part played by the Tanzanian armed forces in the overthrow of President Idi Amin of Uganda. There was widespread sympathy across the board of the geographical groups for the courage and discipline demonstrated by the revolutionaries in their campaign to overthrow the Shah, never a popular figure in UN circles. There was sympathy too for some of their aspirations. But the Islamic Republic was still a newcomer to the non-aligned club and could not expect to receive support or at least avoidance of condemnation regardless of the merits of the case.

Second, in a conclave consisting exclusively of diplomats, the news of the invasion of diplomatic premises, whatever the circumstances, and the early realization that this was no accident quickly to be rectified, created a powerful reaction of shock and hostility which transcended geographical groupings and political differences: in a phrase, the action of the Iranian 'students' was seen as an unforgivable atrocity. Third, as the crisis dragged on, resentment grew on the ground that it was monopolizing the UN horizon to the detriment of consideration of other items to which delegations attached importance, for example the Arab–Israeli dispute, the Soviet invasion of Afghanistan, the progress of the negotiations to solve the problem of Southern Rhodesia, and many others. Fourth, the atmosphere in UN headquarters in New York was inevitably infected by the obsessive preoccupation with the hostage crisis on the part of the American public media and public opinion.

By the end of the Summer of 1980 all these feelings had been intensified by the failure of action by the United Nations to solve the problem, or even to produce progress towards a solution. Security Council Resolution (SCR) 457 of 4 December 1979 and SCR 461 of 31 December 1979, both calling for the release of the hostages, had been ignored: the subsequent American draft resolution calling for sanctions against Iran had secured ten votes but had been blocked by a Soviet veto. Secretary-General Waldheim's visit to Tehran in the New Year had been a publicly humiliating fiasco and the UN Commission of Inquiry in February into Iranian grievances against the Shah's regime, which included distinguished representatives from Algeria and Syria, had proved fruitless. Resentment against Iran for prolonging the crisis was matched by a rare (in United Nations terms) sympathy for the predicament of the United States, bearing in mind that the Carter administration and its representatives in the United Nations had throughout their term of office been more popular with the UN majority than had previous American governments. This sympathy was to some extent offset by a feeling that the United States had been using the mechanisms of the United Nations not so much in the expectation that they would be able to deliver the release of the hostages, but in order to demonstrate to American public opinion that the administration was using every lever available to produce results, i.e. as a defence against the accusation that President Carter was doing nothing to free his compatriots.

When Iraqi forces invaded south-west Iran on 22 September 1980, the Regular Session of the General Assembly had just opened and a number of foreign ministers and heads of government were in New York to deliver their national statements in the annual General Debate. Although there was *ex post facto* recrimination amongst these statesmen at the failure of the United Nations to prevent the war from breaking out, Iraqi pressure succeeded in postponing a meeting of the Security Council for some days, presumably in order to give their forces a free hand in what they hoped would be a blitzkrieg victory. The high standing of Iraq relative to Iran in non-aligned circles prevailed with the seven African, Asian and Latin American members, and the necessary nine procedural votes (out of fifteen) needed to call a meeting and inscribe an item on the agenda were not present. Equally, because of the impact of the hostage crisis the remainder of the Council, including the Permanent Members, were not immediately disposed to make a serious effort to overcome this obstacle.

On 22 September the Secretary-General appealed to the combatants to settle their differences by negotiation and offered his good offices. The next day, acting with the authority of Article 99 of the Charter, he proposed a meeting of the Council. On 28 September, the Council having at last met at the formal request of Norway and Mexico, SCR 479 (1980) was unanimously adopted, calling for a cessation of hostilities, urging the parties to accept mediation and supporting the good offices of the Secretary-General.

However, the fact of the Council's delay in meeting and the failure of the first resolution to call for Iraqi withdrawal from Iranian territory made a profoundly negative impression on the Iranian delegation led by Prime Minister Rajaie. In his long and hard-hitting statement Mr Rajaie castigated the Council for inactivity and bias and stated Iran's war aims, namely the 'identification [presumably by the international community] and punishment of the aggressor'.

In his report to the Council on 30 September the Secretary-General noted that Iraq had agreed to accept SCR 479 if Iran would. But Iran responded on 1 October via a goodwill mission from the Organization of the Islamic Conference (OIC), comprising its Secretary-General and the President of Pakistan, that the government could not consider the Secretary-General's proposals while the war lasted and saw no use in discussing the conflict so long as Iraq was violating Iran's territorial integrity.

On 10 October the Secretary-General appealed to both governments to ensure the safety of peaceful shipping and to allow ships immobilized in the Shatt al-Arab to leave the area. These questions were considered at a series of meetings between the Secretary-General and representatives of the parties, but without positive results.

At the turn of October/November intensive informal consultations took place between the Secretary-General and the members of the Council as a whole. As a result, the President of the Council issued a statement on 5 November on behalf of the membership expressing concern at the continuation of hostilities, urging all concerned to be guided by their Charter obligations to settle their disputes by peaceful means and to refrain in their international relations from the 'threat or use of force against the territorial integrity or political independence of any state'. (This phrase, a direct quotation from Article 2(4) of the Charter, reiterated one of the preambular paragraphs of SCR 479 and was the nearest the Council had come – not very near – to addressing the question of responsibility for the war.) The President's statement noted that the Secretary-General was considering sending a representative to the region 'in order to facilitate authoritative communication with and between the Governments concerned so that negotiations for peace can proceed on an urgent basis'. On 11 November, the Secretary-General told the Council that, with the agreement of Iran and Iraq, he had appointed Mr Olaf Palme of Sweden as his Special Representative with the aim of bringing about a cease-fire and a negotiated settlement.

In the circumstances this was an excellent choice. Mr Palme, the former Prime Minister of Sweden (subsequently re-elected to that office before being murdered in mysterious circumstances in 1984) was a well-known international figure with a reputation for sympathy with the problems of the developing world and their desire for non-alignment, as well as for resolute independence from great powers including the United States with which he was far from popular. He was also known to have been at the least lukewarm towards the Pahlavi Regime in Iran because of its human rights record and to have had contact before the revolution with some of those now holding power. As I came to know him personally up to my departure from New York in the Summer of 1982, I acquired both affection for him as a person and deep respect for his high intelligence and skill as a mediator and negotiator.

However, from the outset I was pessimistic about his chances of success. In my judgement there were two sets of reasons behind the conflict, one a justificatory façade, the other the real cause. On the face of it the purpose of the Iraqi invasion was to recover two areas of land (amounting to about 150 square kilometres) promised to Iraq in the 1975 Algiers Agreement between the Shah and Saddam Hussein but not handed over and, following Iraqi abrogation of the Agreement on 17 September 1980, to restore Iraqi sovereignty over the Shatt al-Arab up to the Iranian shoreline. But the underlying cause was different. Since the success of the Iranian revolution in 1979, Iraq had feared its export to their own majority Shia Moslem community amongst whom Iranian revolutionaries were active. By 1980, the Iraqi government was convinced that it faced a major subversive campaign. It was, so far as most of us in the Security Council could judge, in order to neutralize this threat that the Baghdad regime had decided to take advantage of post-revolutionary confusion in the Iranian armed forces and attack Iran in the hope either of bringing about the collapse of the regime in Tehran or of weakening it to the extent that attempts to export the revolution to Iraq would be abandoned.

From my consultations with Mr Palme in my capacity as a member of the Security Council, I realized that, for obvious reasons of diplomatic behaviour, he felt obliged to concentrate his efforts on the first set of reasons, namely the performance of both parties in terms of implementation of the Algiers Agreement between 1975 and 1980, the merits of each case over the division of the Shatt al-Arab, and so on. I could not bring myself to believe that this approach, correct though it was, touched the true causes of the conflict. I felt that the war was likely to continue until the real war aims of one side or the other had been realized.

Over the next year and a half Mr Palme paid several visits to both capitals and did his utmost to bring the two sides together. His efforts were unavailing, even as regards specific problems such as the release of the merchant shipping trapped in the Shatt al-Arab. After he again became Prime Minister of Sweden he was able to devote less time to his mission and was not replaced by another Special Representative after his murder. Subsequently the Secretary-General carried out his good offices' mission in person or through regular members of the UN Secretariat.

During this period the Council was content to leave matters in the hands of the Secretary-General and his Special Representative notwithstanding the fact that some of the fiercest fighting of the war was taking place, casualties and material damage were mounting alarmingly and the war was presenting a growing threat to the stability of the region.

In July 1982 the Council resumed consideration of the problem and, on 12 July, unanimously adopted SCR 514 (1982). This resolution called for a cease-fire, withdrawal to internationally recognized boundaries, the dispatch of UN observers to verify a cease-fire and the continuation of the Secretary-General's mediation efforts. On 15 July the President of the Council issued a statement expressing the concern of the Council that SCR 514 had not been implemented: on 4 October, SCR 522 (1982) was unanimously adopted. This resolution reiterated the provisions of SCR 514 with an additional paragraph welcoming the readiness of one of the parties (Iraq) to co-operate in the implementation of SCR 514 and calling upon the other to do likewise. In a report of 7 October, the Secretary-General stated that Iraq had agreed to co-operate but that the Iranian government had said that they considered Security Council resolutions on the Iran–Iraq War to be non-binding. On 21 February 1983, the President of the Council issued another statement rehearsing previous statements as well as the terms of SCRs 514 and 522, and urgently calling for an immediate cease-fire together with the withdrawal of forces to internationally recognized boundaries.

This phase of United Nations activity had done nothing to convince the Iranian government of the impartiality of the Council. No attempt had been made to rectify the original omission of exploring the origins of the war (in Iranian terms, the 'identification of the aggressor'). By 1982 Iraq was on the defensive and Iranian forces were established at many points on Iraqi territory. It was therefore no surprise that Iraq should have agreed to co-operate with SCRs 514 and 522. In the Iranian perception the Council had further revealed its pro-Iraqi bias by failing to call for Iraqi withdrawal (SCR 479 (1980)) from Iranian soil at the outset, and only calling for withdrawal when it involved Iranian withdrawal from Iraqi territory.

In the first half of 1983, the Secretary-General addressed two specific manifestations of the war. In March he offered his good offices over the clearing up of an oil spill from the Iranian Now Ruz field, installations having been damaged by Iraqi attack. In the event the Iranians themselves capped the well. The Secretary-General subsequently sent a mission to Iran, at the request of the Iranian government, to inspect areas where there had been civilian war damage. His eventual report presented information provided by both governments.

In October 1983 the Security Council met again, this time on French initiative, and on 31 October, adopted SCR 540 (1983). This was the first resolution not to be adopted unanimously. Malta, Nicaragua and Pakistan abstained, taking the view that the Council had moved to the vote without allowing sufficient time for pre-negotiation with Iran.

This resolution broke some new ground. In its operative paragraphs it condemned all violations of international humanitarian law and called for the cessation of all military operations against civilian targets. It affirmed the right of free navigation and called upon the belligerents to cease all hostilities in the region of the Gulf including sea lanes and shore installations. Furthermore, it included a preambular paragraph 'affirming the desirability of an objective examination of the causes of the war'.

In his subsequent report to the Council the Secretary-General noted that the Iranian government had disassociated itself from SCR 540 on the ground that it was unbalanced. He also noted that the Iranian government had more than once asked for a further UN Mission to inspect civilian areas and that three of these requests had stated that Iraq had used chemical weapons.

Although the activity of the Council in 1983 had taken into account developments on the battlefield, namely the initiation of attacks on civilian targets, the use of chemical weapons and the beginnings of the 'tanker war', and although SCR 540 had made a small gesture in the direction of considering the origins of the war, this was still not enough to persuade Iran that the Council had abandoned what they judged to be its pro-Iraqi bias.

The Iranian government continued to demonstrate its willingness to co-operate with the Secretary-General and his Special Representative and Missions, but their hostility to the Council itself was undiminished. In all these instances, in the Iranian perception, the Council should have apportioned blame to Iraq instead of being studiously non-committal.

For the next two years, although the war continued with unabated ferocity, intensified by the scale of attack and counter-attack in the Persian Gulf itself, the United Nations concentrated on the symptoms rather than the disease. In March 1984, following another mission to Iran, the Secretary-General reported that chemical weapons in the form of aerial bombs had been used in the area inspected. The President of the Council made a statement on 30 March strongly condemning the use of chemical weapons and calling on states to adhere to the 1925 Geneva Protocol (this was the closest the Council had come to a unilateral condemnation of an Iraqi action).

On 1 June 1984 the Council adopted SCR 552 (with Nicaragua and Zimbabwe abstaining) drafted by the Gulf Co-operation Council, expressing concern over recent attacks on commercial shipping *en route* to and from the ports of Kuwait and Saudi Arabia and calling for the right of free navigation to be respected by all states. In his statement to the General Assembly on 26 September the Japanese Foreign Minister proposed that prompt progress be sought on (a) no future violations of the 1925 Geneva Protocol and (b) on ensuring free navigation in the Gulf. The Iranian Prime Minister rejected these plans at a press conference in Tehran the following day. In a statement on 26 March 1985 the Secretary-General expressed, amongst other things, dismay that attacks on unarmed shipping persisted.

Again, in the international diplomatic arena, Iran found herself at a disadvantage over the 'tanker war' which had been initiated by Iraq to weaken the Iranian economy and to involve the outside world in order to maximize pressure on Iran to come to the negotiating table. This imbalance in the international response, as exemplified by SCR 552, persisted. There being no Iraqi shipping in the Gulf, and all Iraqi ports being closed, Iran's only target of retaliation against attacks on shipping on her side of the Gulf was the shipping of 'neutral' nations plying to and from ports on the Arab shore. This inevitably attracted adverse comment and indeed led by 1987 to the presence on the Arab side of the Gulf of a formidable armada of foreign warships. But there was no specific, international condemnation of the Iraqi attacks and no serious attempts made to persuade or coerce Iraq into desisting from them, this in spite of the fact that all members of the international community must have realized that, if Iraq stopped attacking shipping Iran would follow suit immediately. Iran had no interest in endangering the sea lanes through which all her exports and most of her imports passed (in contrast to Iraq whose oil was transported by pipeline and whose imports came in by road).

Meanwhile in 1984 and 1985, the Secretary-General pursued two separate issues, the 'war of the cities' and the treatment of prisoners-of-war. He also continued to address the question of the use of chemical weapons. On 12 June 1984 both sides responded to the Secretary-General's appeal to cease deliberate attacks on civilian targets. They also accepted UN inspection and verification teams in Baghdad and Tehran drawn from the UN Truce Supervision Organization (UNTSO) and the UN Secretariat. The Secretary-General made a further appeal on 29 June, immediately responded to affirmatively by Iran, to both sides not to use chemical weapons. However, in March 1985 the Secretary-General found himself again appealing for a cessation of aerial bombardment of civilian targets and condemning the use of chemical weapons. His earlier efforts had been only temporarily successful.

On 25 October 1984 the Iraqi government asked the Secretary-General to investigate an alleged incident at a prisoner-of-war camp at Gorgan in Iran. A UN Mission visited Iraq from 11 to 17 January, 1985 and Iran from 18 to 25 January. The report of the Mission was transmitted to the Security Council on 19 February. Its overall conclusion was that the existing situation for prisoners-of-war in both countries was a cause for serious concern: it recommended strict respect for the rights of prisoners-of-war under the Geneva Convention. The Security Council met on 4 March at Iraqi request to consider the report. Iran was not represented and there was no conclusive outcome.

At the beginning of 1986 the Council reverted once more to the main issue of the war itself. On 24 February, SCR 582 (1986) was adopted unanimously. Since this resolution (as reinforced by SCR 588 (1986) of 8 October 1986 and by the statement of the President of the Council issued on 22 December 1986 – neither of which was added to the content of SCR 582) formed the basis for subsequent Council action. (See appendices on pp. 27–30.)

In Iranian eyes, SCR 582 added little to previous resolutions. In its preamble it emphasized the inadmissibility of the acquisition of territory by force (a phrase originally enshrined in SCR 242 (1967) on the Arab–Israeli dispute). But to which side did this apply? In its first operative paragraph it 'deplores the initial acts which gave rise to the conflict . . .'. To whose acts did it refer? Here again there was no sign that the international community was drawing closer to the 'identification of the aggressor'. Indeed the preambular paragraph in SCR 540 (1983) already referred to ('Affirming the desirability of an objective examination of the causes of the war') went a little further in the direction of Iranian desiderata than did the language of SCR 582.

The remainder of the resolution, deploring the various aspects of escalation of the conflict, calling for a cease-fire, withdrawal to internationally recognized boundaries, an exchange of prisoners-of-war, etc. broadly speaking reflected the contents of previous resolutions, appeals by the Secretary-General and statements issued by the President of the Council.

On 21 March 1986, following the report of a Mission dispatched by the Secretary-General to investigate further allegations of the use of chemical weapons, the President issued a statement reaffirming much of the language in SCR 582 and containing the following paragraph:

> Profoundly concerned by the unanimous conclusion of the specialists that chemical weapons on many occasions have been used by Iraqi forces against Iranian forces, most recently in the course of the present Iranian offensive into Iraqi territory, the members of the Council strongly condemn this continued use of chemical weapons in clear violation of the Geneva Protocol of 1925 which prohibits the use in war of chemical weapons.

This statement amounted to the second, and most explicit, condemnation of an Iraqi action since the outbreak of the war.

By the first months of 1987 the war had intensified on all fronts. There had been another major Iranian land offensive in the Basra area, Iraqi attacks on shipping and shore installations had increased and, in the light of the Kuwaiti invitation to the United States and the Soviet Union to reflag and escort tankers plying to and from Mina al-Ahmadi, the numbers of foreign warships deployed in the Gulf, principally those of the United States but also including the Soviet Union, Britain, France, the Netherlands, Italy and Belgium, mounted to a total of over seventy. No end to the war was in sight: indeed there appeared to be every possibility that it would both escalate further and spread wider, even engulfing the superpowers.

Against this sombre background, consultations were opened between the Five Permanent Members of the Security Council (China, France, the USSR, the UK and the US) which resulted some months later in the unanimous adoption of SCR 598 (1987) on 20 July. This resolution, the text of which is given in Appendix A, requires detailed analysis. It is thought to be unique in the annals of the United Nations in that, as I am informed, it was drafted collectively by the Five Permanent Members. It also, for the first time, carried the Security Council's deliberations out of the recommendatory area of Chapter VI of the Charter (the Pacific Settlement of Disputes) into the mandatory area of Chapter VII (Action with Respect to Threats to the Peace, Breaches of the Peace and Acts of Aggression). In accordance with the accepted interpretation of Article 25 of the Charter, decisions taken under Chapter VII are binding on the membership.

To begin with, the language of the preambular paragraphs is more resolute than that of previous resolutions, and goes wider. SCR 582 (1986) is reaffirmed and the third paragraph deplores the initiation and continuation of the conflict, thus anticipating the sixth paragraph in the operative section. The fifth preambular paragraph expresses 'determination' (a strong word in the lexicon of the UN) to bring to an end all military actions between Iran and Iraq. The heart of the matter is in the final two preambular paragraphs which first 'determine' that there exists a breach of the peace as regards the conflict between Iran and Iraq and secondly states that the Council is acting under Articles 39 and 40 of the United Nations Charter. To a layman it may seem ridiculous that it should take seven years of bitter warfare to reveal to the Council that a breach of the peace had taken place! But in the arcane procedures of the United Nations, a 'determination' using such language is necessary in order to bring into play the mandatory provisions of Chapter VII of the Charter. In fact the Council took a median line, the title of Chapter VII being 'Action with respect to threats to the peace, *breaches of the peace* [emphasis added] and acts of aggression'.

As regards the operative section of the resolution, the first paragraph 'demands' (a mandatory word) an immediate cease-fire, the discontinuation of all military actions and the withdrawal of all forces to the internationally recognized boundaries without delay.

Paragraph 2 'requests' (a less strong injunction than for example, 'orders') the Secretary-General to dispatch a team of UN observers to verify, confirm and supervize both the cease-fire and withdrawal.

Paragraph 3 'urges' (again a non-mandatory word) the release and repatriation of prisoners-of-war. Paragraphs 4 and 5 respectively 'call upon' (it could have been 'order') Iran and Iraq to co-operate with the Secretary-General's mediation efforts and on other states to exercise maximum restraint. The language in these articles is similar to the equivalent formulations in previous resolutions.

Paragraph 6 picks up, for the first time in four years, the notion expressed in the preambular section of SCR 540 (1983), viz. 'Affirming the desirability of an objective examination of the causes of the war'. It 'requests [again not a very strong injunction] the Secretary-General to explore, in consultation with Iran and Iraq, the question of entrusting an impartial body with inquiring into responsibility for the conflict and to report to the Security Council as soon as possible'.

Paragraph 7 breaks new ground, addressing for the first time the question of post-war reconstruction (reparations). Again the Secretary-General is 'requested' to '. . . assign a team of experts to study the question of reconstruction and to report to the Security Council'.

In paragraph 10 the Council 'decides to meet again as necessary to consider further steps to ensure compliance with this resolution'.

To sum up, SCR 598 moved the international consideration of the Iran–Iraq War into a fresh dimension, that of Chapter VII of the United Nations Charter, thus invoking the possibility of mandatory action against a party or parties in breach of the resolution. It took the preliminary steps of determining that there had been a breach of the peace (Article 39) and calling on the parties to comply with measures laid down in the resolution (Article 40).

It is appropriate at this point to examine the general background to an evolution of this kind. In the forty-five-year-old history of the United Nations the non-military and military measures laid down in Chapter VII have rarely been used. There have been mandatory demands on parties to conflicts for example, for a cease-fire in the first Arab–Israeli War in 1948 and for Argentine withdrawal from the Falkland Islands in 1982. On both these occasions the resolutions did not have the desired effect (although in the first Arab–Israeli War there was a temporary cessation of fighting) and no follow-up measures such as economic sanctions were taken by the Security Council. In theory the Korean War constituted United Nations military action under Article 42 of Chapter VII. But this is a doubtful precedent. The enabling resolution was adopted in the temporary absence of the Soviet Union from the Council, thus avoiding a certain veto. (The Soviet Union at the time was objecting to sharing the Council table with the Taiwan-based 'representatives' of China.) Moreover, although forces deployed in Korea were theoretically 'United Nations' forces', they were under United States', not United Nations', command and control. Between 1965 and 1979, mandatory economic sanctions were imposed against the illegal regime in Southern Rhodesia and, in 1977, a mandatory arms embargo was adopted against South Africa. However, in the former instance, the rebellion was brought to an end, with the independence of the Republic of Zimbabwe in April 1980, by means of negotiations not as a result of the sanctions: in the latter case the capacity and willingness of South Africa to wage war on her neighbours has remained unimpaired. Indeed South Africa, over a dozen years later, has become a major exporter of military equipment.

Hence the conclusion is inescapable that the United Nations has no means at its disposal for the automatic implementation of its decisions, however strongly and unanimously expressed, and that the distinction between resolutions adopted under Chapter VI or Chapter VII is more apparent than real. Only through negotiation, that is, with at least the minimal acquiescence of all parties to a dispute, can positive results be obtained.

In the case of SCR 598 (1987), the first reactions of the parties were predictable in the light of their respective attitudes through the duration of the war. Iraq was quick to accept the resolution provided that Iran did the same. At the time of its adoption, a cease-fire, mutual withdrawal, the interposition of United Nations' observers and an exchange of prisoners-of-war were all favourable to Iraqi interests. Moreover, although the whole resolution was drafted within the framework of Chapter VII, the only unequivocally mandatory injunction in it was the 'demand' in operative paragraph 1 (cease-fire, UN observers, withdrawal). It was therefore logical to assume that these steps must be taken first and that the remainder of the resolution was to be implemented sequentially. Iraq insisted on this interpretation. For Iraq this meant that a UN supervised cease-fire and Iranian withdrawal from Iraqi territory must be completed before the setting up of an 'impartial commission' to consider the origins of the war was addressed or the question of reconstruction (reparations) looked at.

To Iran the resolution had the same pro-Iraqi coloration as its predecessors. As the Iranian government perceived the situation, they were being ordered to lay down their arms and withdraw from the territory which they had won at appalling human cost, with no certainty from the language in paragraph 6 that the 'impartial commission' would even meet, let alone 'identify' Iraq as the 'aggressor', nor that financial reparations would be agreed in their favour, the language of paragraph 7 being equally equivocal. It was therefore no wonder that Iran, without actually denouncing the resolution, should have equivocated.

During the year which elapsed after 20 July 1987, the Secretary-General engaged in intensive consultations with the parties in an attempt to reconcile their positions, without success. The Security Council also consulted frequently about the possibility of imposing a unilateral arms embargo against Iran. But the unanimity achieved in SCR 598 crumbled and no 'further steps' as envisaged in paragraph 10 were taken.

Meanwhile the war continued on land and with greater intensity (and outside involvement) at sea. The 'war of the cities' was resumed in 1988 and chemical weapons were again used. In spite of the virtually universal view that Iraq had used poison gas against the population of the Iraqi town of Halabja in April 1988, the subsequent Security Council Resolution (SCR 612 (1988)), while vigorously condemning the continued use of these weapons, addressed its strictures to both sides.

In mid-July 1988 the Iranian government, for the first time since the war began, took the initiative in calling a meeting of the Security Council. This action following the shooting down, with the loss of life of 290 passengers and crew, of an Iranian civil aircraft on a scheduled flight from Bandarabbas to Dubai by the United States warship USS *Vincennes*.

After some days of inconclusive debate, the Security Council unanimously adopted, on 20 July, Resolution 616, expressing distress at the incident, profound regret over the tragic loss of innocent lives, condolences to the families of the victims, welcoming the decision of ICAO to investigate the chain of events leading to the destruction of the aircraft, and stressing the need for full and rapid implementation of SCR 598 (1987).

Meanwhile, on 18 July, the Iranian government had formally announced its acceptance of SCR 598. This statement was welcomed by speakers in the debate on the airbus incident including the representatives of the United States and the Soviet Union. On 20 July the UN Secretary-General announced at his daily press conference that he was despatching a technical team led by the Chief of Staff of the United Nations Truce Supervision Organization (UNTSO) to Baghdad and Tehran to work out the modalities of establishing an immediate cease-fire.

Iranian acceptance of a cease-fire without the achievement of any of the stated war aims, even the 'identification of the aggressor', took the world by surprise. Ayatollah Khomeini himself conceded that it was like drinking a draught of poison. Several factors appear to have converged. Civilian morale had suffered from the continuing Iraqi bombardment of open cities. Military morale was feeling the effects of chemical attacks. Finance to maintain the war effort was in short supply owing to the fall in oil prices and damage inflicted on Iranian oil installations. Iranian naval strength had been seriously reduced in clashes with United States' forces in the Persian Gulf. In a nutshell, Iran although undefeated, was close to exhaustion and victory was no longer in sight.

It was in this conjuncture that the true importance of SCR 598 emerged. For respective domestic and regional reasons, neither side, when on the defensive, could unilaterally signal to the other that it was ready to end hostilities. But both could, without unacceptable loss of face, accept an internationally formulated peace plan, particularly one couched in mandatory language and strongly supported by the Five Permanent Members. Iraq, still on the defensive in the Summer of 1987, did so immediately. Iran followed suit when the fortunes of war had turned to her disadvantage. Thus the UN Security Council was able once again to fulfil one of its most important functions, namely the provision of a ladder down which parties to conflicts can climb when their positions have become dangerously exposed.

Even so, an uneasy month passed, with Iraq, sensing advantage and wishing to improve her position at an eventual negotiating table, launching probing attacks into Iranian territory. It was not until 20 August that the cease-fire came into effect and the first UN military observers from the United Nations Iran–Iraq Military Observer Group (UNIIMOG) were deployed. Peace talks, under the aegis of the Secretary-General, were opened simultaneously.

On 26 August the Security Council unanimously adopted a further resolution (No. 620) on the use of chemical weapons. Although the advance publicity for the reports on which the debate and the resolution were based heralded a powerful condemnation of Iraq, the eventual text was carefully unbiased. It condemned the use of chemical weapons in the conflict, encouraged the Secretary-General to carry out prompt investigations of future allegations of the use of chemical weapons, called upon all states to strengthen control over the export of chemical products serving to produce chemical weapons and decided to consider 'appropriate and effective measures' should any future use of chemical weapons take place in violation of international law, wherever and by whomsoever committed.

In September, there was pressure from the United States Congress and the European Parliament for Iraq to be arraigned for using chemical weapons against her own Kurdish civilian population. At the time the Iraqis were taking advantage of the cease-fire to crush the rebels in Iraqi Kurdistan just as the Iranians were dealing with supporters of the People's Mujahedin in Iran who had fought on the Iraqi side. Vivid media publicity was given to evidence of Iraqi use of chemical weapons both within Iraq and from the thousands of Kurds who had taken refuge in south-east Turkey. But the Security Council was not reconvened.

For over two years the cease-fire held. There were breaches and the opposing armies continued to be fully deployed, in certain areas in very close proximity. Before the Iraqi invasion of Kuwait tension in the Persian Gulf relaxed and the bulk of the foreign naval forces were withdrawn. But there was no progress towards implementation of the remainder of the SCR 598. Even the withdrawal (almost entirely Iraqi) to internationally recognized boundaries, demanded in the first operative paragraph, did not take place. All that happened was that a handful of prisoners-of-war on both sides was exchanged. The talks themselves continued sporadically, under the chairmanship of Mr Eliassen, Swedish Ambassador to the United Nations and a former aide to Olaf Palme at the time of the latter's mission on behalf of the Secretary-General.

The principal obstacle to progress was the question of the clearance and freedom of navigation in the Shatt al-Arab, namely the re-establishment of a regime over the waterway. Iraq, having denounced the 1975 Agreement prior to invading Iran, refused to reinstate it: Iran would not agree to any other course. It is difficult to see how either side could have given way or how the UN negotiator could have found a means of clearing the path and proceeding with the translation of the cease-fire into permanent peace through the full implementation of Resolution 598. It may well require the full weight of the Security Council to shift the log jam. Meanwhile, with the two armies arrayed against each other and with Iran still in post-revolutionary turmoil, a resumption of hostilities, although unlikely, could not have been excluded. Peace seemed far away.

In more general terms Iran's standing in the United Nations has not improved over the past ten years in spite of the strong ingredients of 'anti-imperialism' and non-alignment in the revolution. From the hostage crisis of 1979–80 to the ferocious reaction to Salman Rushdie's book *The Satanic Verses* in 1989, Iran's behaviour has consistently violated internationally accepted norms and has alienated even intrinsically sympathetic states in the Non-Aligned Movement, let alone in the West. The hostility of the majority of the Arab Group has contributed further to Iran's isolation in the UN which is, at the time of writing, more pronounced than at any time under the monarchy. Not only did this concatenation of circumstances help to sustain Iraq's favoured position throughout the conflict, but Iran is also now under pressure from the UN Human Rights system over alleged mass arrests and executions. It will not be until the revolution settles down and an Iranian government adopts a policy of reconciliation with the outside world that she will regain her proper place in the international community.

APPENDIX A

Resolution 582 (1986) of 24 February 1986

The Security Council,

Having considered the question entitled 'The situation between Iran and Iraq',

Recalling that the Security Council has been seized with the question of the situation between Iran and Iraq for almost six years and that decisions have been taken thereon,

Deeply concerned about the prolongation of the conflict between the two countries resulting in heavy losses of human lives and considerable material damage and endangering peace and security,

Recalling the provisions of the Charter and in particular the obligation of all Member States to settle their international disputes by peaceful means in such a manner that international peace and security and justice are not endangered,

Noting that both the Islamic Republic of Iran and Iraq are parties to the Protocol for the Prohibition of the Use in War of Asphyxiating, Poisonous or Other Gases, and of Bacteriological Methods of Warfare signed at Geneva on 17 June 1925,*

Emphasizing the principle of the inadmissibility of the acquisition of territory by force,

Taking note of the efforts of mediation pursued by the Secretary-General,

1 *Deplores* the initial acts which gave rise to the conflict between the Islamic Republic of Iran and Iraq and deplores the continuation of the conflict;

2 *Also deplores* the escalation of the conflict, especially territorial incursions, the bombing of purely civilian population centres, attacks on neutral shipping or civilian aircraft, the violation of international humanitarian law and other laws of armed conflict and, in particular, the use of chemical weapons contrary to obligations under the 1925 Geneva Protocol;

3 *Calls upon* the Islamic Republic of Iran and Iraq to observe an immediate cease-fire, a cessation of all hostilities on land, at sea and in the air and withdrawal of all forces to the internationally recognized boundaries without delay;

4 *Urges* that a comprehensive exchange of prisoners-of-war be completed within a short period after the cessation of hostilities in co-operation with the International Committee of the Red Cross;

5 *Calls upon* both parties to submit immediately all aspects of the conflict to mediation or to any other means of peaceful settlement of disputes;

6 *Requests* the Secretary-General to continue his on-going efforts, to assist the two parties to give effect to this resolution and to keep the Council informed;

7 *Calls upon* all other States to exercise the utmost restraint and to refrain from any act which may lead to a further escalation and widening of the conflict and, thus, to facilitate the implementation of the present resolution;

8 *Decides* to remain seized of the matter.

Adopted unanimously at the 2666th meeting

* League of Nations, *Treaty Series*, vol. XCIV (1929), no. 2138, p.65.

APPENDIX B

Resolution 598 (1987) Adopted by the Security Council at its 2750th Meeting on 20 July 1987

The Security Council,

Reaffirming its Resolution 582 (1986),

Deeply concerned that, despite its calls for a cease-fire, the conflict between Iran and Iraq continues unabated, with further heavy loss of human life and material destruction,

Deploring the initiation and continuation of the conflict,

Deploring also the bombing of purely civilian population centres, attacks on neutral shipping or civilian aircraft, the violation of international humanitarian law and other laws of armed conflict, and, in particular, the use of chemical weapons contrary to obligations under the 1925 Geneva Protocol,

Deeply concerned that further escalation and widening of the conflict may take place,

Determined to bring to an end all military actions between Iran and Iraq,

Convinced that a comprehensive, just, honourable and durable settlement should be achieved between Iran and Iraq,

Recalling the provisions of the Charter of the United Nations, and in particular the obligation of all Member States to settle their international disputes by peaceful means in such a manner that international peace and security and justice are not endangered,

Determining that there exists a breach of the peace as regards the conflict between Iran and Iraq,

Acting under Articles 39 and 40 of the Charter of the United Nations,

1 *Demands* that, as a first step towards a negotiated settlement, Iran and Iraq observe an immediate cease-fire, discontinue all military actions on

land, at sea and in the air, and withdraw all forces to the internationally recognized boundaries without delay;

2 *Requests* the Secretary-General to dispatch a team of United Nations observers to verify, confirm and supervize the cease-fire and withdrawal and further requests the Secretary-General to make the necessary arrangements in consultation with the parties and to submit a report thereon to the Security Council;

3 *Urges* that prisoners-of-war be released and repatriated without delay after the cessation of active hostilities in accordance with the third Geneva Convention of 12 August 1949;

4 *Calls upon* Iran and Iraq to co-operate with the Secretary-General in implementing this Resolution and in mediation efforts to achieve a comprehensive, just and honourable settlement, acceptable to both sides, of all outstanding issues, in accordance with the principles contained in the Charter of the United Nations;

5 *Calls upon* all other States to exercise the utmost restraint and to refrain from any act which may lead to further escalation and widening of the conflict, and thus to facilitate the implementation of the present Resolution;

6 *Requests* the Secretary-General to explore, in consultation with Iran and Iraq, the question of entrusting an impartial body with inquiring into responsibility for the conflict and to report to the Security Council as soon as possible;

7 *Recognizes* the magnitude of the damage inflicted during the conflict and the need for reconstruction efforts, with appropriate international assistance, once the conflict is ended and, in this regard, requests the Secretary-General to assign a team of experts to study the question of reconstruction and to report to the Security Council;

8 *Further requests* the Secretary-General to examine, in consultation with Iran and Iraq and with other States of the region, measures to enhance the security and stability of the region;

9 *Requests* the Secretary-General to keep the Security Council informed on the implementation of this Resolution;

10 *Decides* to meet again as necessary to consider further steps to ensure compliance with this Resolution.

2 The United States and Iran, 1981–9

Eric Hooglund

During its eight years in office the administration of President Ronald Reagan failed to develop a consistent policy for dealing with Iran. From outward appearances the policies pursued seemed quite contradictory, vacillating from programmes such as Operation Staunch, an effort to isolate Iran internationally by denying it weapons with which to prosecute its war with Iraq, to the initiative of trying to woo Tehran with secret arms sales and high-level negotiations, and culminating with a policy of military confrontation in the Persian Gulf. This ideologically conservative administration's perceptions of and reactions to regional political developments were largely responsible for the pendulum swinging nature of its Iran policy. Initially, it was necessary to adjust to the reality of the Iranian revolution of 1979, a completely unanticipated event that had transformed a dependable regional ally to a seemingly implacable foe. Owing to its preoccupation with the prolonged hostage crisis, which only ended as Reagan was taking the oath of office, the departing administration of Jimmy Carter had not determined how the Islamic Republic, which castigated the deposed monarchy for alleged subservience to US imperialism, related to historic American policy objectives in the Middle East. Thus, the new administration had to figure out the role of an anti-American Iran *vis-à-vis* three broad goals: containment of Soviet influence; maintaining the security of Israel and protecting US interests in the Persian Gulf.[1]

The Reagan administration probably would have preferred to ignore Iran. The memory of the humiliating hostage crisis was too fresh and the continuing anti-American rhetoric emanating from Tehran too irritating. To confine the country, whose government was perceived as irrational and unpredictable, to the back pages of low-circulation papers seemed attractive following the prolonged national trauma of the hostage crisis. Nevertheless, four important reasons made it unfeasible to ignore Iran. First, was the perception that the country was strategically located in terms of vital US interests, i.e. the abundant petroleum resources of the Persian Gulf region. This was not a view unique to conservatives, but one shared by their liberal opponents. Indeed, it was the liberal Democratic Carter administration that had proclaimed 'any attempt by an outside force to gain control of the Persian Gulf region will be regarded as an assault on the vital interests of the United States' and 'will be repelled by the use of any means necessary including military force'.[2] While the Reagan administration was ready to repudiate many Democratic programmes and policies, containing perceived Soviet expansion into the Persian Gulf was one policy it enthusiastically embraced.[3]

The second reason why attention remained focused on Iran was the country's proximity to the Soviet Union. Iran shared a long border with the state Reagan himself referred to as the earthly version of the evil empire. In the east Iran also bordered on Afghanistan, which Soviet troops had invaded during the final days of 1979. The Soviet military intervention in Afghanistan had shocked American politicians of diverse ideological persuasions, but for conservatives especially the invasion confirmed their belief in the ultimate aggressive designs of the Soviets. Some conservatives expressed alarm that Moscow would continue its expansionism by invading Iran. When an expected invasion failed to materialize, these idealogues credited the new US resolve with having deterred the Soviets. Given the strong anti-Soviet mindset of the president and his top officials and advisers, it was thus inevitable that a country so strategically located as Iran should be perceived as having a role to play in the containment of the Soviets in Afghanistan. Tehran's persistent denunciations of the Soviet intervention and its provision of support to Afghan groups organizing to resist the invaders were viewed favourably by the new administration that itself was sympathetic to the resistance forces and advocated policies to help them fight the Soviets.

A third reason why Iran could not be ignored was the attitude of the conservative Arab states of the Arabian Peninsula. In Washington's official jargon, these countries and their leaders were termed 'moderates', and there was a well-established tradition of soliciting their views on regional issues. Saudi Arabia, along with pre-revolutionary Iran, had been considered one of the security pillars of US interests in the region. The Iranian revolution had greatly distressed Saudi and other Arab leaders who complained privately that the United States had failed to protect an ally (the former Shah) during a major – and ultimately fatal – political crisis. Since the Shah's overthrow, these Arab rulers had interpreted Iran's pronouncements about the need for Islamic revolution throughout the Persian Gulf region as very real threats to their own security. The Reagan administration shared the view that its predecessor had abandoned the Shah of Iran when his regime was threatened, and it was determined not to repeat history; if the friendly regimes of these oil-rich countries were endangered by Islamic political forces, the United States had to have the political courage and military means to protect them.

The final reason why the Reagan administration found it impossible to ignore Iran was Lebanon. At the outset of the Reagan presidential term no one thought of associating Lebanon and Iran. However, Israel's 1982 invasion of Lebanon and the subsequent US military intervention there aggravated the country's sectarian civil war and created political conditions favourable for persistent foreign involvement. Iran became interested in the fate of the indigenous Shia Muslims, who were co-religionists. By the end of 1983, many American officials were convinced that Iran was behind the numerous acts of terrorism perpetuated by Lebanese Shia elements against American and European residents in Lebanon.[4]

Although the administration was not able to ignore Iran in formulating its overall Middle East policy, the fact that Tehran and Washington failed to re-establish diplomatic relations meant the absence of any genuine dialogue between the two countries. At least three important consequences resulted from the lack of normal ties. First, the US did not have any reliable intelligence about domestic political forces and personalities in Iran, a situation that encouraged endless speculation about the policies of purported 'moderates' (i.e. pro-West factions) and 'radicals' (i.e. anti-Western, or pro-Soviet, factions).[5] Second, in terms of an Iran policy the US often found itself reacting to unanticipated international and regional developments that directly or indirectly involved the Islamic Republic. Third, the combination of inadequate knowledge and inappropriate policies contributed to the US and Iran misperceiving each other's intentions, fostered inconsistent US policies, and kept mutual relations generally hostile.

The evolution of Reagan's policies can be appreciated if Iranian policy is examined during each of six phases. Since policy toward Iran in the years 1981–9 was inevitably influenced by the Gulf War, these phases correspond to changes in the war situation that stimulated American policy shifts. The first phase began with the inauguration of the Reagan administration in January 1981 and lasted until July 1982. The second phase corresponded with the beginning of Iran's land invasion of Iraq (July 1982) and extended to the terrorist attack on the US Marine barracks in Lebanon in October 1983. The third phase, from October 1983 until June 1985, was the period when the US was most concerned about possible Iranian links to international terrorism. The outstanding characteristic of the fourth phase (1985–7) was Washington's clandestine initiative to engage Iran in substantive dialogue. The fifth phase, from February 1987 to

July 1988, was in sharp contrast to earlier phases inasmuch as the United States actively pursued a military and diplomatic containment of Iran policy. The final phase marked another abrupt, albeit far less dramatic, policy shift as the Reagan administration undertook during its final six months in office a serious but inconclusive re-evaluation of policy toward Iran.

FIRST PHASE, JANUARY 1981 TO JULY 1982

As noted above, the Reagan administration took office simultaneously with the release of the fifty-two US diplomatic and military personnel that Iran had been holding as hostages since November 1979. The fortuitous resolution of the hostage crisis spared the new administration the need to confront an issue that was widely regarded as having been decisive in the political demise of President Carter. Nevertheless, the hostage crisis was a crucial episode in shaping the Reagan vision of Iran as a country ruled by irrational and fanatical forces. Most members of the administration shared a view of Iranian leaders as terrorists and/or sponsors of terrorism. Despite these negative views, the administration did not feel any sense of urgency to formulate policy *vis-à-vis* Iran.

Only four months earlier Iraq had invaded the country and the opposing armies were battling in southwestern Iran. In the early months of 1981 Iran seemed checkmated and incapable of causing mischief. Even though the official US position was that Iraqi forces should withdraw from occupied Iranian territory, the Reagan administration was not interested in expending diplomatic efforts to press this issue at the United Nations or in other forums.[6]

America's Arab allies in the Persian Gulf were not unduly concerned at this time about the war between Iran and Iraq. While the war had not ended as speedily as Iraq had predicted the previous autumn, the fighting did not directly affect the Arab countries of the Gulf and was not interfering with their commercial shipping. Since there were large numbers of Palestinian workers and professionals in all these states, the governments were much more concerned about the political impact of Israel's air raids on Palestinian refugee camps in Lebanon. These views were made clear to Secretary of State Alexander Haig in the spring when he undertook state visits to Saudi Arabia and other countries, with the objective of enlisting broad support for a strategic consensus directed against the Soviet Union. Arab leaders such as the Kings of Jordan and Saudi Arabia stressed their belief that Israel, rather than Iran, posed the most serious threat to regional security.[7]

Washington's primary preoccupation, too, was neither Iran nor the Gulf

War, but rather developments in Afghanistan, Iran's eastern neighbour. A Marxist *coup d'état* had taken place there in April 1978 and Soviet troops had entered the country in December 1979 to end the damaging infighting and to help the new regime suppress a growing resistance movement. Before coming to power, leading Reagan officials such as Secretary of State Alexander Haig and Ambassador to the United Nations Jeanne Kirkpatrick had chided the Democrats for allowing the Shah's regime to fall, arguing that the US lack of resolve in protecting the Shah had convinced the Soviets they could act against American interests with impunity.[8] By 1981, however, Reagan officials did not necessarily see Iran as a strategic loss. Some of them were impressed by Tehran's denunciations of the Soviet invasion and its support of several Afghan resistance groups. Such officials believed the shared US and Iranian interest in opposing Soviet expansionism in Afghanistan could be built upon for a gradual normalizing of relations between Tehran and Washington.

Iran's assistance to Afghan resistance fighters and refugees (several hundred Afghan refugees were entering Iran each day in early 1981) reinforced a view that moderate politicians were trying to regain influence over the country's policies. President Bani Sadr, who had been elected in 1980, was widely perceived as an Iranian leader sympathetic to the West. Although the Carter administration had been disappointed in Bani Sadr's inability to resolve the hostage crisis, the Reagan administration hoped his triumph in the apparent competition with the Prime Minister and Majlis for control of decision making would strengthen the political position of the pro-Western moderates. Thus, there was a general readiness in Washington to bide time *vis-à-vis* Iran until the power struggle in Tehran worked itself out.

The generally complacent attitude about Iran began to change before the end of the administration's first year in office. First, Bani Sadr and the moderates were ousted from power in June 1981, a political move that led to an armed uprising by some political groups who were suppressed in a brutal reign of terror. Then in late September, Iranian forces scored their first major victory by breaking the year-long Iraqi siege of the oil refining city of Abadan. This unexpected development unsettled Arab leaders in the Gulf, who were even more startled four days later when Iranian aircraft bombed oil installations in Kuwait, apparently as a tactical ploy to discourage pan-Arab support for Iraq. This was followed by the assassination in Cairo of Egyptian President Anwar Sadat by soldiers belonging to a Muslim political group claiming inspiration from the Iranian model of Islamic Revolution. Finally in December, Bahraini officials announced the uncovering of a major plot to overthrow the government. The Prime Minister of Bahrain subsequently accused Iran of complicity in the abortive *coup d'état* and sounded the theme that eventually would be embraced by most Arab leaders and the Reagan administration: that Iran through its incitement of local Shia and fundamentalist Muslim populations constituted the main threat to the security of the Persian Gulf and the Middle East.[9]

Iran's continuing battlefield successes during the first five months of 1982 riveted the attention of the Gulf on the war. Washington, however, was preoccupied with the situation in the eastern Mediterranean region, where Israel and the Lebanon-based Palestine Liberation Organization were observing an increasingly shaky cease-fire. An Israeli invasion of Lebanon seemed imminent in the spring, and finally happened in June. The Israeli–Palestinian war in Lebanon dominated American diplomacy and international headlines for three months. During this time, Iraqi forces withdrew from almost all of Iranian territory they were still occupying and Iran launched its own invasion of Iraq.

SECOND PHASE, JULY 1982 TO OCTOBER 1983

Iran's July 1982 invasion of Iraq changed the balance of power in the Iran–Iraq War and forced a re-evaluation of US policy. However, since the sense of crisis surrounding events in Lebanon did not begin to subside until October 1982, the administration's reaction to developments in the Persian Gulf was considerably delayed. By the time Washington was prepared to devote serious attention to this region, Iraq had succeeded in containing the Iranian advance to the border marshes. Although Iran appeared to have the upper hand in the war, Iraq had demonstrated an ability to withstand the offensives. The military situation encouraged a view that the war was stalemated. Many officials believed such an outcome was not necessarily negative in terms of US interests. According to this line of reasoning, a victory by either country could be potentially destabilizing to regional security.

The Reagan administration was still neutral *vis-à-vis* Iran and Iraq because suspicions of Baghdad generally were as strong as those of Tehran. Negative attitudes about Iraq derived from years of American–Iraqi hostility. Ever since it had come to power in 1968, the Ba'th government had been regarded as a radical (i.e. anti-American) regime on account of its support for the PLO and denunciations of Israel. Additionally, many of the conservatives associated with the administration considered Iraq, which had signed a 1972 treaty of friendship with the Soviet Union, to be Moscow's surrogate in the region. Conservatives and liberals alike had long believed Iraq sponsored terrorism in the Middle East. US antagonism toward Iraq was so strong that even when Israel undertook the unprecedented action in 1981 of bombing a nuclear reactor construction site near Baghdad, the administration, with the support of Congress, had done little more than issue an ineffective verbal protest. Nevertheless, attitudes about Iraq were in the process of changing. The regime of Saddam Hussein had been gradually aligning its foreign policies with pro-Western Arab countries such as Egypt, Jordan, and Saudi Arabia, and these American regional allies were influencing Washington to view Iraq more positively.

Unlike the US, the Arabs in the Persian Gulf were alarmed by the reversal in military roles and felt threatened by the war's continuance. They tried to convince the administration that Iraq wanted to negotiate an end to the conflict. They argued that Iran was unnecessarily prolonging the war in order to achieve a punishing victory. They viewed the prospects of an Iranian victory with dismay and hinted darkly at the terrible consequences in the area if Iran were triumphant and Iraq defeated. The Arabs in the Gulf believed the ideal solution to the war would be a negotiated peace in which neither of the two regional superpowers achieved a major victory nor suffered a humiliating defeat.[10] The Kuwaitis and Saudis were especially vocal in expressing these views in late 1982 and early 1983. Since Kuwait and Saudi Arabia were regarded as allies, there was sympathy within the administration for their proposals. Additionally, the US' continued involvement in Lebanon, where a contingent of Marines had been sent as part of a multinational peacekeeping force, made the prospects of a negotiated settlement to the Iran–Iraq War attractive. Thus, in the spring of 1983 the administration adopted the Arab suggestion of international pressure as a means of coaxing Iran toward negotiations, Iraq had already announced its willingness to negotiate, by formulating a policy, publicly proclaimed as Operation Staunch, to dissuade neutral countries from selling arms to the belligerent undertaking offensives in the war, i.e. Iran. The policy was not successful in terms of halting arms sales, not even those to Iran from US allies. Operation Staunch did, however, satisfy friendly Arab regimes who wanted Washington to pay some attention to the war. Conversely it provoked Iranian antagonism and confirmed persistent suspicions in Tehran that the US supported Iraq.

Although Operation Staunch tilted US policy towards Iraq, the administration was not ready to accept the full implications of the policy shift. Despite genuine misgivings about Iran's motives in the Persian Gulf, some officials remained optimistic that Tehran's and Washington's mutual interests in getting Soviet troops out of Afghanistan would eventually facilitate better relations. Even as policy analysts were in the process of planning Operation Staunch, Iran had initiated a major crackdown on leftist parties. The Tudeh, the country's oldest Marxist party, was banned and most of its leaders arrested. Some of those arrested were featured on state television where they confessed publicly to having been spies for the Soviet Union. These developments in Tehran cheered the anti-communist ideologues of the Reagan administration and revived hopes that moderate political forces were regaining control of the government. During the summer discussions took place within the State Department on ways to encourage better ties with Iran, but no conclusive policies were formulated.

THIRD PHASE, OCTOBER 1983 TO MAY 1985

The administration's hopes of a more moderate Iran were dashed as a consequence of developments in Lebanon. In response to the international outcry following Israel's occupation of Beirut in September 1982, the US had dispatched 1,000 Marines to Lebanon as part of a US-sponsored multinational peacekeeping force. Within a year, Lebanese Shia militias had come to regard the Marines as partisans supporting the rival Lebanese Christian militias. Skirmishes between Shia militia units and Marines increased in September and October, and culminated on 23 October with the deaths of 241 Marines when a suicide driver ploughed an explosives-laden truck into the Marines' Beirut headquarters.[11]

The Shia militias received moral support, and probably financial and military assistance as well, from their co-religionists in Iran. Some officials, including the Secretaries of Defence and State, were unable to believe that the Lebanese Shia had legitimate grievances or that they acted independently. In their view the Shia militia were terrorists directed from Tehran. As the situation in Lebanon deteriorated, blame and hostility were focused increasingly on Iran.[12]

Following the withdrawal of the Marines from Lebanon in February 1984, a new threat to US and Western interests emerged in the guise of kidnappings of American and European citizens working in Beirut. A total of seven Americans were abducted and held as hostages in a fifteen-month period. The groups claiming responsibility for these abductions generally identified themselves as affiliated with a Shia militia group known as Hizbullah. Iran, through a contingent of its Revolutionary Guards who had been stationed in Lebanon since the summer of 1982, had direct contacts with Hizbullah and was even credited with having organized the group. The Reagan administration was distressed by the turn of events in Lebanon, but it had no effective counter strategy to the new wave of terrorism other than verbal condemnation.

The most serious incident was the March 1984 kidnapping of the CIA station chief William Buckley: memories of Iran's holding of American hostages for 444 days were revived. Alarmed officials were convinced that

Iran was behind the abductions, and rumours permeated the national security agencies of Buckley's incarceration and torture in Tehran. Unable to appreciate how Lebanon's sectarian intolerance was spawning religious violence in all communities, the administration tended to attribute the rapid breakdown of law and order there to Iranian machinations. The US became increasingly concerned, even fearful, about Iran's spread of Islamic revolution throughout the Middle East. These fears encouraged a containment of Iran mentality and tended to inhibit the kind of rational discussions essential for the development of policies that would permit Washington to take advantage of diplomatic opportunities for rebuilding its relationship with Iran.

The main beneficiary of Washington's increasing anti-Iranian hostility was Iraq. Saddam Hussein's efforts to cultivate a new image of Iraq as a member of the camp of moderate Arabs had begun to reap diplomatic dividends. Significantly, Iraq was removed from the list of countries that the US had identified as sponsors of international terrorism. This paved the way for greatly expanded economic and political contacts, a process that culminated in November 1984 with the re-establishment of formal relations between Baghdad and Washington after a seventeen-year break. Iraq also escaped international censure when it initiated the 'tanker war' in the Persian Gulf by attacking Iranian and neutral shipping carrying Iran's sea-borne trade. When Iran responded to these attacks by launching its own assaults on Kuwaiti and Saudi ships that it said carried goods for Iraq, the United States expressed concern over Tehran's interference with the freedom of commerce in the Gulf and through the strategic Strait of Hormuz. The American response to this new threat was to send naval ships to patrol the Arabian Sea, the body of water into which empties the Gulf of Oman and the Persian Gulf. Aircraft based on these ships were sent on reconnaissance flights over the Gulf. By early 1985, few people doubted that US policy had definitely tilted towards Iraq.

FOURTH PHASE, JUNE 1985 TO FEBRUARY 1987

Despite the obvious emergence of an anti-Iran bias in US policy, there were officials within the National Security Council and the CIA who believed that the isolation of Iran was potentially harmful to long-term American interests. They continued to view the country as the region's strategic prize on account of its proximity both to the oil-rich Persian Gulf states and to the Soviet Union. They believed the Islamic Republic was naturally anti-Soviet and expressed concern that current policies antagonized its leaders and could drive Iran to seek the very alliance with Moscow that the United States wished to prevent. They foresaw a power struggle following the inevitable death of the aged leader, Ayatollah Khomeini, and wanted the United States to position itself in a way that it would benefit from the new political climate. The United States could help strengthen the influence of Iran's moderates, they argued, by selling desperately needed weapons to the Islamic Republic. If the moderates demonstrated their ability to obtain arms, they could more easily consolidate power after Khomeini, would be receptive to normalizing relations with the US, and Soviet ambitions would be thwarted.[13]

The circulation of these ideas within the administration during June and July 1985 was controversial because they were in such stark contrast to the basic thrust of Iran policy as it had developed over the preceding eighteen months. Influential members of the administration lined up on opposing sides to argue for (NSC Adviser Robert McFarlane and CIA Director William Casey) or against (Secretary of State George Shultz and Secretary of Defence Caspar Weinberger) a fundamental policy change. Even the views of Israel, the United States' closest ally in the Middle East, were solicited by proponents of a new policy because Israel advocated better relations with Iran and may have originated the idea of selling it weapons.[14] Iran itself contributed to the internal debate when it used its influence among Lebanese Shia to secure the release of a hijacked American airliner and its passengers.[15] Nevertheless, the administration failed to achieve a consensus on changing the direction of policy. Consequently, a two-track policy was adopted. The public policy remained one of opposition to Iran's continued prosecution of the war with Iraq, involvement in Lebanon, and export of revolution. Simultaneously, the NSC initiated a clandestine policy that had the objective of seeking a *rapprochement* with the Islamic Republic. The main feature of this secretive initiative was a US willingness to sell Tehran weapons, ostensibly for defensive uses only, in return for Iran's assistance in getting the release of American citizens being held as hostages in Lebanon.

An American hostage actually was released in September 1985 after Israel, with US approval, had shipped missiles to Iran. Following a second and third shipment of arms, hopes that more hostages in Lebanon would be freed were not fulfilled. The general disillusionment with the secret initiative almost caused its cancellation in December. Officials who had opposed the policy argued that Iran's failure to get the hostages freed was evidence of its unreliability and urged an end to contacts. Proponents insisted that the intent of weapons sales was to establish a political opening to Tehran and not to trade arms for hostages. The secret policy was continued only because it received the personal sanction of the President. Nevertheless, during all of the next year (1986) just two additional hostages were released.

The more significant aspect of the covert initiative was not the haggling over arms for hostages, but the covert meetings that culminated in McFarlane's secret trip to Tehran in May 1986. Although the Iranians permitted the visit to take place, albeit under conditions of strict secrecy, and authorized representatives from the Majlis and the Prime Minister's office to talk with McFarlane's delegation, they were not as prepared for substantive, high-level discussions as the Americans had anticipated. McFarlane had hoped to get the hostages issue cleared up permanently so that talks could focus on other issues of mutual concern. The Iranians, however, were unable or unwilling to use their influence to get the hostages in Lebanon freed. The results of this first official dialogue between the Reagan administration and the Islamic Republic were thus disappointing. Nevertheless, the fact that officials of both governments had actually conducted talks was an important precedent and set the stage for future continuation of contacts.

Prior to the implementation of the two-track policy, some administration officials had been contemplating strategies to contain Iranian radicalism. Their conviction that Iran supported or even incited all manner of political turmoil in the Persian Gulf and Middle East had not been shaken; even though from mid-1985 until the end of 1986 plans to deal with Iran-inspired mischief were necessarily held in abeyance. Initially, it seemed appropriate to stop focusing on Iran because the regional situation, apart from the war in the Gulf, was relatively calm. In Lebanon, no additional Americans were taken hostage after June 1985. In the Persian Gulf, Tehran was diplomatically courting the Arab states. Relations with Saudi Arabia had improved to such an extent that each country's Foreign Minister made an official visit to his counterpart's capital.[16] Under the circumstances, Arab pressures on Washington to do something about the war decreased considerably. The United States retained the goodwill of the Arabs by continuing to pursue Operation Staunch; the Arabs were unaware, of course, that the Americans also were secretly abetting Israel's sale of American-made missiles and spare parts to Iran.

The Iran–Iraq War had experienced intermittent periods of high- and low-intensity fighting since its beginning in 1980. The summer and early autumn of 1985 was one of the phases of relative calm, at least on the ground. By November, however, both sides had resumed major offensives. Iran generally maintained its superior strategic position, and, in February 1986, achieved one of its most important victories, the capture of Iraq's Fao Peninsula. To compensate for its battlefield losses, Iraq intensified the air and sea warfare, theatres in which it had an advantage over Iran. As the volume of Iran-related shipping hit by bombs and missiles increased (a total of sixty-six in 1986 compared with only thirty-three the previous year), Iran stepped up its own assaults on commercial vessels calling at ports on the Arab side of the Persian Gulf. Iran attacked forty-five ships during the year, three times the number hit in 1985. Thus, throughout 1986 fears mounted in the Gulf about the likelihood of an Iraqi defeat and the consequences of an Iranian victory.

The November 1986 revelations about the secret US–Iran contacts and arms sales came at a most inopportune time. Saudi Arabia and Kuwait were trying to persuade Washington to intervene more forcefully to protect freedom of navigation in the Gulf. They naturally were stunned to learn that the United States was selling Iran arms while discussing with them means to contain Iranian aggressiveness. Their sense of betrayal was as acute as Washington's sense of embarrassment. The State Department, which had consistently objected to the secret initiative, believed the folly of the two-tract policy had been exposed with disastrous consequences for the reputation of the United States. Proponents of the covert policy were equally dismayed by the revelations, but they also hoped to salvage the fragile relationship with Iran. For several weeks they sought to keep the now public initiative alive, but further revelations that profits from the sale of arms to Iran had been diverted to fund the Nicaraguan Contras in violation of a Congressional ban, brought the whole policy into disrepute. By the beginning of 1987, the dismissals and resignations of senior personnel associated with the Iran initiative had left the policy without any influential defenders in the administration, and thus it died unmourned.

FIFTH PHASE, FEBRUARY 1987 TO JULY 1988

In early 1987, officials who had been advocating the containment of Iran for three years got an opportunity to formulate a more activist policy. The impetus came from reports that Kuwait was negotiating with Moscow an agreement to reflag some of its oil tankers with the Soviet hammer and sickle as a means to protect the vessels from Iranian attacks. Kuwait had also requested permission to re-register part of its tanker fleet under the American flag, but initial administration support for this proposal had not been enthusiastic. When the request was first made in the Autumn of 1986, there was no evidence that Kuwaiti ships were being singled out for attacks at any greater rate than those of other Arab states. Under these circumstances, policy makers reasoned that allowing Kuwaiti vessels to fly the stars and stripes could make them eligible for protection from the US Navy, a situation that Washington preferred to avoid.[17] News that the Soviets had agreed to assist Kuwait followed by a few weeks' announcements that both Oman and the United Arab Emirates had established diplomatic relations with the Soviet Union led to the perception within the

Reagan administration that Moscow was on the verge of increasing significantly its presence and influence in the Persian Gulf. Questions were no longer raised about the implications of re-flagging Kuwait's ships. Rather, questions focused on what steps could be taken to counter Soviet threats to US prestige and influence. By the end of February the decision was made to accede to the Kuwaiti request; within two weeks the United States had agreed to reflag eleven oil tankers owned by the Kuwaiti government.[18]

In the early spring of 1987 few administration officials anticipated that the reflagging decision would lead to major military intervention in the Persian Gulf or confrontation with Iran. The policy was perceived as an effective means of countering the Soviets, redeeming the US' tarnished reputation among its Arab allies, and generally diverting attention away from the covert policy which was still causing domestic and international embarrassment.[19] From the Iranian perspective, however, the new US policy represented exactly what it did not want to occur: the internationalization of its war with Iraq. Tehran's denunciations of the reflagging helped to firm up Washington's resolve to protect any 'American' ships that might be threatened as they transited the Gulf. By May, when an Iraqi pilot strafed the USS *Stark*, claiming he had mistaken it for an Iranian ship, the administration was ready to blame Iran's rhetoric and attacks on neutral shipping as the cause of the incident. During the following weeks the US found itself reacting to rapidly escalating events which had not been foreseen: mines, believed to have been planted by Iran, were discovered in the waters off the coast of Bahrain and Kuwait; one of the re-flagged Kuwaiti tankers was severely damaged when it struck a mine; mines were discovered in the waters of the Gulf of Oman; and several European allies of the US agreed to dispatch minesweepers and other naval craft to the area. In response to these developments, the US decided to increase significantly its naval presence in the region. By the end of the summer, the US had deployed twenty-eight ships in the Persian Gulf, Gulf of Oman, and Arabian Sea, the largest naval armada it had assembled in one area since the Second World War.

The US military intervention was clearly directed at Iran which Washington accused of interfering with the rights of neutral ships to travel freely in international waters. The recent efforts to woo Tehran were forgotten in a new determination to compel Iran to end its war with Iraq. In tandem with its military policy, the Reagan administration also went on the diplomatic offensive, focusing on the United Nations (UN) where it hoped to garner international support for sanctions against the Islamic Republic. The American UN delegation took the initiative in rewriting a draft resolution that won unanimous Security Council support in July 1987.[20] Resolution 598 called upon Iran and Iraq to follow a step-by-step peace process beginning with a cease-fire and withdrawal of forces to international frontiers; it also provided a mechanism for the Security Council to impose sanctions on whichever country refused to comply. Both Washington and Baghdad assumed Tehran would reject Resolution 598 because Iran, which occupied Iraqi territory along the two countries' common border, had strongly opposed consideration of troop withdrawals as an initial issue in several unsuccessful earlier efforts by third parties to mediate a cease-fire. Although Iraq accepted Resolution 598 immediately, Iran quite unexpectedly declined to accept or reject the resolution. Instead, Tehran expressed its willingness to discuss with the UN Secretary-General the order of implementation of the resolution's separate steps. Washington, which had not foreseen the possibility of such a response, was less than happy with this outcome and tried unsuccessfully to convince the other permanent members of the Security Council to vote on sanctions.

Outwitted by Iran at the UN, the US policy focus turned to the military option. Although the ostensible motivation for the military intervention was to protect neutral shipping, the US Navy made no efforts to protect from Iraqi attacks neutral ships transporting goods to and from Iranian ports. Iran believed the American presence gave Iraq a virtual green light to attack its shipping, a perception that was reinforced by the major escalation in the number of Iraqi attacks beginning in September 1987. Iran responded by increasing the numbers of its retaliatory strikes although it was careful to avoid ships flying the American flag. Nevertheless, the significant increase in military activity in the Persian Gulf inevitably involved Iran and the United States in direct confrontations. Iran fared badly in skirmishes between its forces and American vessels during the autumn and spring, primarily because its poorly equipped navy was no real match for the US armada. The most serious incident occurred in July 1988, when the USS *Vincennes*, following an exchange of fire with Iranian gunboats that had attacked a Danish tanker, mistook an Iran Air civilian passenger jet for an attacking F-14 and shot it down killing all 290 people aboard.

SIXTH PHASE, JULY 1988 TO JANUARY 1989

Iran's unexpected announcement on 18 July 1988 that it would accept UN Security Council Resolution 598 surprised the Reagan administration which was discussing how and when to respond to a variety of terrorist incidents that officials believed Iran would undertake in retaliation for the shooting down of the Iran Air plane. Once the reality of this unexpected development had sunk in, the administration attributed Iran's decision to the success of its own policy of military intervention. Feeling a sense of victory, the administration agreed to support the UN which had responsibility under the resolution for organizing a multinational observer force to patrol the cease-fire lines; a military group actually was organized quickly and dispatched to Iran and Iraq in August. US officials were not ready, however, to order a sudden withdrawal of the American armada. They reasoned that the naval presence was necessary because the cease-fire was a temporary measure and threats to free navigation in the Gulf existed as long as Baghdad and Tehran refrained from negotiating a comprehensive peace agreement.

By the time the cease-fire came into effect (mid-August 1988), the Reagan administration was in its last months of office. Despite the cessation of fighting and the start of UN-mediated peace talks, there was no mood within the administration to consider a reappraisal of policy toward Iran. Even though the President himself had supported the initiative of 1985–6, probably because he hoped to include a political opening to Iran as part of his legacy, the political damage of the Iran-Contra scandal had left him with little enthusiasm to tackle Iran. The attitude during the final weeks of the Reagan presidency was similar to that in the early weeks eight years ago: to ignore Iran as much as possible. In the intervening years Iran had been an important focus of US policy in the Middle East, but the net result of eight years of reacting to Iran was that the Reagan administration left office with an Iran even more hostile toward the United States than when its term started. Nevertheless, that was not a subject on which officials dwelled. They were content that the Iran–Iraq War was over, or at least in a state of respite, and quite willing to leave the seemingly intractable problem of normalizing relations to a new administration.

3 The Soviet Union and Iran, 1979–89

Manshour Varasteh

Iran derives much of its geo-political importance in the Middle East from its position as a neighbour of the Soviet Union. Their mutual borders stretch for approximately 1690 km (1,050 miles),[1] a critical factor of Soviet foreign policy in the light of the historical Soviet preoccupation with border security and the various ethnic and Muslim minorities whose homelands straddle the border. The strategic value of Moscow's relations with Tehran lie to a large extent in Iran's outlets onto the Persian Gulf and its oil (and natural gas) production and export capacity. It has been said that Iran is to the Soviet Union what Mexico is to the United States – a 'backyard' neighbour.

In the decades before the Iranian revolution, the Soviet Union had cultivated Iranian trade and joint ventures, notably in chemicals, mineral prospecting and agriculture. In 1970 a fifteen-year trade agreement provided for natural gas to be sold to the Soviet Union from Iran in return for Soviet investment in and expansion of the Isfahan Steel Mill. The relationship was, however, limited by Iran's increasing ideological and political proximity to US interests in the region. As the Shah directed Iran increasingly into the US' sphere of influence, Moscow was faced with the foreign policy dilemmas inherent in the superpower struggle for 'clients' and influence within the Middle East region as a whole.

As internal turmoil developed within Iran during 1978, Moscow chose to take a cautious line, refraining from open criticism of the Shah yet clearly in sympathy with the 'revolutionary' opposition. At the same time the Soviet Union was anxious to prevent any repetition of the 1953 CIA intervention which re-established the Shah's reign and determined his pro-Western orientation. On 19 November, an official Soviet statement with regard to the events in Iran reported that:

> The Soviet Union, which maintains traditional, neighbourly relations with Iran, resolutely states that it is against foreign interference in Iran's

internal affairs by any one, in any form and under any pretext.

The events taking place, these constitute a purely internal affair, and the questions involved in them should be decided by the Iranians themselves.[2]

Furthermore:

It must be made clear that any interference, let alone military intervention in the affairs of Iran – a state which has a common frontier with the Soviet Union – would be regarded by the USSR as a matter affecting its security interests.[3]

By late 1978 to early 1979, however, the Soviet Union decided that it was time to come out clearly on the side of the Iranian opposition. They began to emphasize the anti-imperialist nature of the opposition and the Soviet media started to attack the Shah, denouncing him as a corrupt and brutal dictator who had oppressed the Iranian people.[4] Evidently the increasingly obvious instability of the Pahlavi regime presented the Soviet Union with a good chance in terms of the possibility of undermining American influence and prestige in the region. According to one Western observer:

At some point between the appointment of the military government in early November and the second week in December, when the chances of the Shah's survival began to be questioned in the Soviet media, Moscow had come to the conclusion that it must prepare itself for a possible change of regime in Iran.[5]

EXPANDING RELATIONS 1979–82

To some extent the Soviet Union was as unprepared as the United States for the new regime which took power after the revolution in Iran. The prospect of an Islamic fundamentalist entity on its back doorstep was not entirely welcome, but the strategic and economic losses which it represented for the US most certainly were. The US lost its 'Gulf Policeman' and with it a vital network of electronic monitoring and information gathering stations positioned on the Iran–Soviet border. More intangible, but perhaps more importantly, its reliability and prestige as a superpower patron suffered serious setbacks in terms of credibility. In zero-sum terms, the US' loss was a definite gain for the Soviet Union. The Soviet conclusion was summed up thus:

The reality today is that whatever the outcome of Iran's internal political struggle, which is of unprecedented scale, Washington will hardly be able to count on continuing to use that country as a reliable guardian of US Imperialism's interests.[6]

Anti-American slogans put forward by the Islamic Republic encouraged the hope for the Soviet Union that Moscow could step in and fill the gap left by America. It therefore based its foreign policy towards Iran on the following two premises:

1 The Soviet Union considered the new regime in Tehran to be fundamentally anti-imperialist and therefore was a possible instrument for Soviet interests in the region.
2 That the Soviet Union should avoid repeating the mistakes made with the Mossadeq government (1951–3) when their opposition to a regime which was not wholly to their own taste had made that regime vulnerable to ultimate CIA intervention.

The path chosen by the Soviet Union to capitalize on the new revolutionary government was to provide support, and channel influence through, the Tudeh (Communist) Party. Under the Shah's regime the Tudeh Party had been illegal but the revolution provided it with the opportunity of once more moving to the political centre stage. For the Soviet Union it represented a neat way of combining ideological preference with political necessity.

All was not well, however, for the Soviet Union as Bazargan's government appeared to be making overtures to the West. Their suspicions were raised by the meetings of Iran's Foreign Minister, Ibrahim Yazdi, and US Secretary of State, Cyrus Vance in October 1979 and between Bazargan himself and Zbigniew Brzezinski (President Carter's National Security Adviser) in November 1979 in Algiers.[7]

On 3 November 1979, Bazargan's government unilaterally cancelled Items 5 and 6 of the Agreement signed in 1921 between the Soviet government and Iran. This treaty authorized the Soviet Union to occupy Iranian soil if another foreign army invaded or occupied that country. As part of the new 'neither East nor West' foreign policy orientation, Bazargan also cancelled the 1959 Treaty between Iran and the USA.[8]

Tensions were exacerbated by disputes between Iran and the Soviet Union over the Kurdish ethnic question.[9] Tehran accused the Soviet Union of stirring up trouble among the Kurds on its norther borders and of sending arms and back-up support to the Kurdish Democratic Party (KDP). Abdol Rahman Ghasemlou, leader of the KDP, denied any supply of arms was forthcoming from the Soviet Union, but welcomed Soviet support for Kurdish autonomy:

We have 50 kilometres of common border with the Soviet Union, where 20,000 Kurds live mostly in Armenistan. We have natural mutual concern and sympathy with all Kurds anywhere, but we are an Iranian party. The Soviets are our friends and we need their political support, but only political.[10]

On 12 June 1979, the Soviet Ambassador in Tehran, Vladimir Vinogrado, met with Khomeini and personally denied any Soviet intervention in Iran.[11] The denial was repeated after Khomeini openly criticized the USSR for its support of leftist political groupings on 31 August, this time by the Iranian Ambassador to Moscow, Mohammed Mokry, who announced that, 'So far there was no proof of Soviet intervention in Kurdistan'.[12]

An attempt was made by the Soviet Union to restore goodwill to the relationship in November 1979 when radical students occupied the US Embassy in Tehran, taking the resident staff as hostages. The Soviet Union hoped to capitalize on the anti-imperialist elements among the students[13] and their antipathy for the Bazargan government. Indeed, the hostage issue was eventually to lead to the resignation of Bazargan, the liquidation of his government and its replacement by the Revolutionary Council.[14] Ironically, Moscow was aligning itself with the most reactionary elements of the revolution, those most clearly opposed to secularism and modernization; clear evidence of national interest taking precedence over ideological commitments. At this point, however, these reactionary elements had much in common with the virulently anti-Western Tudeh. The position was succinctly stated by the Tudeh leader, Kianoori in 1980:

As long as we keep the hostages we will prevent a normalisation of relations with the US, a condition which some Iranian politicians are dreaming of.[15]

Indeed, what could have suited the Soviet Union better?

This hopeful innovation in Soviet–Iran relations was to be severely tested by the Soviet invasion of Afghanistan in December 1979. For Iran, which bordered both countries, the invasion caused considerable alarm, creating the possibility of a similar Soviet attack on the Islamic Republic. The new regime was well aware of the Soviet desire for access to warm-water naval facilities as well as the strategic gains that could be made from control over the Strait of Hormuz.

Yet parallel to its fears, came the opportunity for Iran to unite with the Afghanistan resistance and establish itself as a leader of the Pan-Islamic Movement. Despite the knowledge that there was little that Iran could really do to save Afghanistan from occupation, Tehran became still more vocal in its anti-Soviet (and anti-American) sentiments. As the Iranian–Soviet differences escalated, Foreign Minister Gotbzadeh announced the closure on 2 July of the Iranian Consulate in Leningrad.

Simultaneously the Soviet Consulate in Rasht (at the centre of the Guillan Province where the Tudeh Party were considered to be most influential) was closed.[16]

Iran also joined in the boycott of the Olympic Games in Moscow as a protest against the invasion and occupation of Afghanistan.

THE IRAN–IRAQ WAR

The Gulf War presented a series of severe dilemmas for the Soviet Union, preoccupied as it was with the war in Afghanistan and problems in Poland.

Having cultivated both Iran and Iraq as assets in the region, it was far from keen on the development of a polarization among the Arab states, replacing the previous alignment of Arab states and USSR versus the United States and Israel. Moreover, it was clear to the Soviet Union that the United States would be quick to exploit the war with some form of intervention in the region under the excuse of containing the conflict.

While the Soviet Union was far from happy at the prospect of a victorious Islamic entity on its southern borders, inciting the Muslim minorities of the USSR, it was still less enthusiastic about a Western-backed Iraqi victory which would make the prize of a regionally powerful Iran under a Soviet umbrella impossible to attain.

Thus, while the Soviet Union expressed concerned neutrality in the war, it tended in the early phases to favour the Iranian side while emphasizing that only the United States could benefit from continued hostilities.[17]

According to Moscow:

> Iran was the more important country and that its potential gain or loss would lead to fundamental change in the geo-strategic environment in the area.[18]

As a sign of goodwill towards the Islamic Republic, the Soviet Union halted arms sales to Iraq and offered arms shipments to Iran. Despite verbal expressions of gratitude to the USSR for its stated neutrality and its support of Iranian rights to territorial integrity, Iran was not particularly impressed since it had already side-stepped the need for arms from the Soviet Union by receiving shipments from Soviet allies like Syria, Libya and North Korea. Moscow's concern at what it saw as a move towards the West by the government of Bani Sadr was manifested typically in anti-Bani Sadr broadcasts by Moscow Radio's[19] Persian section. Bani Sadr and his government remained, however, suspicious of the motives behind the Soviet gestures of support in terms of arms supplies and declarations of neutrality, and wary of the political obligations that might accompany any arms deals.

It is worth mentioning that Soviet favouring of the Iranian line was as much due to Soviet disenchantment with the regime of Saddam Hussein as with warmth for that of Tehran. Saddam Hussein had shown a worrying tendency to encourage Western support. The Soviet Ambassador to Iran was quoted as saying:

> But we are also keen to achieve the political result that is important to you (Iran) – Saddam Hussein's downfall . . . he shows all the symptoms of the evil syndrome which seized the Egyptian President Sadat in 1975.[20]

If Soviet efforts did not pay off in the political field, they can be said to have met with more success in the economic sphere. By 1981, Iranian imports from the Soviet Union, which had not exceeded 6 per cent during the Shah's reign, reached 15 per cent, while 21 per cent of Iranian total imports came via either the Caspian Sea or the Soviet Union. In 1981 USSR trade with Iran reached a record total of $1,100 million. Iran exported 15 million barrels per day of crude oil to the Soviet Union as well as quantities of lead, copper and fruit. Exports of natural gas, however, suffered since Moscow refused to pay the prices set by Tehran.[21]

In February 1982, Iran and the Soviet Union signed a trade agreement under which the Soviet Union was to build two new gas power-stations at Ahvaz and Isfahan. Meanwhile Iranian trade with Eastern Europe was also flourishing with one deal with Romania alone being worth $1,000 million.

STAGE TWO: 1982–4 (GROWING STRAINS)

It became clear towards the end of 1982 that the Soviet Union and Iran had entered a complex game whereby both sought to advance their own interests through covert acknowledgement of one another's needs. The Soviet Union was not unaware of the arms trading between Iran and its own client states (Syria, Libya and North Korea). Indeed the rejection of the Soviet offer of arms in October 1980 was not the end of the Soviet involvement in arms sales to Iran. Its acceptance of the participation of its clients in such deals provided it with a lever over Iran. Furthermore, the Soviet Union did actually provide material support for Iran in the form of jet-fuel supplies. It guaranteed a peaceful border so that Iran could concentrate on its own borders with Iraq. The USSR also supplied satellite pictures of the war front which included the Iraqi positions.

In return, the Islamic Republic paid a minimum price of restraint in its dealings with the Afghan resistance.

The period from 1982 to 1984, however, witnessed a growing tension between Iran and the Soviet Union as the former's fortunes in the war were improved. The Soviet Union had grown impatient with Iran's seeming ingratitude for her friendly gestures, while the latter was unhappy at the constant 'wooing' into the Soviet sphere of influence. Indeed, Khomeini's government was increasingly vocal in its hostility towards its northern neighbour, just as Radio Moscow was bitterly critical of Tehran. As Iranian forces moved into Iraqi territory, the Soviet Union began to 'revise' its supposedly neutral position. Soviet arms sales to Iraq recommenced, partly as the Soviet Union grew alarmed at the possibility of a loss of its own oil supplies from Iraq. Additional strains were put on Moscow's relations with Tehran when the Vice Consul of the Soviet Union in Tehran defected to Britain, taking with him documents regarding the activities of the Soviet intelligence community in Tehran and including the names of members of the Tudeh Party. The British handed these documents over to the Iranian government who promptly began to arrest the members of the Tudeh Party and to close the lines of Soviet influence in Tehran. On 6 February 1983 Noredin Kianoori and some other Central Committee members were arrested and accused of spying for the Soviet Union.[22]

Banning the Tudeh Party

The revolution represented an opportunity for the previously banned Tudeh Party to become actively involved in the politics of government in Iran. Having been seriously injured by the arrest of many of its leaders and members after the Shah was reinstalled in 1953, it had been left to those who had escaped to Eastern Europe, such as Ehsan Tabari, Iraj Eskandari and Kianoori, to carry on left-wing opposition to the Shah.

After the revolution, the exiled leaders returned to Iran and reopened the Tudeh offices. Supporting Khomeini's anti-imperialist stand, they gradually built up their influence and began to infiltrate the different government organizations. It is necessary if one is to understand the position of Tudeh officials, to see the relationship between the Tudeh Party and the two dominant political trends within the Iranian regime in their proper context.

The first line, that of Hojattieh, which is itself split into various factions (including the Ebadiol Salehin and the Mujahedin Engelab Eslami), follows extreme religious fundamentalist beliefs and is extremely conservative on issues such as private ownership, economic control and the superiority of religious over political leadership.

By contrast, the so-called 'Imam's line', believed to have been nourished ideologically and politically by the Tudeh Party, supported the idea of exporting revolution, the continuation of the Iran–Iraq War and the pursuance of anti-imperialist policies. It could be said that while the

Hojattieh line is more concerned with economic and internal issues, the Imam's line considers more political and international issues.

It should be noted that one of the most influential of the Soviet Union's allies who followed the Imam's line was Mussavi Khoeinia, later the Attorney General. He was one of the leaders of the 'Group of Students Following the Imam's Line' which affected the seizure of the US Embassy in Tehran and the holding of US hostages for more than sixteen months.

Other influential patriots of Lumumba University in Moscow included ex-Deputy Foreign Minister, Sheikh Oleslam, also of the Imam's line. It was due to such connections with students of the Imam's line that the Tudeh Party took the supporting positions that it did over the hostage-taking crisis and other regime policies such as:

1 The suppression of the Kurds by the central government.
2 The disposal of Bani Sadr as President.[23]
3 The declaration that the People's Mujahedin Organization of Iran (the main opposition to the government) were traitors and should be arrested.[24]
4 The continuation of the war with Iraq.

The involvement of Soviet personnel in internal affairs became a particularly delicate subject when eighteen Soviet diplomats were expelled from Iran, accused of 'activities incompatible with Iranian affairs' in May 1983. Thus, as the Iranian governing regime cracked down simultaneously upon both Soviet-supported Tudeh activists and Soviet political intervention, the political tensions and strains between the two countries became rife. This came about despite the improvement of trading relations which resulted in 1983 in agreement regarding the Soviet construction of the Arak Dam, and a series of talks and Soviet visits aimed at solving the shipping problem in the Caspian Sea.[25]

AN UP-TURN IN SOVIET–IRANIAN RELATIONS, 1984–9

The expulsion of Soviet diplomats from Iran marked the lowest point in relations between the two countries. In June 1984, the Director General of the Iranian Foreign Ministry, Seyad Mohammed Sadr, headed a group of Iranian diplomats on a visit to Moscow, going some way towards improving relations.[26] The gesture was returned at the end of the month with a visit by the Soviet Deputy Minister of Energy, Alexei Makukhin, to Iran.[27]

The Soviet responsiveness was somewhat forced upon it by events in the Gulf War. Iran had launched an attack south of Basra and was threatening to close the Strait of Hormuz if Iraq was to obtain Super Etendard fighter planes. This posture was bound to antagonize American naval forces in the region, a prospect which worried Moscow since it would inevitably bring with it an intensification of those forces and a growing US presence in the region.

The Iranian move towards restoring good relations with the USSR was the product of contradictions within the Iranian leadership. On the one hand, Prime Minister Moussavi was eager to establish a closer relationship with Moscow, if only to ensure the completion of the Isfahan power station.[28] The head of the Iranian parliament, Hashemi Rafsanjani, was however, seeking rather to develop links with Beijing with a visit to China and the purchase of Chinese missiles.[29] Sharam Chubin[30] has remarked on Soviet concerns over the drawing in of the PRC into the Gulf conflict, in particular the strategic implications of an Iran–China alliance of sorts. However, the ideological competition between the two Communist states was reason enough for Soviet concern. The possibility was interesting as far as Iran was concerned since it provided for the co-operation of two powerful non-aligned countries, maintaining the anti-imperialist stance without owing political obligations to the Soviet Union.

Soviet–Iranian relations were still at this fragile stage when the General Secretary of the USSR, Chernenko, died. In March 1985, Mikhail Gorbachev was elected as leader of the Communist Party and consequently took over the helm of the Soviet Union. He brought with him the remarkable transformation of both the Soviet Union's internal structure and its foreign policy which were to be come known as *perestroika* and *glasnost*.

As far as the Middle East was concerned, Soviet policy was redirected in favour of bettering relations with Israel and the conservative Arab states. The new approach to the Arab–Israeli conflict reflected Gorbachev's view that regional conflicts inhibit East–West relations and should be contained.

Soviet policy towards Iran was more or less the same as before, although severely critical of Iran's determination to continue the war. The Islamic Republic was concerned by developments in radio broadcasts by 'The National Voice of Iran' which operated from Baku, within Soviet territory. The radio station began for the first time to demand the overthrow of the Islamic regime.

In February 1986, the Soviet Deputy Foreign Minister, Georgi Kornenko, visited Tehran during celebrations for the seventh anniversary of the revolution. According to Iranian sources, the discussions were based around four main points: Afghanistan; the purchase of arms from the Soviet Union; the position of the Tudeh Party; and improving economic relations. Topmost on Iran's agenda was the re-establishment of relations which would distance the Soviet Union from Iraq, perhaps the reasoning behind the new determination to purchase arms directly from the Soviet Union rather than through its client states, thus creating a certain awkwardness in Soviet arms sales to Iraq.

In August 1986, the Iranian Energy Minister visited Moscow and promised the reopening of the Igat I gas pipeline to the Soviet Union. Despite this sweetener in political relations, economic relations had clearly suffered from their problematic relations, as can be seen from Table 3.1.

Table 3.1 USSR trade with Iran

Soviet imports	(million roubles)
1981	470
1982	189
1983	377
1984	242
1985	144
1986	18
Soviet exports	(million roubles)
1981	409
1982	577
1983	599
1984	242
1985	204
1986	58

Source: 'Vneshnyaya Torgovlya 84'; Business International p. iv, 51, 54; F. Halliday, 'The USSR and the Gulf War', Washington, MERIP, September and November 1987

Gorbachev's determination to help 'contain' the Gulf War was manifest in mid-Summer 1986, to Iran's displeasure, in the positive Soviet response in the United Nations to Kuwaiti requests for protection for her oil tankers against Iranian attack. The seizure of a Soviet cargo vessel in the Gulf by the Iranian Navy in September 1986 did little to improve relations.

In January 1987, the Soviet Union again made clear in the United Nations that it viewed with deep concern the continuation of the war which was threatening international sea-lines and vessels not belonging to either of the belligerents. Even when the Iranian Foreign Minister, Velayati, visited Gromyko in Moscow, he was faced with Soviet criticism of Iranian war policies:

Our assessment of the war and your view of it do not coincide . . . commonsense suggests that primary attention should be focused on the future and not the past – on putting an end to the war . . . the only ones who gain from the continuation of military conflict are the imperialist forces for whom this war is profitable.

It would appear that, while both Iran and the Soviet Union were aware that relations had to be improved, and while they were both willing to make the effort to do so in the economic sphere, they were unable to reconcile this with their contrasting views on the continuation of the war. The primary dilemma for the Soviet Union has been the choice between its desire to develop friendly relations with its southern neighbour and its need to contain the war so as to limit the opportunities for the expansion of American influence in the region and, latterly, so as to minimize tensions between US and Soviet interests in the region for the sake of a general thaw in the Cold War.

This last intention was somewhat thwarted, therefore, when revelations of the US arms deals with Iran came to light in April 1987.[31] Parallel to Soviet displeasure over Iran's covert operations with its own 'Great Satan', was Iranian displeasure at a visit by the Soviet Deputy Foreign Minister, Mr Dennicgov, to Iraq, also in April. During this visit he reassured the Iraqis of continued Soviet support for their territorial integrity and of further arms sales. Soon after, on 7 May 1987, Iranian naval vessels attacked a Soviet ship which was protecting Kuwaiti oil tankers.[32] Ironically a wave of anti-Soviet feeling spread through Iran, despite the fact that the Gulf War still represented the sharp-end of USSR–USA rivalry in the region. If anything, Iran's hostility to the Soviet Union at this point reinforced the few common priorities shared by the superpowers. Both were hostile to the prospect of an Iranian victory and the expansion of Islamic fundamentalism in the region. By 1987 the Soviet Union was reversing its previous position and stating that:

The US has no stake in the continuation of the Iran–Iraq War.[33]

In July 1987 the Soviet Union supported the American attempt to secure an immediate cease-fire in the Gulf. They tried simultaneously to improve their relations with Iran and to assure the Iraqi government that they would never allow its total defeat. Rafsanjani's attempt to 'play the Russian card' by intimating that he was to be invited to Moscow was seen as a gross miscalculation, since the Soviet Union evidently had no intention of antagonizing the United States or of allowing the escalation of the conflict. Gorbachev was in fact at that time trying to secure the Medium-Range Nuclear Missile Treaty, as well as a dignified solution to the Afghanistan problem. He was certainly not going to risk these far more precious efforts for the sake of advancing relations with Iran.

Some reassurance was given, however, in the form of further trade agreement to cement existing ties. On a visit to Tehran by the first deputy from the Soviet Foreign Ministry, Yuli Vorontsov, the following trade items were agreed:

1 The export of 100,000 b/d of oil through a gas pipeline to the Soviet Union.[34]
2 A joint exploration for oil in the Caspian Sea.[35]

On 20 July 1987, the United Nations Security Council passed Resolution 598, calling on both Iran and Iraq to implement a cease-fire and start immediate negotiations to end the hostilities. Significantly the superpowers had agreed to pass the burden of resolving an international dispute, vital to their own interests, on to the shoulders of the UN.

The crucial factor in the ending of hostilities, temporarily at least, was the acceptance by Iran of Resolution 598 on 18 July 1988. The acceptance was forced upon it by a series of military setbacks, notably in Fao, by intense international pressure, including the fear of an escalated US military involvement, and by internal turmoil.

The cease-fire left Iran with the critical task of reconstruction of its damaged economy. Since foreign investment was obviously going to be crucial, the Iranian leaders saw fit to redefine their foreign policy so as to decrease their isolation and improve relations with the 'countries with the capital'. The Soviet Union gained a new importance, both as a source of investment itself and, more importantly, as a lever to threaten the West into providing an alternative source of capital. Moreover, it was hoped that warm relations with the Soviet Union would enhance Iran's bargaining position as it fought for concessions at the peace table.

A high-ranking official trade delegation was dispatched to Moscow, headed by the Iranian Minister for Finance, to meet with the Soviet Prime Minister. Emphasis was put by the Soviets on trade co-operation and better political relations.[36] During this visit a treaty was signed committing Iran to the export of 3 billion m^3 of natural gas through a pipeline to the Soviet Union.[37]

THE ISLAMIC REPUBLIC MAKES AMENDS

In January 1989 Khomeini sent, for the first time, a message via his special envoy, Javad Amoly, to the Kremlin. His message explained the Islamic ideology to Mr Gorbachev but added that 'we are willing to learn from our past mistakes and are willing to have a better relationship'.[38] The message opened a new era in Iran–Soviet relations. On 25 February 1989, the Soviet Foreign Minister, Eduard Shevardnadze, met personally with Khomeini. He in turn passed on a message from Gorbachev to the effect that the Soviet Union gave its support to the Iranian revolution and its aims. An intelligence 'offering' was made when the Soviet Foreign Minister informed Tehran that the CIA had established a spy ring within the Iranian armed forces, in particular within the ranks of the navy. The information had been passed to the KGB from the East German secret services who had been monitoring the activities of the CIA's special Iranian cell in Frankfurt. The Iranian government arrested the members of the ring, including several senior naval officers in late April 1989.[39]

Relations were further improved by the Soviet commitment to withdrawal of its forces from Afghanistan. This new warmth was consolidated by the visit by Ali Akbar Hashemi Rafsanjani, then Parliamentary Speaker of Iran, to Baku within weeks of Khomeini's death. He sealed the new relations with an economic and trade agreement worth $15 billion. The trip served also to consolidate Rafsanjani's own position within Iran as presidential elections loomed. The agreement provided for ten years' of economic co-operation beginning in 1990 with the resumption of Iranian gas exports to the Soviet Union. Yet despite this considerable advance in their relations, the Soviet Union could never hope to compete with the West in terms of offering capital investment to Iran.

It must be said, however, that the Soviet Union has proved her worth to Iran over the years in another field, that of arms supplies. By 1984 the Soviet Union had supplied the Islamic regime with surface-to-surface missiles[40] and by 1985 there were 5,000 Soviet advisers stationed in Iran. In August 1986, the Soviet Union delivered $18.64 million worth of advanced weapons. The Islamic Republic also agreed to purchase 400 SAM-7 anti-aircraft missiles and 100 launchers, withdrawn from the Warsaw Pact arsenals in Eastern Europe, as well as Soviet anti-tank grenades and artillery ammunitions. The significance of these deals becomes apparent when one considers also two agreements between Iran and Czechoslovakia and Iran and Romania. According to the agreement with Czechoslovakia the Islamic regime would obtain more than 180 Soviet-made tanks whose parts had been assembled in Czechoslovakia. Czech technicians and engineers would assist the Iranians in the construction of an anti-tank and anti-aircraft missile factory in Isfahan. They would also train the IRGC and regular armed forces in the operation and maintenance of such missiles. As a result of the agreement with Romania, a tractor manufacturing factory would be converted into an armoured- and transport-vehicles factory. Romanian technicians and engineers would assist in the construction of a new naval facility near the Strait of Hormuz.

There were also rumours before Rafsanjani's trip to Moscow that the Iranian regime was seeking to buy arms valued at around $3 billion from the Soviet Union. Items sought included 200 MiG-29s, 300 T-72 tanks, 150 mortar launchers and 2,000 tank carriers. The Soviets proved reluctant to make such sales in light of their developing relations with the United States and chose rather to assure the Iranian government that they would have full Soviet co-operation in construction projects such as foundries, a power station and other technological endeavours.[41]

CONCLUSION

Any military and economic co-operation between the Soviet Union and Iran must be viewed from within the regional geo-strategic and global economic environment.

Iran regards it as essential that it be able to attract Western investment in order to allow for the reconstruction of the post-war economy. To that extent relations with the Soviet Union are inevitably limited. Likewise the ideological differences of the two regimes, Iran's anti-communist, anti-secular and Muslim fundamentalist ideology can barely compromise itself with Soviet-style socialism, however moderated its present foreign policy stance may be. Finally, from the Soviet point of view (but this applies equally to the Western countries), the internal problems of Iran and the conflicts within its leadership make any investments uncertain and any commitments unstable.

On the other hand Soviet foreign policy is no longer constrained by rampant fear of American expansionism. The thaw in the superpower Cold War has relieved the region of the competitive jostling which made regional allies, at any cost, so important. The Soviet Union seeks good relations with the Islamic Republic more for the sake of comfortable southern borders and good neighbourliness than for reasons of anti-imperialist investment.

Clearly the Soviet Union has proved itself willing to sacrifice ideological considerations for national interests and pragmatic policies in its relations with Iran. Yet the Soviets still demonstrate a lack of creativity and imagination in their dealings and understanding of Iranian internal politics.

4 Iran and the European Community

Anoushiravan Ehteshami

The Iranian revolution of 1979 shocked the Western world. The Soviet Union, although concerned about the implications of an Islamic order emerging in place of the Pahlavi regime, openly rejoiced in Washington's and her European allies' 'loss' of a reliable friend in as sensitive a region as the Persian Gulf. The international implications of the anti-Shah revolution though were not confined to the political realm, nor indeed calculated in wholly strategic gains and losses. The social upheavals of the 1977–9 period soon developed sharp after-effects in the country's economic life, initially affecting only the West's energy supplies and the price of hydrocarbons. With the Shah gone in the first month of 1979 and the Islamic Republic ushered in within the next few, serious reservations about the economic orientation of the new regime were expressed. Its cancellation of some $10 billion worth of civilian and military contracts with Western countries (and the suspension of a few Eastern European agreements) within weeks of the Shah's departure, and the emergence of the provisional government appeared to have put the writing on the wall: another lucrative Third World market spinning out of the capitalist orbit.

Although the republic's leaders stressed their desire to maintain correct, close and mutually advantageous economic relations with all, including Iran's capitalist suppliers, many in the West feared the worst. The worst, however, never happened and when the Iranian market for Western goods and services finally shrank, it happened years later and then only as a consequence of sharp falls in the price of crude oil in 1986 and the prohibitive cost of the war with Iraq. It transpired also in the life of the provisional government (February–November 1979) that far from aspiring towards a centrally planned, Eastern European-oriented economy, the country's new leaders (clerical and non-clerical) were in broad agreement over Iran's role in the global relations of production and exchange. It was demonstrated time and again, in spite of the slogan 'neither East nor West' and despite their populism, that they did not envisage the economic substance of the new republic to be dramatically different from that of the *ancien regime*; that they hoped that wealth and income would be distributed more fairly was in little doubt; that it was deemed to be less luxury-goods oriented is not really questionable; that they expected their new regime to be less dependent on the West is also appreciable. But it was clear from the early days of its life that, far from actively seeking to opt out of the capitalist world economy (assuming that this feat were to be achievable), the Islamic Republic would ultimately merely remould its relationship with global economic processes. Also, it was made plain that Iran under its 'new management' would no longer chase the shadow of Japan but, if anything, would try perhaps to emulate the post-War West German economic success story. Prominent in this school of thought were the France-educated Bani Sadr and his colleagues.

These points underscored, there is little doubt though that Iran's domestic system of production and exchange has undergone some appreciable changes since 1979 (the nationalization of almost all of the country's modern industrial units and financial sector, implementation of the Islamic banking system and so on) and, by the same token, so too has the country's foreign economic relations. The pertinent question, however, is in what ways?

Back in 1981 an Iranian economist, Nassouri, predicted that in the last analysis the Islamic Republic's trade ties would reveal a pattern not too dissimilar to that of the *ancien regime*:

> Iran's trading relations with the West will remain more or less unchanged, whatever anti-Western noises may emerge from Iran from time to time. But the volume of this trade is likely to be far lower than it ever was under the Shah, and there could be significant changes in the share of that trade taken by the various countries of the West.[1]

His insight was born out of his perceptive analysis of the Islamic Republic:

> [the] picture of the political structure indicates that the major socio-political elements in Iran will continue to trade with the West. Having followed capitalist routes to development, they have no choice but to continue traditional trading relationships and indeed are happy to do so.[2]

Although some may disagree that the element of choice never existed or that harsher trading regimes could not have been implemented because of the need to export hydrocarbons and import Western consumer and capital goods, Nassouri's overall conclusions, in my view, cannot be overlooked. It emerges from this perspective, based on the Iranian example at least, that political change in the Third World, even when violent, does not necessarily or automatically culminate in the emergence of anti-capitalist pro-Communist ruling elites and economies. The development and expression of some degree of hostility is unavoidable but in this case appears largely to have been confined to the political arena. Iran, despite Tehran's struggles against greater and lesser 'Satans', has continued its trade with the West more or less unabated. What has changed appreciably is the pattern of that trade and here political calculations and diplomatic relations have certainly played their part.

THE ISLAMIC REPUBLIC'S TRADE STRATEGY

The vision of the new elite in Iran varied from that of the Shah only as far as the country's relations with the United States (and to a lesser extent the Soviet Union) were concerned. Iran continued to court the European Community (EC), Japan and other OECD (Organization for Economic Co-operation and Development) countries, the People's Republic of China, a number of Eastern European countries and of course many developing countries for the supply of arms, technology, expertise, food, capital and general consumer goods. Other factors being equal, in isolating the 'usurping powers of world-devouring USA' the new elite in Iran was at least in part responding to Beijing's elevation of the Soviet Union as the rising imperialist threat for the best part of at least two decades. A true strand of pragmatism, helped in no small way by the close proximity of the USSR, was also visible beneath the revolutionary regime's ideological opposition to both Western capitalism and Soviet-style Communism; relatively mild anti-Soviet propaganda was in sharp contrast to the uncompromising anti-Americanism found in virtually all aspects of the Islamic Republic's public life.

It emerged over time that the prudent application of the Republic's slogan of 'neither East nor West' provided an ideal conduit for US bashing without necessarily alienating Iran economically from the other OECD (particularly EC) countries, nor distancing Iran too much from the Soviet Union or her Warsaw Pact allies.

More than any other factor, the war and its longevity brought Iran closer to Europe, Japan and the newly industrializing countries (NICs). She needed their markets for her crude oil exports and was badly dependent on their manufactured consumer and capital goods and management and industrial services. The war itself of course made continuous demands on the new elite to seek and activate military relationships with as many countries as possible. If they possessed compatible US military hardware all the better. If not, Tehran was still willing to sell to them her crude oil on a barter basis and to receive in exchange whatever lethal and non-lethal military equipment available. In this context the Western European connection was vital. It combined 'under one roof' not only the official suppliers and the clandestine arms dealers, but also provided the customer with a network of shipments facilities and outlets, and expert accounting and financial services. Thus many Western European countries came to serve Tehran as her military supermarket.

Additionally, in the aftermath of the US hostage crisis the philosophical prospects of emulating the Western European economic experience was also postponed, reducing Iran's ambitions to one of survival against great odds through public and secretive collaboration with the 'Second World' powers. The new leaders, of necessity, had postponed their, and the Shah's, ideal of creating a European-size power in the Middle East indefinitely. Western Europe and Japan were to provide the badly needed inputs of Iran's Western-dominated economy. Particularly after the US hostage crisis and the severing of formal ties between Tehran and Washington, this stop-gap measure became an established policy of the Islamic Republic, still in place even without the war.

Tehran did aim to diversify her trading partners and has made concerted efforts towards increasing her commercial ties with the developing countries. Although she has not been very successful in significantly expanding her commercial ties with the Islamic states, she has none the less made some gains in her overall South–South trade. As Table 4.1 shows, in 1977 only 22 per cent of her exports found their way to other developing countries. The share of developing countries in Iran's exports, however, rose sharply from about 25 per cent in 1978 to 34 per cent only two years later. The figure for 1988 (42 per cent) leaves one with little doubt as to the success of the Islamic Republic in finding export outlets beyond the industrialized countries.

A close scrutiny of her imports and their countries of origin, however, would reveal the cracks in the Islamic Republic's trading strategy. From around 11 per cent of Iran's total imports, South's share has more than doubled in the life of the Republic but remains less than half of that of the OECD's total. Furthermore, Iran's Third World partners have not changed markedly since the revolution; the volume of South–South trade has increased appreciably, but not the number of her Southern partners.[3] For example, economic relations with Argentina, Brazil, India, Malaysia, Pakistan, the PRC, South Korea, Thailand and Turkey have either been maintained or expanded over the last eleven years, but available data supports the view that little expansion in Iran's trade with other Third World countries has taken place.[4] This said, South–South trade and diplomatic relations will continue to figure highly in Iran's international posture, serving the needs of both sides. As the developing countries

Table 4.1 Patterns of Iran's trade with the West and the LDCs (%)

	1977		1980		1983		1985		1987		1988	
	E	I	E	I	E	I	E	I	E	I	E	I
OECD	78	86	65	66	67	65	58	61	65	66	58	61
EC	36	43	32	42	39	38	35	38	36	41	41	39
Other												
OECD	42	43	33	24	26	27	23	23	29	25	17	22
LDCs	22	11	34	25	33	29	42	32	35	27	42	30

Source: Based on IMF, *Direction of Trade Statistics Yearbook* (various years) and A. Ehteshami, 'The Islamic Republic of Iran model: a new alternative to Socialism in the Third World?', paper presented at the European Consortium for Political Research Joint Sessions, Bochum (FRG) 2–7 April 1990

industrialize, their demand for sources of energy and fuel rise. But Iran will be amongst the handful of countries able to meet these needs over the next century. The energy/fuel relationship can serve as a push-factor in the economic relationship between Iran and the fast-industrializing developing countries. Iran's own interests in expanding her economic ties with these same countries, her willingness to barter her oil for goods and services and her need for industrial expertise available from these NICs (and NECs) can be said to serve as pull-factors. This industrial relationship will provide Iran with cheaper manufactured and capital goods and industrial services (and perhaps fewer political restrictions) than available from Western countries and, at the same time, make available rich markets for the products and services of the beleaguered NICs, which are simultaneously subject to fierce competition in world markets and faced with the spectre of protectionism in the Western countries.

More qualitative changes are still in store, therefore, as far as Iran's economic relations with the developing countries (and particularly with the NICs) are concerned.

But as far as the country's trade relations with the industrialized countries are concerned, significant changes are already discernible.[5] There is a significant expansion of the Republic's ties with the number of Eastern European countries. Of this group of states the most active traders with Iran have been the following: Czechoslovakia, the GDR, Hungary, Romania, the Soviet Union and Yugoslavia. It is as yet too early to predict precisely the impact of regime changes in these Eastern European countries and their progressive Westernization on the two sides' trading relationships. The two scenarios predicting either a decline or a rapid expansion in the trade relations do remain plausible, but for the most of the

1980s it is clear that the Islamic Republic exercised her Eastern European option for two over-riding reasons. First, as an alternative supplier of industrial goods and other manufactured products. Second, the centrally planned economies of Eastern Europe provided Iran with a convenient bargaining chip against the EC countries as a means of extracting maximum benefit from the latter. In a sense then, the Republic's Eastern European trading strategy was contingent upon the state of play with the EC. Furthermore, in the context of the Islamic Republic's world view, some members of the OECD (and Japan, Canada and Australia) came to be regarded as non-hostile and economic partners with whom correct relations could be maintained. Ultimately though, the expansion of economic relations between Iran and the 'Second World' powers could be attributed partly to the Republic's ideological orientations and partly as an illustration of her desire to isolate the US – Iran's traditional trading partner – to the benefit of Washington's other Western allies and many foes. The significance of this strategy was not lost on Iran's Western trading partners, for throughout the 1980s Iran remained in the top six OECD markets in the Middle East. Since the second half of the 1980s, on average, some 8.5 per cent of total OECD Middle East exports have gone to Iran.[6]

Table 4.2 Total OECD exports to selected Middle Eastern countries, ($billion)

	77	78	79	80	81	82	83	84	85	87	88
Saudi Arabia	12.2	16.6	19.8	23.3	27.4	31.3	30.3	24.9	18.9	17.7	17.8
Iran	12.1	15.4	5.9	7.6	8.0	6.4	12.2	9.7	7.2	6.0	5.6
Egypt	3.9	4.6	6.0	8.3	9.2	9.9	9.9	10.3	9.3	8.2	8.2
Algeria	6.0	6.6	6.9	8.8	8.7	8.3	8.2	8.0	7.3	5.8	6.3
Iraq	3.7	4.3	6.9	10.0	14.3	14.8	7.1	6.4	7.0	4.5	6.1

Sources: OECD, *Statistics of Foreign Trade, Series A* (various years) and COMET

Over time the composition of the OECD exporters has changed to reflect Iran's political preferences. As Table 4.3 reveals, on balance, the greatest loser of Iran's international trade strategy has been the United States and the overall beneficiaries, Japan, the FRG and the smaller OECD countries. By the second half of the 1980s the latter set of countries accounted for about 40 per cent of Iran's OECD imports.

Table 4.3   OECD market shares in Iran, mid-1980s (%)

	FRG	Japan	Italy	UK	France	USA	Other OECD
1984	23.1	17.5	9.8	9.7	1.9	1.7	36.4
1986	22.5	17.3	9.8	8.8	1.2	0.5	39.7

Source: Calculated from OECD, Statistics of Foreign Trade, Series A (various years)
Note: A downturn in trade occurred after 1986, reflecting the collapse of the price of oil and Iran's inability to import all its consumer and industrial needs as well as maintaining the war effort.

A more disturbing blow still to US commercial interests has been the emergence of virulent Third-World competition in the potentially rich markets like Iran. It is debatable whether Washington can afford to overlook indefinitely the challenge of the NICs in such important markets, as the following example illustrates. In 1988 Iran's total trade with the US stood at $88 million, just under a sixth of Brazil's total figure of $517 million for the same year.[7] Furthermore, since 1985 Iran's imports from Brazil have on average been four times those from the US.[8]

Within the OECD group the demise of the US export preference was matched by the consolidation of Japanese and West German exporters, with the UK and Italy holding on to their shares of the market. The reduction in France's role can largely be attributed to political factors; Paris' consistent support for the Iraqi war effort, her involvement in the Lebanon and EC-orchestrated counter-terrorism strategies, her harbouring of Iranian dissident organizations and personalities, her unwillingness to repay her large financial debt to Iran and her boycott of Iranian crude oil exports.

Within the ranks of the OECD countries though the four prominent EC countries as a group have accounted for the bulk of Iran's imports in recent years. The shift thus in the Iranian strategy is clear; a preference for EC trade, augmented by Third World and Eastern European commercial ties, is increasingly detracting from the US' historical economic foothold in Iran. But how have the EC states viewed the situation?

THE VIEW FROM THE EUROPEAN COMMUNITY

The EC's 1980 Venice Declaration marked a watershed in the nine's involvement with the Middle East. It illustrated the concerted effort of the Community to adopt an active and independent foreign policy towards the Arab–Israeli conflict and, as many hoped, other regional issues. Of the EC states' unilateral interests in the Middle East there is little doubt. Their diplomatic and military preparedness to intervene in all four Middle Eastern sub-theatres (the Persian Gulf, the Levant, the Horn of Africa and North Africa) since de-colonization is too well documented to need further elaboration here. But the various crises of the 1980s, coupled with the expansion of the EC from nine to twelve (adding three more Mediterranean countries to the total) held promise of a more active involvement in the Middle East. The multiple crises in the Gulf, however, unveiled a more disturbing trend: the pursuance of the 'national interest' at the expense of the collective's. With hindsight, it can be said that this tendency had already surfaced at the outbreak of the Gulf crisis at the turn of the 1980s.

In the aftermath of the Iranian revolution and the outbreak of hostilities between Iran and Iraq, four powers stationed naval forces in the Persian Gulf and the Sea of Oman: alongside the two superpowers' contingents present were naval detachments from the Community's leading military powers, Britain and France, operating independently of one another. By November 1980 Britain and France had ten and fifteen naval vessels respectively in the area, compared with thirty-five ships each from the US and the Soviet Union. By no means however could it be maintained that in practice the combined British and French naval vessels in the Gulf in the early 1980s represented an EC force dispatched to protect the Community's interests there. The vigorous French drive to expand her Persian Gulf arms markets in the 1980s served notice that not only was Paris prepared to compete in Gulf markets within the superpowers' spheres of influence, but she had few reservations about undermining the favoured position of her Community partner, Britain, in her traditional arms markets in the Middle East. It emerged at about the same time that France had targeted the three Gulf countries of Iraq, Qatar and Saudi Arabia for her military export drive. The choice of countries was farsighted; the war with Iran would guarantee France a captive market in Iraq (a country flushed with petro-dollars at this time, able and willing both to expand her military capabilities and augment her Soviet-made weaponry with sophisticated Western arms, and in contrast to Iran not already dependent on other Western military equipment). Saudi Arabian willingness to expand and modernize her armed forces in response to the Iran–Iraq War, coupled with the emergence of an informal security pact (later to be formalized in the form of the GCC) amongst the smaller Gulf states, would ensure a high-profile French presence in other Gulf markets too. Thus, what characterizes the early 1980s is the French reluctance to concentrate on the Iranian arms market (despite her favoured status having hosted Ayatollah Khomeini and his entourage before their triumphant return to Iran aboard an Air France 747) on the one hand, and on the other her drive to penetrate the Persian Gulf's Arab arms markets at a time of heightened tensions.

From here on the EC would be divided over the treatment of the crises in the Gulf. Increasingly the interests of the Community's leading powers conflicted with each other and with those of the collective. This was so until the internationalization of the conflict became a reality.

The EC's position on the US hostages issue, on the other hand, paradoxically both confirmed and undermined the vision of an independent and united Western European voice in the Middle East. It confirmed it with the pointed European deliberations over imposing complete US-inspired sanctions against Iran. Yet it also undermined this vision in the almost blanket support given to the US' position. By the mid-1980s, however, very clear and vocal opposition within the Community to the British-endorsed US position in the Middle East had emerged again raising the vision of a co-ordinated EC foreign policy. It was lost to many observers, however, that while Europe appeared to speak with one voice over the US bombing of Libya for instance, it remained firmly divided over the Gulf crisis, where France supported Iraq, West Germany drew closer to Iran, Britain and Italy tried to maintain a balance between Tehran and Baghdad, and the smaller EC members got involved only when profits were to be made.

Tensions within the Community over political and economic sovereignty and security issues have continued to undermine the unifying thrust of the dynamism of a united European position on regional problems. These tensions become contradictory precisely over what may appear to be good for Europe, counters the national interests of the prominent EC member-states. Nowhere can these contradictory tensions be better illustrated than in the crisis-ridden Middle East in general, and over the treatment of revolutionary Iran in particular.

I would maintain that, in the case of Iran, while the latter had been prepared and willing to expand her economic and political relations with the EC, albeit even as a counter-weight to US influence in the region, the Community was unable to respond consistently in kind and in a co-ordinated manner. Certainly instances of co-ordinated action in the Gulf can be mentioned. These, however, could be said to be the exceptions and not the rule. Interestingly, these exceptions have occurred where security concerns have been high on the Community's agenda. This is not to say that the EC responds unitedly only to security threats, but that it seems to take crisis of some magnitude before the Twelve can be expected to speak with one voice.

It is clear, for instance, that over the issues of Middle Eastern-originated terrorism and negotiations with hostage-takers in the Lebanon and their backers, the EC has been unable to speak with one voice. Through direct negotiations Paris and Bonn have been able to secure the release of their citizens from the Lebanon, while Britain has refused categorically (at least in public) to follow suit. In the second half of the 1980s, Britain led the EC into breaking off diplomatic relations with Syria and Libya for their supporting of terrorists, and with Iran over the Rushdie affair and Tehran's role in international terrorism. At the turn of the 1990s, however, it was Britain which stood isolated in the Community while the other member-states proceeded to mend fences with all three culprits. Britain, until late 1990, was the only EC partner with no representation in three important Middle Eastern capitals. The others did not even seem to be protecting her interests: in Iran she was represented through the Swedish mission – a non-EC Western European state! Indeed far from maintaining solidarity with London, some of her partners at times proceeded to exploit Britain's vulnerabilities to their own advantage.

Such an anarchic behaviour (undertaken by both sides to the negotiations debate) over such issues as the hostages, therefore, do little to improve the image of a divided European Community. Despite the advances in the institutional integration of the EC certain aspects of foreign policy appear at times to have remained totally untouched by decades of 'community-building'. Yet, under certain circumstances, a remarkable level of co-ordination in foreign policy matters is in evidence. This will be illustrated through a brief examination of the Western naval build-up in the Persian Gulf in the late 1980s. In response to the 'internationalization' of the conflict between Iran and Iraq, and the increased threats to free navigation in the Gulf, many Western countries agreed to send some naval vessels (and to co-ordinate their naval efforts) to this part of the world. But in sharp contrast to the Western naval build-up of 1980, the 1987 presence included a substantial EC contingent. As Table 4.4 shows, on the latter occasion the total EC naval deployment was greater than those of the superpowers, and resembled remarkably a Western European Union contingent rather than an alluded to NATO force.

Even here though, the absence of naval detachments from Portugal, Spain and Greece – the EC late-comers – was conspicuous. The FRG incidently pleaded constitutional constraints on out-of-area military deployments, but none the less helped to relieve the pressure on NATO through increasing her naval presence in the Mediterranean. This Western

European involvement in the Persian Gulf, alas, further antagonized Tehran. The Islamic Republic immediately linked the WEU naval deployment in the Persian Gulf to the aggressive American posture there, and thus regarded it as a hostile gesture.

Table 4.4 Foreign naval deployment in the Persian Gulf, 1980, 1987

	UK	France	Italy	Belgium	Holland	EC	US	USSR	Total
1980	10	15	–	–	–	25	35	35	95
1987	10	13	8	3	2	36	28	6	70

It was also seen by the Republic as another facet of the US-orchestrated drive to isolate Tehran internationally. In the context of the on-going war with Arab Iraq, furthermore, these Western European moves were viewed as a sign of general pro-Arab leaning within the Community, at the expense of Iran. The cumulative effect of these interpretations served as a blow to those in Tehran who had painstakingly argued that in order to prevent the Islamic Republic's anti-US strategy from back-firing it would be essential for the country to maintain close relations with Washington's allies in Europe. But the EC's readiness eventually to put its eggs in the American basket in the Gulf indicated to Tehran that: (a) their strategy of European appeasement had failed; (b) it was futile to attempt to drive a wedge between the US and her NATO partners; and (c) the time had come to treat the EC 'activists' with the distaste usually reserved for Washington.

Willingly or otherwise, thus, the EC had sent an uncompromising signal to Tehran, just at the time when the latter would have been expecting the Community to continue distancing itself from the American military activities in the Persian Gulf. This perception would have resulted in Iran seeking closer ties with another global giant, the Soviet Union. Except of course the USSR itself was in the throes of implementing Gorbachev's *perestroika* and thus in no mood to exploit fully the situation against the West.

The deterioration in overall Iran–EC relations, however, continued with the aid of the increasingly militant stance adopted by some European institutions against the Islamic Republic. This was done in two ways: unconditional support afforded to the main opposition groups, including the Mujahedin-Khalq-dominated National Council of Resistance (and its army, the NLA) and Bakhtiar's Namir; and the condemnation of the Iranian regime in international circles. On numerous occasions since the mid-1980s the European Parliament has explicitly condemned the regime for its appalling human rights record, and has objected strongly to those in the Community and elsewhere who have covertly helped the regime. In February 1990 this same body debated the conditions in Islamic Iran again and went as far as passing an extraordinary resolution with 65 per cent (114 MEPs) of the vote in favour, calling for the immediate expulsion of the Islamic Republic from the UN. Such efforts at isolating Tehran, while helping to raise public awareness, would have been more effective if the governments of the member-states could be seen endorsing their passage.

In fact the activities of the MEPs, and others within the institutional framework of the EC, have by and large served to embarrass the member-states themselves. It emerged during the Iran-Contra affair, for instance, that this uniquely Israeli-American operation had indeed involved the EC on a number of levels. First, over eight major EC ports, including Bordeaux, Hamburg, Lisbon, Zeebrugge and Las Palmas, had been used as supply routes. Second, many EC companies had helped in providing arms for this operation. The European Parliament went as far as singling out three European explosives manufacturers for criticism; Muiden Chemise, Dinamiet Nobel and Poudreries Reunion de Belgique. Third, vessels of at least three EC countries, including those of Denmark, Portugal and Greece, had been used to ferry arms to Iran. And last, private financial institutions of some member-states had been involved in funding or underwriting parts of the operation. Besides its embarrassment potential, this episode highlights better than any other the inherent links that seem to tie Iran and the EC together.

IRAN–EC RELATIONS IN PERSPECTIVE

It appears that at times both sides have deliberately been trying to disrupt the apparently smooth path towards a mutually advantageous relationship. Lack of sophistication in the Islamic Republic's foreign policy decision-making machinery would undoubtedly have adversely affected the equation. But so too would the EC have itself. Part of the problem could be said to be that the EC is still very much divided over its own identity (its expansion southwards since 1980 and the historic changes in Eastern Europe have not helped of course), and therefore can hardly project a single voice over crucial matters of interest to its member-states in a consistent fashion. The effects of these confusions can be seen over the EC's relations with Iran over the recent years. It would appear that wherever the nation has been challenged the state has erected the 'national interest' factor – the dissension factor – at the expense of the wider EC identity. The unity has been remarkably successful in its East–West context, but as soon as relations with other parts of the world come to the fore the system faulters. Indeed as the diversifying Third World throws-up new challenges the EC is found to be increasingly at odds with its North American and Japanese partners (which may be a good thing in the long run) as well as with its own constituent parts. And yet the relentless pursuit of the national interest has brought significant collective gains too.

It is clear also that the balance between the internal forces for unity and the external incentives for dissent are continually tested in the Middle East. This chapter will, I hope, have exposed some aspects of the so-called contradictory tensions within the Community itself and those in the latter's relations with a turbulent Iran. It is clear from the data that Iran is heavily dependent on EC trade, and that the Community is also dependent on crude oil imports from Iran. Economic interdependence, thus, provides an ideal prerequisite for improvements in bilateral relations. The prospects for economic expansion, underscored by the political changes in Tehran since Ayatollah Khomeini's death, furthermore, ought to secure a marked improvement in the pre-conditions for better relations between the two sides into the 1990s.

Clearly the EC also carries with it a considerable diplomatic weight which could be utilized to serve the collective's interests in Iran, and in the Persian Gulf generally. There are few insurmountable obstacles in the way of expanding the Euro–Arab dialogue or the EC-GCC conferences to include the issue of Gulf security peace talks, for instance. Indeed the EC is likely to be called upon more frequently in the future, by both the international community and the regional actors themselves, to exercise its influence in regions such as the Middle East. To name but one such instance, more can be made of the fact that military contingents from three EC countries (Denmark, Ireland and Italy) have already been directly committed to peaceful reconciliation in the Persian Gulf, if nothing else, by the virtue of their participation in the United Nations Iran–Iraq Military Observer Group (UNIIMOG). But perhaps the Community members themselves must become more aware of their international role and their collective responsibilities before sufficient action from them can be expected. In the last analysis, the case of Iran–EC relations since the overthrow of the Shah could be investigated meaningfully only in the context of the historical changes which engulfed the two sides on their 'home turfs'. Ultimately, then, only if the two sides can learn from their past mistakes and accept the limitations on each other's respective positions will the burgeoning economic relationship of the 1980s between them translate into meaningful political dialogue and mutual trust in the 1990s.

5 Iran, the southern Mediterranean and Europe: terrorism and hostages

George Joffe

Over the past decade, Western Europeans have constructed a paradigmatic vision of Iran as a focus of Islamic antagonism towards the secularism of the West. Its manifestations have been the spectacle of Shia activism in Lebanon and the Gulf, the chiliastic millenarianism of Iran's own leaders and the hostage-taking and terrorism practised against Europeans under the assumed direction of Iran. Even though the Gulf War seems to have ended and a more pragmatic government seems to have come to power in Tehran in the wake of the death of Ayatollah Khomeini in June 1989, the stereotype persists.

It has been fed by incidents such as the Lockerbie disaster in December 1988 – when an America-bound PanAm airliner from Heathrow was destroyed by a bomb in mid-flight; the Rushdie affair in February 1989 – in which the Indian-born British author of a controversial novel was condemned to death for apostacy by Ayatollah Khomeini; and by repeated reports of bloodletting on a massive scale in Iran itself during mid-1989, as the various factions settled their differences. Overarching all of this, however, is the persistent collective memory of Western hostages held in Beirut or elsewhere in the Lebanon by groups which are popularly believed to act at the behest of Iran.

Little attention has been paid, however, to the real nature of Iran's involvement in the waves of disruptive violence that have flooded across the Middle East and, on occasion, have flowed over into Europe as well. Nor has much significance been placed on the general political and cultural environment in which this has occurred. Equally, most Western commentators have tended to dismiss the complex and complicated political developments *inside* Iran that have powerfully affected aspects of its overt and covert foreign policy.

Any proper evaluation of the significance of Iran's involvement in international terrorism must, however, consider these factors. Equally, it must include an evaluation of Western national attitudes towards Iran over the past decade, for it is evident that the patterns of terrorist events in

Europe reflect the diplomatic attitudes adopted towards Iran by different European states. Ironically enough, despite these differences in European approaches towards Iran, the Iranian responses have done much to coalesce the European response and to channel it increasingly through the European Community[1] – as the Rushdie affair made clear.

There is an additional factor to be considered in this connection, however. This is that terrorist acts in Europe, particularly in France, which have been linked to Iran have usually involved persons from North Africa. Necessarily, therefore, the effect of the Islamic revolution in Iran on North Africa, particularly on popular support for Islamist movements, needs to be considered in this context. It is important to determine to what extent Islamist developments in North Africa have been stimulated by the Iranian example or have been materially aided or organized by Iranian organizations.

It is also important to see to what extent North African involvement in Europe is a consequence of Iranian organization of Islamist movements there, rather than in their places of ethnic origin. In fact, the evidence seems to suggest that links across the Mediterranean have played little part in terrorist events inside Northern Europe – unlike the situation with Libya, for example. Instead, Europe-based terrorism apparently linked to Iran is very much a consequence of the nature and evolution of Muslim migrant communities in Europe. In this connection, the Iranian presence in Europe may well have played a vital organizing and directive role.

European attitudes towards Iran

There is little doubt that the Islamic revolution in 1979 caused considerable anxiety in Europe. Although European states were not involved in Iran in the same way as the USA, for example, they were certainly affected by the general panic over the implications for Western energy consumers which caused a doubling of oil prices as a result of the revolution. Equally, companies in most European states had also become involved in the massive development plans proposed by the Shah in 1975, in the wake of the 1973 oil price shock.

For some states, particularly the UK and France, these economic interests went hand-in-hand with longer-term political concerns in the region. For others, such as West Germany and Italy, economic considerations were paramount. Whatever the reason, there is little doubt that the Islamic revolution rocked Western political assumptions about the Middle East. This was reinforced by parallel events in Saudi Arabia, the Levant and North Africa.

It appeared to many Western commentators that a massive swell of anti-Western, anti-secularist Islamism had swept through the region. They pointed to the Grand Mosque attack in Mecca in December 1979, the consequent riots at *Ashura* in the Eastern Provinces of Saudi Arabia; powerful anti-regime tensions created by the Ikhwan Muslimin in Syria; similar movements in Egypt and Turkey; and the growth of Islamist movements in North Africa. The timing of these events did not seem to be coincidental but implied, instead, a common causal link. They seemed to confirm that, under Ayatollah Khomeini, revolutionary Iran was at the crest of an anti-Western wave of political activism throughout the Middle East.

ECONOMIC RELATIONS

What was not clear, however, was to what extent the revolution in Iran was an event as profound in its implications as the French and Russian revolutions, or whether it was merely a reshuffling of the political elites in Tehran. Most European states seem to have concluded, once the dust of revolutionary events had settled, that a pragmatic approach was the most appropriate. It was a sentiment that was powerfully reinforced by the outbreak of the Gulf War in September 1980 – just eighteen months after the revolution began and before the revolution inside Iran itself was complete.

The result was that European states soon shrugged off the ideological implications of the revolution as they began to reconstruct their economic links with Tehran. There were significant changes in the nature of these links, however. Companies in countries such as West Germany, Italy and France had been involved in major development and construction contracts which had been discontinued by the revolutionary authorities. They now had to seek roles as suppliers instead, alongside Japan and the UK.

Two countries, however, had special problems. Japanese companies, particularly Mitsui, were heavily engaged in the massive petrochemicals project at Bandar Khomeini, which was costed at around $3 billion and which was 80 per cent complete when the war broke out. Unlike their attitude towards other major projects, the new Islamic authorities were insistent that the Bandar Khomeini project should be completed, despite repeated Iraqi bombing damage. In fact, Mitsui was only able to arrange its withdrawal from the project in late 1989.[2]

France, on the other hand, found its supplier role to Iran severely curtailed by the support it continued to give to Iraq. Since the 1970s, France had been a major arms supplier to Iraq and had also constructed the Tammuz nuclear reactor for the Saddam Hussein regime. By 1981, Iraq owed France around $2 billion for arms supplies, a figure that was to rise to around $7 billion by 1983, when Iraq was taking up to 40 per cent of all French arms exports.[3]

Table 5.1   Iran: major suppliers, 1982–7 ($ million)

	1982	1983	1984	1985	1986	1987
West Germany	1,536	3,310	2,518	1,812	1,649	1,740
Japan	1,033	2,102	1,862	1,496	1,270	1,160
Turkey	870	1,197	862	1,187	621	484
Italy*	796	994	1,039	672	715	556
UK*	635	1,047	1,030	745	645	556
USSR	712	676	608	548	438	394
Netherlands*	298	460	417	298	254	315
Spain*	361	452	327	312	188	112
France*	367	408	201	176	108	198
TOTAL[†]	11,161	18,989	14,829	11,622	9,527	8,981

Source: IMF, *Direction of Trade Statistics*, 1988
* EC member states
[†] Total also includes countries not listed

None the less, as the figures above show, Europe soon established a powerful position as a major source of imports during the war. Even France managed to maintain a position, despite its prior links to Iraq, while countries such as West Germany, Italy and the UK enjoyed considerable success. Indeed, even in 1988, Iran was still the UK's second most important Middle Eastern market, despite the political tribulations through which diplomatic relations had passed. At the same time, the evident neutrality and political disinterestedness of countries such as West Germany, Spain and, to a lesser extent, Italy, encouraged the Islamic regime in Tehran to favour commercial links with them.

Diplomatic relations

The diplomatic picture was not so smooth, however, for, as the Gulf War continued, Iranian frustrations began to impinge ever more powerfully on European sensibilities. What is striking, however, is how long it took for these problems to affect commercial relations. With the UK, for example, it was only in 1987 that the Iranian Majlis attempted to impede trading relations and it was only in 1989, as a result of the Rushdie affair and the UK government's reaction to it – which was judged insulting in Tehran – that commercial links were seriously damaged.

In fact, two countries – France and the UK – have suffered serious disruption in their diplomatic relations with Iran during the past decade. In both cases, this arose because of Iranian activities within their national territories. Italy and West Germany also suffered from diplomatic problems with Iran as the war moved towards its close, mainly because of what Tehran considered disrespectful media attention accorded to Iran and its institutions. The result was that diplomatic representation was cut back in both cases. However, the problems they faced were minor, compared with those that confronted France and the UK.

FRANCE

France's problems arose in part because of French hostages taken in Lebanon and in part because the Chirac government attempted to alter France's established policy of co-operation with Iraq in favour of better relations with Iran after it came to power in March 1986. Premier Chirac tried to use a $1 billion loan, made by the Shah's government before the revolution for a uranium separation plant (the Eurodiff project), as a bargaining counter for the release of the hostages. This was coupled with the expulsion – in June 1986 – of Massoud Rajavi, the leader of the anti-Khomeinist Mujahedin Khalq movement who had escaped to France in 1981.[4]

The attempt did result in hostage releases – three hostages in November and December 1986, a further two hostages in November 1987 and the final three French hostages in May 1988. France repaid a $330 million tranche of the Eurodiff loan in early 1987, with a further sum being repaid after Jacques Chirac left power in May 1988. However, the experiment in improved relations also resulted in a diplomatic breach in July 1987.

The reason was quite simple – an Iranian had been implicated in terrorist activity in France and had claimed diplomatic immunity. He took refuge in the Iranian Embassy in Paris at the end of June 1987. The French authorities, exasperated by the affair, tried to insist on interviewing him and blockaded the embassy. Iran retaliated by arresting the French consul in Tehran and the issue was abruptly ended by a breach of diplomatic relations on 17 July 1987.

It took a further four months for the affair to be finally sorted out, with the expulsion of Vahid Gurdji, the Iranian involved, at the end of November 1987, two days after the French consul in Tehran was allowed to leave on 27 November. His departure coincided with the release in Lebanon of two French hostages, in a move that seemed, by implication, to underline the links between Iran and the hostage-takers of Islamic Jihad and the Revolutionary Justice Organization, the two clandestine groups apparently involved.[5] A few days later, apparently in a move to further pacify pro-Iranian opinion, twenty-six anti-Khomeinist Iranians and Kurds were expelled from France to Gabon. The affair ended in considerable damage to French prestige, however, because a public outcry in France forced the repatriation of those expelled.

By then, however, French patience had already worn thin and a powerful French naval detachment, including the aircraft carrier *Clemenceau*, had been sent to the Gulf area. This has been intended as a deliberate warning to Iran that France's tolerance of its attacks on French shipping had been exhausted. It was also meant as a gesture of support for the US naval units which had ben engaged in protecting Kuwaiti oil and gas tankers since July 1987. It was, indeed, the first such gesture by a European power after the initial European reluctance to become involved in what was seen as a dangerous US policy initiative.

The apparently inevitable diplomatic confrontation between France and Iran was typical of the way in which Iranian intransigence destroyed the advantages the Islamic Republic had enjoyed in Europe. By failing to limit its objectives, and allowing mutually exclusive policies of diplomatic confrontation and support for terrorism to operate simultaneously and in mutual contradiction, Tehran threw away the advantages implied by the French willingness to change its policies in the Gulf after the conservative Chirac government came to power. Admittedly, this confusion in foreign policy corresponded to in-fighting between different factions within the regime in Tehran. That, however, was quite irrelevant to the Matignon, the Elysée and the Quai d'Orsay.

It was quite evident in 1986, for example, that the conservative Chirac government was prepared to abandon the carefully developed policy of support for Iraq, fashioned by its socialist predecessor with the full support of France's wily socialist president, François Mitterrand. It was also evident that the French government was prepared to adapt its policies towards Iran in order to maximize domestic support. It was also prepared to bypass elements within the administration that would object, including the president himself. The negotiations over the hostages and the repayments of the Eurodiff loan were not entrusted to the Quai d'Orsay, for example. Instead, they were controlled by the powerful Minister of the Interior, Charles Pasqua, and his Corsican associates. It was a close friend of his, Jean-Charles Marchiani, who handled the actual discussions and it was Pasqua who took the credit.

It was also evident that both major strands in French political life were anxious to exploit the Iranian connection in the presidential campaign in 1988. Jacques Chirac, the challenger, was anxious to ensure the release of the remaining three hostages. François Mitterrand, the incumbent, was equally anxious to prevent this occurring before the elections. There were ugly rumours that his representatives had offered up to $10 million to the Lebanese captors not to release the hostages.[6] Mr Chirac's supporters were little better – a previous hostage negotiator, Omrane Adham, who had criticized Mr Chirac was expelled from France by an obliging Mr Pasqua just before the elections.

Indeed, the release of the hostages just before the elections ensured that the new socialist French government would reluctantly fulfil the promises of its predecessor. It paid a second tranche of the Eurodiff loan, recalled the *Clemenceau* naval group and refused to supply promised Mirage aircraft to Iraq. However, that was as far as it was prepared to go, and relations with Iraq were quietly repaired. Tehran was now seen as unreliable and unpredictable.

This had not been inevitable, however. There were many people in French political life who would have preferred to maintain the Iran link, had the Islamic Republic showed some coherence and restraint in its foreign policies. It was clear that, despite the firm actions of the previous year, Iran could have played on French sensibilities to improve its position in Europe, at a time when it was under heavy and ultimately successful US pressure to end the war. The arrogant ignorance of the clerical leadership in Tehran, however, wasted the opportunity, as it had earlier with the UK.

THE UNITED KINGDOM

Revolutionary Iran's relations with the UK were clouded from the start by the long and unhappy history of British intervention in Iranian affairs ever since the late nineteenth century. After Ayatollah Khomeini returned to Tehran in February 1979, London soon acquired the status of a 'minor satan' in Iranian eyes. The British Embassy in Tehran, although not occupied as had happened with the US Embassy on 4 November 1979, was considered to be sufficiently under threat for most of its staff to be withdrawn. Thereafter, the Iranian authorities insisted that UK diplomatic representation should be limited to a British interests section in the Swedish embassy. The mutual antagonism was reinforced by Iranian irritation with the UK over the violent end of the occupation of the Iranian embassy in London in 1980.

The UK government, however, soon realized that it had little to gain from confrontation with Iran. It therefore chose to follow a policy of strict neutrality, particularly after the Gulf War broke out. The result was that, quite apart from the latent hostility between the two governments, commercial contacts continued to flourish. Even more significant was the fact that Iran continued to use London as a focal point in its own commercial contacts with the West. London was the major centre for Bank Melli, the foreign agent for Iran's Central Bank, for the National Iranian Oil Company which handled foreign hydrocarbon sales, and for the arms procurement agencies.

The relatively calm diplomatic scene was hardly ruffled by isolated terrorist incidents in London, as Iranian factions settled their differences. Even the fact that one Briton, Roger Cooper, was held without trial in Evin prison, or three Britons were held hostage in Lebanon did little to change matters, not least because the UK government rigidly refused to negotiate over the issue, unlike the Chirac government in France. However, growing Iranian frustration over the Gulf War and its international isolation eventually provoked a major diplomatic crisis.

In late May 1987, an Iranian diplomat was arrested in Manchester for a minor offence. The response in Tehran was immediate, officials of the Ministry of Islamic Guidance arrested a British diplomat in return. Eventually, the matter was resolved by the reduction of each country's diplomatic presence to one representative each and the Iranian Consulate in Manchester was closed. The UK government was extremely irritated by the incident and further difficulties were not long delayed.

Although the UK, in common with other European countries, initially refused to participate in the US naval operations in the Gulf in July 1987, the situation soon changed. Iranian frustration over the US operation began to be vented on the shipping of other nations. On 11 August, after evidence that Iran had mined the Sea of Oman, London decided to provide the naval support that Washington had requested the previous month. The 'Armilla Patrol', which had been escorting UK shipping in the Gulf since 1984, was reinforced with mine sweeping units.[7] Then, after a British vessel was attacked on 23 September, the UK government ordered that the Iranian arms procurement offices in London should be closed.

The Iranian authorities wisely did not over-react to the British actions. As a result, the diplomatic environment gradually improved during the latter part of 1988 and negotiations over the full restoration of diplomatic relations began. All the efforts, however, were aborted by Ayatollah Khomeini's sudden condemnation of the Indian-born British author, Salman Rushdie, in February 1989, for his novel, *The Satanic Verses*. The resultant death threats against Mr Rushdie and the UK government's refusal to act against continued sale of the book in question caused outrage in Tehran. Diplomatic and commercial relations were ended at Majlis insistence so that the breach between the UK and Iran was finally complete.

3 EUROPEAN RESPONSES

The most striking feature of the general trend of European policies towards the Islamic Republic of Iran was the fact that, initially at least, every European state was prepared to accept the implications of the revolution in 1979. US anger over the occupation of its embassy on 4 November 1989 and the consequent economic embargo received much public sympathy in Europe but little official support. The outbreak of the Iran–Iraq War in September 1980 was met, after the initial panic, with diplomatic disinterest and commercial anticipation.

Even though an arms embargo was supposed to be in force, Europe was soon heavily involved in supplying the belligerents. France clearly did not observe the embargo, given its supplies to Iraq and the UK did little, until 1987, to interfere with Iranian arms purchasing activities in London. Equally, little was done to impede the activities of the Luchaire company in France and its associated companies in Belgium, the UK, the Netherlands, Sweden, Italy and West Germany in supplying Iran with massive quantities of explosives.[8] In any case, neutral European states outside the European Community (EC), were not bound by the embargo and profited from the limited restraint shown by EC member-states.

Issues such as hostage-taking in Lebanon after 1985,[9] the earlier attacks on the multinational force (involving French, US, Italian and UK troops) in Beirut in December 1983, and terrorist incidents in Europe produced gusts of rhetoric but did not significantly disrupt relations with Iran. European states did concert anti-terrorist measures through the Trevi Group, but this was as much in response to their perceptions of Libyan- and Syrian-backed terrorism as it was directed against Iran. It seemed, in effect, as if European states were not prepared to make a common stand over Iran, as they had in 1980, in the Venice Declaration, over the Arab–Israeli conflict.

In large measure, this reluctance reflected the very different views European states took of their national interests. It also reflected their reluctance to allow pan-European organizations, such as the EC, to usurp the prerogatives of national sovereignty over matters of foreign policy. In addition, there was also a strong component of anxiety over being too closely associated with US policy towards Iran and the Middle East. This reflected another anxiety, that of being too closely associated with the UK, given its evident muscularity over Middle Eastern affairs and its closeness with the Reagan administration in Washington. The reluctance was only reinforced by the revelations of the Irangate and Contragate scandals in Washington in 1986.

As a result, it took a long time before something resembling a common European attitude towards Iran emerged. When it did, it was not events on the European continent that stimulated the move, but the issue of the Gulf War. For the first five years of the war, European states took the attitude close to that immortalized by the former US Secretary of State, Henry Kissinger, when he commented, 'Too bad they can't both lose'.[10] Most European politicians felt that the Gulf War was one that Iraq could not lose and Iran could not win. It was a belief that was maintained despite occasional anxieties caused by periodic massive Iranian offensives, particularly that launched in December 1986–January 1987 against the defences of Basra.

The situation changed as a result of the Kuwaiti appeal for protection from Iranian attacks on its shipping at the end of 1986 and the renewal of the 'tanker war' in 1987. It was the Iranian decision in mid-1987, frustrated by Iraqi air attacks on Iranian oil terminals at Kharg, Larak and Sirri islands and on tanker traffic from them, to turn on all shipping in the Gulf that caused the change of heart. It was first demonstrated by the unanimous support accorded in July 1987 to the UN Resolution 598 calling for a cease-fire in the war, even though there were national disagreements over the issue of a concomitant arms embargo in January 1988.[11] It was soon followed by ever wider support for the US naval action in the Gulf. It seemed to be justified by the virtually universal Muslim condemnation of Iran over the riots during the annual *hajj* in Mecca in July 1987.

The simple fact was that European powers had decided that Iran's attitudes towards the maritime conflict in the Gulf now threatened their own vital national interests. The result was that, for the first time since 1979, they seemed to be acting in concert – although not through the EC. Instead, the basic organizational structure for concerting naval strategy turned out to be the wider Western European Union forum.

It was a solidarity that was to prove illusory, however, for, nine months later, the apparent EC unanimity over rejecting Ayatollah Khomeini's condemnation of Salman Rushdie soon gave way to national anxiety over commercial access to Iran in the wake of the cease-fire. EC ambassadors who had virtually all been withdrawn from Tehran began to trickle back several weeks later, as individual states moderated their stances in terms of perceived national interest. United European attitudes over terrorism and hostage-taking had already broken down a year earlier, as first France and then West Germany negotiated separately for the release of their nationals.

HOSTAGES IN LEBANON

Indeed, the issue of Western hostages held in Lebanon was one of the two major ways in which European states came into contact with the radical aspect of the Islamic revolution in Iran. It was evident from the very earliest days of the revolution that at least one of the factions closest to Ayatollah Khomeini was anxious to encourage the spread of Islamic radicalism beyond the borders of Iran. For his close clerical collaborators, it was inherent in the very process of the Islamic revolution that its success could not be confined to Iran but would inevitably have to be emulated on a wider scale.[12]

The organizational background

Soon after the revolution, the new religious regime created the Vahdat (the Islamic reunification movement, under the Council for the Islamic Revolution), an organization dedicated to overseeing the growth of a pan-Islamic movement stimulated by the force of the Iranian example. It was eventually placed under the control of Ayatollah Hussein Ali Montazeri, who was also appointed Ayatollah Khomeini's putative successor in 1986. The movement had little to do with terrorism, however,[13] for its main function was propaganda. Indeed, Ayatollah Montazeri was eventually removed from the succession process because of his open opposition in late 1988–early 1989 to illegal and unrestrained oppression inside Iran. He objected, in a powerful open letter, to a wave of executions designed to destroy domestic opposition elements.

At the same time, it was clear that the radicals in the revolution would not necessarily abide by conventional diplomatic process and that the new clerical leadership under Ayatollah Khomeini would not necessarily reject them.[14] The US Embassy siege in November 1979, for example, was spearheaded by a radical Islamic leftwinger, Dr Habibollah Peyman, who believed in popular revolution and was profoundly anti-Western. He was supported by a radical mullah, Mussavi Khoeinia, and the two were able to persuade Ayatollah Khomeini to support the siege – albeit, eventually for his own ends – despite the fact that the action was completely illegitimate under international law.[15] Populist Islamic support was the sole justification and legitimization required, in the eyes of the new regime.

The result was that Islamic revolutionary Iran entered the 1980s with two aspects of its foreign policy clearly defined. It intended to encourage the Islamic revolution elsewhere and it was quite prepared to ignore the conventional niceties of diplomatic convention to achieve its policy goals. The only issue that was still in doubt was whether 'export of the revolution' was to be carried out by example or by direct intervention in suitable areas.

In the event, both policies seem to have been adopted. The revolution had occurred at a time when, for quite different reasons, Islam had become a political and ideological rallying cry elsewhere in the Middle East. The previous decade had seen the popular rejection of secular Arab nationalism and its replacement by renewed hope in Islamic paradigms in the Levant and in North Africa.[16] The result had been the growth of Islamist movements amongst the Middle East's Sunni majority and this, in turn, had coincided with the Iranian revolution. The events in Iran seemed to justify the general belief that Islam was a viable political alternative[17] and, not surprisingly, Sunni Islamists began to beat a path to Tehran's door.

These foreign groups were controlled in Tehran through the *Pasdaran* (Revolutionary Guards) and the Ministry of Foreign Affairs. In theory they came under the Council for the Islamic Revolution, controlled by Ayatollah Montazeri. In reality, control of the operation seems to have been seized by some unsavoury kinsmen of his, centred around the shadowy figure of Mehdi Hashemi, who was to figure briefly in the Irangate revelations of 1986 before being arrested and executed the following year.

Their activities – largely linked to propaganda and ideological education – were part of the major propaganda effort which the Islamic Republic undertook from 1980 onwards. It became particularly important after March 1982, when a seminar held in Tehran on the ideal Islamic government concluded that Islam was a ' . . .weapon in revolutionary wars against the rich and corrupt'.[18] It was then that operational control of these groups seems to have been taken over by Hizbullah. This had been revived in 1979 as a radical political movement which had originally been used to establish the Khomeini regime firmly in place in Iran. Now it was to become the standard bearer of radical, revolutionary Islam abroad as well.

At the same time, another organization within Hizbullah apparently began to be set up, under a committee of three persons appointed by Ayatollah Khomeini – Hojatolislam Fazlallah Mahalati who had been active in Iman Musa Sadr's Amal movement in Lebanon in the 1970s and who had been Defence Minister in the early days of the Islamic Republic, and Ali Akbar Mohtashemi, future ambassador to Syria and, later Interior Minister. The committee was charged with creating an effective commando within the Hizbullah movement. The commando was designed to use foreign recruits for activities, including those conventionally construed to be terrorist in nature, directed towards the spread of the Islamic revolution abroad and against its perceived enemies and dissidents.[19]

There were many elements within the new Iranian regime that were strongly opposed to policies of this kind. They included the secularist elements originally associated with the Bazargan government (the first government in revolutionary Iran that was forced from office by the US Embassy seizure) and the Bani Sadr presidency. They also included elements from the pragmatist mullahs that began to come to the fore after 1984. One of the leading members was Hojatolislam Ali Akbar Rafsanjani who began to dominate the governmental structure after 1985.

Increasingly, the radical hardliners linked to Hizbullah attempted to use the movement's revolutionary interests abroad, particularly in Lebanon, to embarrass the pragmatists in the domestic political arena. This was part of the reason for the Irangate revelations in 1986 – the Hashemi group appears to have tried to discomfort Hojatolislam Rafsanjani, who was by then dominant within the power structure, but to have been eventually outflanked by him. It was also why Mr Rafsanjani was so reluctant to respond to Western demands for hostage releases after the end of hostilities in the Gulf War. To have done so too readily would have made him vulnerable to attack by the radical factions, even after his election as President of Iran under the new post-Khomeini constitution in September 1989.

THE MOVE INTO LEBANON

The best opportunity to test the viability of radical policies was provided in 1982 by the Israeli invasion of Lebanon in June 1982. Immediately after the invasion, a detachment of Revolutionary Guards from a unit committed to supporting Islamic activities abroad was sent to Zebdani, on the Syrian–Lebanese border. Other detachments soon followed and links were made with Shia militants in the Bekaa valley around Baalbeck. Eventually, Iran had a detachment of around 2,000 *Pasdaran* located in Lebanon and Syria as an advance guard for the Islamic revolution abroad.[20]

The units found a fertile ground awaiting them. Not only had the majority Shia population been radicalized during the 1960s and 1970s by the activities of the founder of Amal, Imam Musa Sadr,[21] but the Israeli invasion had prompted a split within the movement. The leader of Amal's militia, Hussein Mussavi, had rejected Amal's attempts to support US mediation in trying to persuade the Israelis to withdraw and was soon persuaded to found a new radical Shia militia, Islamic Amal. At the same time, a parallel Shia movement, under the spiritual leadership of a well-known mullah, Sheikh Fadlallah, who had outflanked the major Shia conservative religious leader, Sheikh Mohammed Mahdi Shamseddin, emerged as a Lebanese version of Hizbullah.

Iran's support for both movements was to be critical. The operation appears to have cost around $70 million annually, but it provided considerable diplomatic advantage initially. Hizbullah soon began to act as an umbrella organization for other Shia factions, such as the Mughniya group with its links into the Gulf. Because of this loose structure, it was never under direct Iranian control, although there was often close collaboration between its component groups and the Iranian embassies in Beirut and Damascus. At the same time, as its activities expanded, so its component groups, which often engaged in autonomous activities which were only loosely co-ordinated, began to operate under a series of different names, such as Islamic Jihad and the Revolutionary Justice Organization, to name but the best known.

Other links were also created – with the Syrian intelligence services, for example, since Syria controlled access from Iran to Lebanon, and, eventually, with Palestinian extremists, such as the Popular Front for the Liberation of Palestine-General Command (PFLP-GC), a pro-Syrian group under Ahmad Jibril, which, by 1988, had moved very close to Hizbullah and Iran. The result was a degree of loose co-operation between Syria, Hizbullah and Palestinian extremists.

Collaboration was not consistent – Syria backed Amal for example, and Hizbullah and Amal were frequently in conflict over the control of Lebanon's Shia community. None the less there could certainly be close co-operation on occasion. This was well demonstrated by the increasingly close collaboration between Hizbullah and Palestinian groups in attacks on the Israel security zone in Southern Lebanon which was nominally under the control of Antoine Lahad's South Lebanese Army, an Israeli-backed Christian militia.

The US position

The taking of hostages became an acute diplomatic issue for two simple reasons. First, the USA became heavily involved in attempts to extricate Israel from Lebanon in 1983 and, in the process, became identified in the Shia mind with the Maronite community. Second, the pursuit of a radical Islamic state in Lebanon presupposed the removal of the significant Western community there, on the grounds of removing Western corruption from the Islamic environment and destroying imperialism. However, the actual process of hostage-taking might never have begun, had it not been for the US membership of the multinational force (MNF), introduced into Beirut in the wake of the Israeli siege of the city.

The problem was that the US contingent soon became associated with the discredited Christian-dominated Lebanese government. This had begun when the Lebanese army and the two Shia militias – Amal and Hizbullah – became locked in battle at the end of August 1983. US marines intervened to stop the fighting, which involved Christian Lebanese army units which US instructors had been retraining. It became far more serious after the Druze militias in the Chouf mountains forced the Lebanese army back into Souk al-Gharb, just above the Beirut suburb of Babda. US naval units provided covering fire for the embattled Lebanese army and the US MNF contingent was blamed.

Soon after came the bombing of the US marine headquarters and the start of the wave of assassinations and kidnappings of US citizens, all clearly organized by Hizbullah under one of its many guises. That was accompanied by a growing series of aircraft hijacks, usually linked either to a previous bombing outrage or to official retaliation. The major targets were US and Kuwaiti aircraft, largely because the sequeliae of the original attack on the US marine headquarters involved US reactions to it and, later, the Kuwaiti arrests of those responsible for the December 1983 bombings of the US and French Embassy buildings there by associates of the Mughniya faction of Hizbullah.

The French experience

Although French troops in the MNF had also been attacked by Hizbullah because of French support for the Christian-dominated Lebanese government, Europeans only really became targets of Shia hostility later on as the determination to force foreigners out of Lebanon became greater. There were also ancillary factors involved that often had nothing to do with religious or ideological imperatives. Autonomous groups who had no religious status often saw the commercial value in hostages, for example. They kidnapped individuals either for ransom or to sell on to clandestine Shia groups associated with Hizbullah

It became increasingly clear that the activities of clandestine Shia groups in Lebanon were not consistently, nor directly, linked to events involving Iran, as the continuing chaos inside the country and conflicts with neighbouring countries provided its own rationale for them. Thus French support for Iraq in the war did not, in itself, stimulate hostage-taking of French citizens in Lebanon. Far more important was the perception of France as a former colonialist ruler still pursuing neo-colonialist policies which were also identified as anti-Islamic. In addition, there was the factor of what was perceived in the Muslim world as generalized and exclusive Western support for Israel.

European interests also became a major target for Shia hostility by 1985 because the US presence in Lebanon had been dramatically reduced. By October 1984, the official US presence in Lebanon had been reduced to six persons, compared with 190 persons a year before.[22] Thus Europeans now became hostage victims, both as a means of removing the remaining Western presence from Beirut. French nationals became particular targets as hostage-taking became a technique to apply pressure to the French government.

In this latter respect, there were three competing motivations. The primary one was the attitude adopted towards the French presence in

Lebanon by Shia extremists. Second to this came the issue of France's antagonistic attitude towards Iran. Thirdly, there was also the fact that Syrian intelligence sources were not averse to using Hizbullah, over which Syria had some control because of its military presence in Lebanon, for its own complex diplomatic ends. The Syrians were certainly to be involved on several occasions later on in arranging hostage releases – a clear indication of the contacts they had with the various groups involved.[23]

During 1985 five French citizens were taken hostage. Two were diplomats; another, Gilles Peyroles, was the head of the French cultural centre in Tripoli; another, Jean-Paul Kauffmann, was a journalist; and the fifth, Michel Seurat who was the only Frenchman to die in captivity, was a researcher living in Lebanon who had been investigating Islamic fundamentalism.[24] This has been suggested as a reason for his capture, particularly because of his interest in the Ikhwan movement in Syria. One other additional reason for the kidnappings seems to have been a desire to force the French authorities to release Lebanese prisoners in France accused of terrorist activities.

In March 1986, four hostages were taken, all of them members of an Antenne-2 television team. Four more French citizens were taken during 1986 and January 1987, nearly all of them as a result of a French decision in February 1986 to expel two pro-Iranian Iraqis to Baghdad. The two individuals concerned were eventually returned to Paris, after being pardoned by President Saddam Hussein of Iraq as a result of desperate French diplomatic intercession because of the kidnappings in Lebanon.

By this time, the French presence in the Muslim areas of Lebanon had practically disappeared. In any case, the change in government in France – the Chirac government came to power in March 1986 – presaged a change in policy, in which Iran was to be encouraged to dissuade their Lebanese clients from attacking France. The result was that, by May 1988, all the French hostages in Lebanon had been freed.

There is little doubt, however, that the weapon of hostage-taking had been – and was perceived in Lebanon to have been – successfully used. The French community had been effectively forced out of Muslim-controlled West Beirut and from other Muslim areas of Lebanon. France had changed its policies towards Iran (a switch in which the hostages issue had played a minor part). It had reversed its expulsion policies as far as pro-Iranian Iraqis were concerned. It had also reversed its refugee policies as far as the MKO were concerned. Finally, it had had to come to terms with the reality of Syria's link with Iran and control of Lebanon in its policies towards the Middle East.

Other European hostages

The French government had succeeded in obtaining the release of its hostages by a carrot-and-stick policy and by trying to persuade Tehran into pressuring its own clients in Lebanon. Other countries were to succeed in exactly the same way. Indeed, the preferential links between Tehran and countries such as West Germany and Italy meant that it was to prove relatively easy for them to obtain hostage releases. West German statesmen, for example, were particularly careful to maintain good relations with Tehran and to balance them carefully with their relations with Iraq.[25] The real difficulties were encountered by the US and the UK.

After the US military and diplomatic departure from Lebanon, more US hostages were seized. In 1986, as a result of the Irangate negotiations, several hostages were released, but at massive US diplomatic cost. It was clear that the same technique could not be used for the remaining US hostages who now numbered nine persons. Instead, the US, in pursuing an antagonistic and confrontational policy towards Iran, seemed to accept that it would have effectively to abandon its citizens held in Lebanon.

Even the end of the Gulf War did little to help the US position. The Iranian authorities made it clear that they could and would do little. This continued to be true even after the death of Ayatollah Khomeini in June 1989. The new authorities in Tehran made it clear that they were not prepared to help until Washington unfroze the $5 billion worth of Iranian funds that had been held by the USA since the US Embassy hostage crisis in 1979 and until the USA delivered arms paid for by the Shah's regime but never delivered. Even then, it was clear that Tehran could guarantee nothing and that any solution to the problem would also have to involve Syria as the dominant power in Lebanon.

The implications of this for the three UK hostages held in Beirut – Terry Waite, Brian Keenan and John McCarthy – were bad. John McCarthy was a journalist who disappeared in April 1986, just after Brian Keenan, a teacher at the AUB, had been kidnapped. They, like Alex Collet, another journalist who had died during his captivity which had begun in March 1985, seem to have been part of the wave of kidnappings designed to force Europeans out of the Lebanon.

The case of Terry Waite, the Archbishop of Canterbury's special envoy, was different. He had been an experienced negotiator with Middle Eastern governments and with terrorist groups. In the early days of the Iranian revolution he had successfully negotiated the release of Christians held in Iran, in February 1985 he had persuaded the Qadhafi regime in Libya to release four Britons and in 1986 he had been instrumental in the release of two US hostages from Lebanon.

Indeed, that may have been his undoing, for it was on his return to Lebanon to negotiate further US releases in January 1987 that he was kidnapped. It has been surmized that Islamic Jihad suspected him of being too closely involved with the USA and no longer accepted him as a valid negotiator. It was also apparently felt that he had failed to deliver on promises to persuade the Kuwaiti authorities to release seventeen prisoners held after the attacks on US and French diplomatic buildings in December 1983. However, no details have ever come to light, despite repeated efforts by the Church of England to negotiate on his behalf, both in Lebanon and with Iran.

The UK government had consistently refused to discuss, let alone negotiate, with any government or group that it construed to be involved in terrorist activities. It even condemned other governments for doing so. Quite apart from the French government's behaviour, which London found easy to condemn, the British government even tried to organize a boycott of Algeria, after the Algerian government had successfully brought a hijack of a Kuwaiti airliner to a successful conclusion in April 1988. British attitudes were deeply resented in Algiers and the result was that Algeria ceased to be a potential intermediary for the UK, despite its good relations in Tehran and in Beirut. The British government was virtually the only government to adopt such a hardline stance. It was, as a result, the only government unable to achieve any releases from the shadowy hostage-takers in Beirut.

None the less, UK officials clearly hoped that Iran, at least, would use its good offices in persuading Hizbullah in Lebanon to release British hostages, once diplomatic relations had been restored. However, they overlooked the problem that they would also have to deal with Syria – with which diplomatic relations had been broken in late 1986 in the aftermath of the attempted bombing of an El Al airliner at Heathrow. In any case, relations with Iran remained very poor in the wake of the Rushdie affair and no quick solution to the plight of the UK hostages could therefore be expected.

TERRORISM IN EUROPE

The issue of Iranian-backed terrorism in Europe, even though it exercised European minds, seems to have played a subsidiary role in Hizbullah strategy. Although French, West German and Italian security officials are said to have planned a common strategy in anticipation of Iranian-backed terrorism in March 1983,[26] Iranian concerns in Europe were far more linked towards propaganda on behalf of the Islamic Republic. None the less, over the next few years, considerable numbers of Iranian diplomats, businessmen and students were expelled.

In France seventy persons were expelled between 1982 and 1986 and the Islamic Cultural Association was disbanded. In 1987, a further sixteen members of a group linked to Hizbullah were expelled.[27] Several Iranian diplomats in Italy and twenty persons in Spain were expelled in 1984. In the UK, a further twenty-three militants were expelled in 1984[28] and there were new expulsions in 1988. One of the reasons for the expulsions was the belief that Iranian embassies abroad were being used as a cover for activities connected with terrorism.

At the same time, European states began to formulate a unified response towards terrorism which culminated in the Trevi Group contacts from 1986 onwards, in which common anti-terrorist measures were developed. The range of terrorism involved was far wider than just that connected with Iran or the Middle East, for the Trevi Group was also concerned with the IRA, ETA, and the various urban groups linked to France, Belgium, West Germany and Italy. None the less, there is little doubt that Iran played a central role in their deliberations.

In fact, the major activity in which Hizbullah was involved was propaganda amongst Muslim students and migrants abroad. This included the preparation and dissemination of publicity materials and the organization of tours to Iran. Under the cover of these tours, a small number of persons were recruited into the more clandestine activities of Hizbullah. These, in turn, often became the agents of Iranian terrorist attacks on opponents of the Islamic regime abroad.

One of the earliest cases of such activities was the assassination attempt in Paris on Shapour Bakhtiar, the last prime minister under the Shah. Those involved were often Lebanese, no doubt because of the traditionally close links between the Shia community there and Iran. Indeed, attempts to achieve the release of one of them – Anis Naccache – became a *cause célèbre* for Hizbullah in Lebanon. Hizbullah's obsession with this was closely paralleled by a similar obsession on the part of the Mughniya faction in the organization over the release of the seventeen Shia prisoners held in Kuwait as a result of the December 1983 bombings there. It was this concern that was responsible for the repeated hijacks of civilian, particularly Kuwaiti, aircraft during the remainder of the decade.

There were also attacks (later shown to have been carried out by groups linked to Syria) on other former officials of the Shah in France and elsewhere. Indeed, in the early days of the revolution, it is believed that pro-Syrian groups frequently operated on behalf of the Islamic Republic in eliminating its dissidents. Pro-Bani Sadr and MKO dissidents were also the subject of attack. In the UK, a dissident was killed by a bomb in 1986 and there were several other attacks as well.

Terrorism in France

France was a particular target of terrorism, not only because it was a haven for anti-Khomeinist Iranians, but also because of its large Muslim migrant population. The terrorist groups involved were not only Iranian, or linked to Iran, although this was certainly the case with the Naccache group. Other groups stemming from Lebanon were secular in nature and were often linked to other issues than the Lebanese civil war or Islamic fundamentalism.

One such group from Lebanon – the Georges Abdallah group, all of whose members came from a single Maronite village – was Marxist in inspiration. It took part in activities that supported Iranian objectives only because of a perceived common purpose of confronting US imperialism.[29] None the less, the release of its members from French prisons became part of the demands of the Committee for the Liberation of Arab and Middle Eastern Political Prisoners (CLAMEPP). This shadowy group carried out a series of serious bomb attacks in Paris and elsewhere in February and September 1986.

Several of its presumed members were arrested in March 1987, including one Mohammed Mouhajer, a French citizen born in Lebanon and a member of a prominent Bekaa valley family. Interestingly enough, although Mr Mouhajer would have appeared to be an ideal candidate for Hizbullah, he was discharged as not guilty one year later. Charges were levelled, instead, against five North Africans from Tunisia. Fouad Ali Saleh, Abdelhamid Baddaoui, Fehti Bourguiba, Hassan Aroua and Omar Agnaou were also accused of having planted a devastating bomb in the *Tati* store in Rue du Rennes on 17 September 1986.[30]

The fact that those involved were North African was significant. The majority of Muslim migrants in France come from North Africa. They number about 1.5–2 million. Many of them have been radicalized by their experiences in France and, with the advent of the 1980s and the success of the Iranian revolution, many of them turned to Islamic fundamentalism, rather than the secularist values of European socialism, to express their resentments. They had available to them not only the mosques and immigrant organizations already created in France, but also new, radical organizations.

Some of these were linked to Iran and Hizbullah or were sympathetic to it. The former Algerian president, Ahmad Ben Bella, for example, quickly became notorious for his pro-Iranian sympathies. Other groups, such as the

Radical Islamist Movement led by the Algerian, Rashid Ben Aissa, in Paris was linked to pro-Iranian groups in West Germany. Contacts were maintained through formal conferences, such as one held in 1983 in Dusseldorf, in the Ruhr. West Germany was apparently chosen as a meeting place because Iranian access there was much easier than elsewhere in Europe as a result of the good relations between Bonn and Tehran.

Meetings such as these were dominated by Iranian representatives and organizers. Their overt purpose was to popularize the achievements of the Islamic Republic, discussion of the political and ideological implications of Islam and exchanges of information on matters of importance to Islamists, particularly those in the migrant communities in Europe. They also, however, provided the setting in which the types of terrorist network like CLAMEPP that appeared in France in 1986 could be covertly organized.

Indeed, the combination of relatively easy Iranian access to West Germany, because of the careful diplomatic links preserved by Bonn with Tehran, and of a large, discontented North African migrant community in France nearby, offered an ideal opportunity for the organization of terrorism. There is little doubt that Iran was involved in these activities. In June 1987, the French police arrested and expelled fifty-seven Middle Eastern nationals for being involved in terrorism and attempted to arrest an Iranian, Vahid Gurdji, for organizing terrorist incidents. It was an action which, even though it caused the rupture of diplomatic relations with Iran, none the less ended the threat of Iranian-inspired terrorism in France.

Links with North Africa

It seems most likely that the involvement of North Africans, particularly Tunisians, in terrorism in Europe linked to Iran was the result of propaganda and organizational activities based in Europe. None the less, there are several long-established Islamist movements in North Africa itself, some of which certainly have links with Iran. The evidence, however, suggests that there is no significant connection between Islamists in North Africa and Iranian-inspired terrorism in Europe.

Morocco

In Morocco, for example, there has been an active Islamist movement since the early 1970s. In 1973, the Ikhwan Muslimin – the Egyptian fundamentalist movement created in the early 1920s by Hassan al-Banna, with Sayyid Qutb as its major ideologue – were accused of being responsible for the murder of a leading left-wing politician, Omar

Benjelloun. Abdulkrim Muta'i, a former administrator in the Moroccan education system, was held responsible – he was also said to have acted with official connivance because of governmental exploitation of the nascent Islamist movement against the secular left-wing opposition.

He fled to Saudi Arabia where he later became involved in the Grand Mosque attack in 1979. On escaping from Saudi Arabia, he set up the Jam'iyyat al-Shabab al-Islamiyyah. It soon split, with a separate organization, al-Mujahedin, being formed under Abdesslam Na'amani. Four other splinter groups appeared at the same time, one of them amongst Moroccan migrant workers and students in France.[31]

Both of the major groups associated with Muta'i are radical, clandestine and sympathetic to Iran. They both operate, however, quite independently from Iranian influence and compete for popular Moroccan attention against the preponderant official Islam as typified by King Hassan II[32] – the king is a descendent of the Prophet and has caliphal status in Morocco – and against two non-terrorist strands. One, the Jam'ah group, was founded by a former schools inspector, Abdesslam Yacine, in 1980. The other is a more inchoate strand of local preachers, such as Sheikh Zamzami of Tangier. In effect, these groups are marginalized within Moroccan society, even though they are sometimes linked to long-standing sufi orders, such as the Bushishiyya order, or apolitical movements, such as the Jam'at al-Tabligh wa al-Daw'a.[33] New factions constantly appear – the most recent, in Ksar al-Kabir, openly espouses Iranian concepts of the Islamic state but without any contact with Iran itself.

They were prominent, however, in the January 1984 riots in Morocco which resulted from a sudden rise in retail food prices as a result of the suppression of price subsidies in accordance with IMF demand. King Hassan insisted that those responsible were 'Khomeinists'.[34] However, although there is plenty of evidence that Iranian propaganda was available in Morocco, it seems unlikely that the riots were in any way inspired by Iran.

There have been suggestions, but with little evidence, that the Hizb al-Tahrir al-Islami (the Islamic Liberation Party) has been trying to organize within the Moroccan armed forces since 1986.[35] The Hizb al-Tahrir al-Islami was originally an offshoot of the Ikhwan Muslimin and was founded in the early 1950s in Jordan, in the wake of the creation of Israel. Its aim was to recreate the Islamic ideal of the Muslim state under the first four 'Rightly Guided Caliphs' and its *modus operandi*, in Egypt, Libya and Tunisia, has been to operate through the armed forces.

Nevertheless, the government took stern action. Abdesslam Yacine was arrested and imprisoned for two years for insulting the government in his review *al-Sulh*; sixty-one persons were tried in Casablanca in July and thirteen death sentences were handed out[36] (although none have been put into effect). The result has been a far more circumscribed attitude on the part of Islamists since then. Support still exists, not least because of the continuing economic difficulties faced by the majority of the population. As recently as May 1990, 2,000 Islamists supporting the Yacine group, now renamed al-'Adl wa-l-Ihsan and recently banned by the government, were arrested in central Rabat after a demonstration. Iran, however, is too remote from the majority to serve as a guide and is condemned as obscurantist by most elements of minority opinion, not least because of the competing religious status of the Moroccan monarchy.

Algeria

The Algerian state is based on an inherent contradiction, which stems from the original nature of the Algerian national liberation movement, the FLN.[37] Since the FLN had to incorporate a range of segments of Algerian political opinion, it laid claim to Islamic legitimacy as well as to socialist orthodoxy. The same duality has been transferred into the constitutional makeup of the Algerian state.

In 1972, the Boumedienne regime cracked down on nascent Islamist movements, while giving the regime a more austere Islamic face. Islamist sentiment was channelled into the clandestine Ahl al-Daw'a movement which replaced the original officially tolerated Qiyam movement. Within six years, however, Islamist agitation appeared again, articulating the frustrations of the new Algerian working class and petty bourgeoisie in suburbs of Algiers, such as Kouba, Bir Mourad Rais and Hussain Dey, and in smaller provincial towns, such as Blida, Larbaa, El Oued, Biskra and Laghouat.

In Algiers the movement was dominated by Sheikh Ahmad Sahnoun in the La Concorde district of Bir Mourad Rais. Sheikh Sahnoun had always rejected government pretensions of control over the activities of imams and refused to publish the official khutbas issued by the Boumedienne regime for use during Friday prayers. Although this had frequently meant arrest, Sheikh Sahnoun had always sought a tolerant accommodation with the modern secular world.

This approach, however, increasingly isolated him from the more extremist Sheikh Abdellatif Sultani. By the mid-1970s, the two had split, with the more extremist Islamist wing being focused on the mosque in Algiers university. Here supporters of Sheikh Sultani, who was normally based in Hussein Dey, were in control. Sheikh Sultani's major supporter was Abbasi Madani, a former student who had studied in Europe and who gave the extremist wing of the Islamist movement a more modernist tinge.

Sahnoun, however, still commanded widespread respect, even amongst the more extreme Islamists.

In the early 1980s, the new Chadli Ben Djedid regime attempted to use the Islamist movement, by then close to the Ikhwan, against its opponents – supporters of the austere state capitalism of the former President Houari Boumedienne: supporters of the outlawed Algerian communist movement; the PAGS (Parti de l'Avant-Garde Socialiste); and members of the Berberist movement, centred in Kabylia and the Chaouia. By 1982, however, the dangers of this kind of policy were evident, and the movement was suppressed after a series of clashes with Berberist elements led to the death of a student at the University of Algiers. The urban fundamentalist movement persisted, however, particularly in Hussein Dey under its charismatic leader, Sheikh Sultani. A measure of its strength was provided in 1984, when Sheikh Sultani died and, within hours, there was a spontaneous 25,000-strong demonstration, despite an official information blackout.[38]

The increasing economic crisis in Algeria after 1982 stimulated discontent and Islamist agitation. By 1985, a small group in the Blida area had decided to take more violent action. In August of that year it attacked a police centre at Soumaa in order to capture weaponry. Bank robberies and bombings followed, despite gendarmerie and military action and, eventually, the group was dispersed close to Larbaa on 3 January 1987, with its leader, Mustafa Bouali, being killed.

Mustafa Bouali and his nine associates had been guerillas during the Algerian War of Independence. Their Islamism was a purely indigenous product, being borne out of their frustration with the development of the independent Algerian state. They had all become active in the late 1970s and were among the 135 Islamists arrested during disturbances in 1982 and tried in April 1985. Although sixty were acquitted and forty-four others were freed, five persons, including Bouali, were sentenced to life imprisonment *in absentia*. It was clear that his activities had little to do with Iranian influence, apart from the generalized stimulus to Islamist sentiment from seeing the Iranian revolution create an Islamic Republic in 1979.

Similar conclusions must apply to the more recent outburst of Islamist activity in the wake of the October 1988 riots throughout Algeria. Contrary to many press accounts, these were not Islamist-inspired, nor dominated by Islamist groups. There is considerable evidence to show that the riots were originally initiated by pro-Boumediennist and pro-PAGSist groups within the FLN. The role of the Islamists, particularly the groups around Ali Bel Hadj in the Bab el-Oued quarter of Algiers, became important only in a local sense as a result of repressive army action in Central Algiers and in Kouba.

Bel Hadj represents the most violent and extremist aspect of the new movement which has otherwise coalesced around the person of Abbasi Madani who leads the Front Islamique du Salut (FIS). Abbasi Madani has sought to take up the mantle of Sheikh Sultani and, apart from his powerbase in the outlying Algiers suburb of Bou Douaou, now seeks national stature. Madani is believed to depend on advisers who have extensive contacts abroad and is expected to attain a similar national status to that of Rashid al-Ghannushi in neighbouring Tunisia. There is no evidence to suggest, however, that these links are Iranian-inspired. There may be, none the less, indirect links with Iran through Algerian fundamentalists based abroad, such as Rashid Ben Aissa. However, even the evidence to support this thesis is very tenuous.

The older figure of Sheikh Sahnoun still really dominates the Islamist horizon, together with his relatively tolerant vision. During the October 1988 riots, it was Sheikh Sahnoun who was approached by the government with requests to call for calm. Indeed, it was his calls that were subsequently heeded. In the same way, it was Sheikh Sahnoun who was able to bring together different Islamist groups – such as the FIS and Al-Ishrah wal-Islah – together under the umbrella of the Da'wa al-Islamiyyah at the end of 1989 in major street demonstrations.

The conclusion must be that, even in the current situation where new prominence has been given to the Islamist movement, its inspiration is still essentially confined to the Algerian political and social environment. Even the legitimization of the Islamist movement, the FIS, as a political party in 1989 is unlikely to alter this, for, by being forced to participate on the formal political stage, the Islamist movement will find itself increasingly distracted by temporal issues. In such a context, the likelihood of a significant Iranian role seems increasingly remote.

Tunisia

The activities of the Islamist movement in Tunisia are very similar to those in Morocco and Algeria. The role of Iranian influence, despite government claims, has been minimal and has been confined to providing a stimulus by example as a result of the Iranian revolution. In all other respects, however, the mainline fundamentalist movement has depended entirely on domestic inspiration, even when offshoots from it carried out violent clandestine activities. The only outside influences of note have been the Qadhafi regime in Libya and the Hizb al-Tahrir al-Islami.

The movement was stimulated by the abandonment of the co-operative movement of the 1960s in Tunisia and the creation of a free market economy under the premiership of Hedi Nouiria. Its founders came basically from educated groups within Tunisian society and it has appealed to the new working class and the petty bourgeoisie. Since the start of the 1980s, however, it has become particularly effective within the University of Tunis, where there have been regular confrontations with the authorities.

The radicalization of the movement and its increasing politicization came about because of three inter-related factors. These were the influence of the secular European-style left in the late 1970s, combined with increasing government repression of the trade union movement after the riots of January 1978 and the example of the Islamic revolution in Iran in 1979.[39] Since then it has depended on support from the university student body, the teaching profession, the urban proletariat and the lower ranks of the administration.

The main ideologue of the movement, Rashid al-Ghannushi, and his aides, such as Abd al-Fattah al-Muru, have, however, been inspired by the Qutbist ideology of the Ikhwan Muslimin. The role of Iran in their political development has been simply to persuade them in 1981 to form an organized movement, the Harakat al-Ittijah al-Islami (also known as the Mouvement de la Tendence Islamique – MTI). Even more radical factions, such as the 15/21 movement of Sheikh Hamida Enneifer, adhere to the same ideological principles.

Furthermore, both movements have always looked for legitimate political positions inside Tunisia, despite repeated attempts at government repression and accusations of links with Iran. This was particularly the case in 1981, when the leadership and 100 members were imprisoned for up to ten years. They were released in August 1984, after the bread riots in January of that year, in which grassroots Islamists were much in evidence. None the less, a further forty-eight members had been imprisoned in 1983. The Bourguiba regime decided, however, to seek a degree of reconciliation in 1985, and the MTI was allowed to register as a cultural association

To a large extent, however, the Tunisian authorities did accept that the MTI and its associates were not attempting violent overthrow of the regime. It followed, therefore, that the attempted rebellion in Gafsa in January 1980, in which Libyan-backed Tunisian dissidents, said to be Islamist, were involved had nothing to do with the MTI. Equally, the activities of the Hizb al-Tahrir al-Islami, were quite separate from the main movement. On 19 August 1983, thirty members of the movement were put on trial. They included nineteen members of the Tunisian armed forces and eleven civilians and had been members of the organization since 1981. No further evidence of the movement has since appeared.[40]

The Bourguiba regime was unable to preserve this degree of objectivity, however. In March 1987, the authorities moved against the MTI again. Over 1,000 persons were arrested during the year and the government increasingly tried to link the MTI with Iran. The accusations were prompted by arrests in Paris that month of five Tunisians in connection with the CLAMEPP movement which was linked to Iran. The evidence connecting them with the MTI was irrelevant, however.

In September 1987, ninety MTI activists, including Rashid al-Ghannushi, were accused of planting bombs. This came in the wake of bombs that were planted in tourist resorts on 2 August by six persons who had no connection whatsoever with the MTI.[41] The government, however, insisted on the MTI being responsible and President Habib Bourguiba began to insist that the MTI leaders should be condemned to death. In the end, however, he was forced from power by a legal *coup d'état* in November 1987, organized by the premier, Zine el-Abidine Ben Ali.

Since the Bourguiba regime was overthrown, the new Tunisian government has tried to find a basis for accommodation with the Islamist movement. That, in turn, has split into three factions of which the MTI is still the most important. It has now renamed itself as the Nahda Party, in accordance with government regulations which require that political movements are not based on religion or language. However, the Ben Ali regime has not yet been able to bring itself to legalize the movement.

The attitude of the Tunisian government appears to be rather blinkered. It seems to be satisfied that Iranian influence is virtually non-existent within the movement, although diplomatic relations with Iran, broken off in March 1987, in the wake of the arrests of the CLAMEPP activists in Paris, have not been renewed. It is also clear that the Tunisian Islamists seek legitimate participation in a pluralistic political system. The timidity demonstrated by the Tunisian authorities seems calculated to create the very danger, through frustration, that it appears most anxious to avoid – namely, an extension of disenfranchised support for the Islamist movement.

The Rushdie affair

The most public evidence of Iran's ability to affect the situation in Europe came, not from terrorism inspired by Iran and organized in Europe, but from a call from Ayatollah Khomeini to declare the British writer, Salman Rushdie, an apostate. Yet, even here, the real purpose behind the call seems to have been far more closely linked to Iranian domestic and regional concerns than it was to the European scene.

Rushdie's book, *The Satanic Verses*, was published in October 1988 and was immediately available in Iran. Rushdie's previous work had been extremely popular in the Islamic Republic and had received official approval. The latest work was clearly controversial, however, and a review in *Kayhan* during the same month warned the Iranian public not to read it, on the grounds that it was blasphemous.

In the UK, meanwhile, the book had become a *cause célèbre* with the Muslim community, which is largely Sunni in belief. This was because the offensive passages in it were circulated amongst the various mosques by two missionary organizations, one Saudi-backed and the other Iranian-backed. In short, Rushdie's work had become a weapon in the struggle between the two organizations for control of the UK Muslim community, now numbered at around 1.5 million persons.

Much of the community in the UK, however, comes from the Indian sub-continent and demonstrations took place in Lahore and Bombay in early February. In Pakistan, police intervention caused several deaths during the demonstrations and popular anger, both in the sub-continent and in the UK, began to mount. At this point, however, the demonstrations over the book coincided with two issues in Iranian domestic policy.

The first was that Ayatollah Khomeini had been horrified by certain aspects of Iranian Television which seemed to him to indicate that Western-style corruption was creeping back. He had threatened severe disciplinary measures to restore Islamic order in Iran, but had been dissuaded from putting the threats into practice. The second was that remnants of the Mehdi Hashemi group, radicals who had been ousted by Hojatolislam Rafsanjani in the Irangate scandal in 1986, complained to Ayatollah Khomeini's son, Ahmad, over *The Satanic Verses*. They asked him to persuade his father to issue a *fatwa* condemning it. Their purpose appears to have been to discredit the pragmatists, who were having a powerful moderating effect on Iranian foreign policy and seemed likely to dominate any post-Khomeini government.

Just after the riots in Lahore, the Ayatollah was asked to pronounce on the book and issued his famous *fatwa*. The result was catastrophic, for no-one could then proffer an alternative view of the situation, particularly when large reward payments were offered for Mr Rushdie's execution. Both Hojatolislam Rafsanjani, the Majlis Speaker, and Iran's president, Ayatollah Khomeini attempted initially to play down the seriousness of the situation, in order to save the precious recovery in diplomatic relations that Iran had begun to create in the wake of the cease-fire in the war. Both soon realized that this would not be possible.

Despite attempts by the UK government to find mediators and to cool the situation, the Iranian authorities proved obdurate. The Majlis was enraged by the UK government's response. In two quick measures it first placed an embargo on economic relations with the UK and then broke diplomatic relations between Tehran and London. The intensely public nature of the breach made it far more difficult to heal than is usually the case when relations are broken as the result of administrative fiat.

CONCLUSIONS

The result has been that, for domestic reasons, Iran created a political fact that cannot now be easily reversed. The practical consequence for Iran is that its own interests have been damaged and that little has been achieved to alter European attitudes in any significant way. Even though EC diplomatic solidarity was not long sustained, European states did nothing to accommodate Iran's demands that *The Satanic Verses* be banned. Indeed, European attitudes towards Iran and Islamism seem, if anything, to have stiffened, as the French controversy over the use of *chadors* and scarves in the school system indicates.

The Rushdie affair could stand as a suitable epitaph for the progress that Islam has achieved as the guiding principle of Iran's foreign policy over the past decade. Other states have been prepared to accommodate Iranian attitudes to the degree that it suited their own foreign policy objectives. They have not, however, been prepared to incline to Iranian demands if this condition were not satisfied. In short, the Rushdie affair is a paradigm for the success of diplomacy based on Islam, where short-term gains lead only to long-term disadvantage.

6 The GCC and the Islamic Republic: towards a restoration of the pattern[1]

Gerd Nonneman

Amid the flurry of activity and expectations in the aftermath of the cease-fire in the Gulf War, this chapter will examine more closely the attitudes of the Arab states in the Gulf (those states making up the Gulf Co-operation Council (GCC) since May 1981) towards their western neighbour, the Islamic Republic of Iran. It will be argued that a number of limitations on the foreign policies of these six states steer them naturally in an accommodating direction; that the initial developments of the Iranian revolution, and the resulting Iraq–Iran War, introduced a perceived level of threat temporarily high to push these political attitudes off course; and that the end of the war, and growing evidence of Iranian goodwill towards these states, will eventually lead to a restoration of the 'natural' pattern.

LIMITATIONS ON THE FOREIGN POLICIES OF THE GULF ARAB STATES

Two basic characteristics of the foreign policies of the six monarchical systems on the Arab side of the Gulf are: (1) that they are continually striving towards a secure, predictable regional environment; and (2) strong links between foreign policy and domestic security. This results from a vulnerability which is twofold: military-economic and ideological. Both of these concern three main issues. On the whole, the six states are militarily weak, with the relative exception of Saudi Arabia. They are dependent on utterly exposed oil fields and installations, and on fairly vulnerable oil export channels. In the case of the UAE, and to a certain extent also Bahrain and Qatar, they are linked to Iran by trade relations. In addition, there is a significant part of the population (in Bahrain a majority) which is Shia and/or of Persian extraction. This final point is linked to the second set of vulnerabilities, the ideological. Three powerful issues are involved: Islam, Arabism, and political participation. On all three counts the six have been vulnerable to external and internal criticism to varying degrees. Islam, for instance, ostensibly the main legitimizing factor for the Saudi regime, became especially resonant with the advent of the Iranian revolution. Given these vulnerabilities, a protective American umbrella, if kept relatively discreet, has remained an asset to be appreciated, most clearly so by the regimes in Saudi Arabia, Bahrain, Oman, and Kuwait.

In this context, mishandling of foreign policy can have highly dangerous consequences for domestic survival, both directly because of the ideological issues which may be involved; and indirectly because of the potential upsetting of regional security. Hence, the Gulf six in their regional foreign policy have generally been concerned to maintain bridges to all, to promote consensus, and not be too overtly active when such activity could draw anyone's ire. In the conduct of foreign policy, *domestic* security is ultimately paramount. If this latter factor at any time does necessitate coming off the fence, then there will generally be an effort to do so covertly and to try to balance words and actions in different fora. An example of the latter would be the divergence between positions adopted by the six individually, and the positions expressed by the GCC, once it was formed.

Partly as a symptom of the above, partly as a consequence of the structure of the domestic political system – particularly in Saudi Arabia – policy is liable to waver, to be unclear, sometimes of course intentionally so. Focusing on the Saudi case for a moment, three traits stand out. The decision-making process is diffuse; there is a continual seeking for compromise within the royal family; and there are greatly varying personalities among the senior princes, each with their own backgrounds.[2] An example would be the outspoken pro-Iraqi attitude of Prince Nayif, the Minister of the Interior.

Combined with the features mentioned before, this results in a predisposition against any strong long-term commitments to alliances or enmities. The normal policy output will, rather, be one of careful manoeuvring, staying in the safer channels of the stream; it will be a policy dictated by a pragmatic concern for domestic consensus and political stability, as well as regional security.

Unfortunately for the six, they are borne down upon by two regional giants, both violently opposed to the other and both very different from the conservative monarchical systems.

The Iranian revolution and its radical, expansive aftermath appeared to present these six states with a totally new, and potentially threatening, environment. The threat from Iran, which appeared to become a regional, military *and* domestic one, was confirmed by a number of declarations on the part of members of the Iranian leadership in 1979 and 1980. These statements made clear that powerful quarters in Iran did not consider the conservative leaderships at all legitimate. Indeed, the ruling families were depicted on these and later occasions as despotic and, worse, un-Islamic.

This external threat merged with the domestic one in a very direct way, because of the Shia factor on the Arab side of the Gulf. Some 65 per cent of Bahrainis are Shia, as well as some 30 per cent of Kuwaitis, 15 per cent of Qataris, 7 per cent of Saudis and 10 per cent of UAE citizens.[3] By the Summer of 1980 the perceived threat had become overpowering.

On the other side of the equation, the potential ally against this threat, Iraq, had moved away from its erstwhile radicalism. From the mid-1970s a shift in overall Iraqi foreign policy had been visible. This had been strengthened with the formal take-over of power by Saddam Hussein in 1979. By 1980 the six conservative Gulf states could look upon Iraq with less apprehension than had been their wont. Economic and socio-cultural links with Baghdad were growing. It appeared that the leadership in Baghdad had become more clearly pragmatic and now accepted existing Arab states as a given, no longer insisting on the abolition of borders and regimes in pursuit of Arab unity. In short, many believed that Iraq had become a more predictable power, behaving largely according to its pragmatic state interests.

This power, Iraq, was subject to precisely the same threat as that which the Gulf monarchies perceived themselves to be under, only more directly and intensely so. The resulting covert alliance between Baghdad and the Gulf's ruling families, therefore, was not particularly surprising. Although they all kept up a neutral front (in obeisance to the determinants listed earlier), the regional and domestic threat presented by Iran was too great to be left unchallenged, particularly when the actual challenger was at hand, and Iran itself appeared to be in chaos. At least Saudi Arabia, Kuwait, Abu Dhabi, Ras al-Khaima and Qatar, but probably the others as well (possibly excepting Dubai and Sharjah), supported the Iraqi invasion of Iran in September 1980, albeit reluctantly, as the only means left at their disposal. They were expecting a quick Iranian defeat and a subsequent return to a more settled, less threatening environment.[4]

Before considering subsequent developments, it must be stressed that the six states which today make up the GCC are by no means uniform – neither has their foreign policy output been. A brief scan reveals some of the particular features relevant for the purposes of this article. In Kuwait, the Arab nationalist issue has long been especially potent and its population relatively politically articulate. Both are to some extent rooted in the emirate's position next to Iraq, with the strength of the nationalist movement in Iraq forcing a political opening-up in Kuwait in the 1930s, as a counterweight against the call for Kuwait's integration into Iraq. In Saudi Arabia, Islam is ostensibly the main legitimizing force for the regime, necessitating close attention to the maintenance of Islamic credibility domestically and internationally. Another element distinguishing the Kingdom is its relatively greater military power. Bahrain and Qatar are both extremely weak and exposed, as well as being dependent on Riyadh. The UAE, apart from being a rather loose federation, is also characterized by a large reliance on offshore oilfields which are particularly vulnerable to Iranian action, and even has some joint oil fields. The state, but particularly Dubai, has long had a strong trading relationship with Iran (both official and unofficial) and much of the commercial activity around Dubai's harbour depends on people of Iranian extraction. Finally, there is Oman, which is saddled with a geographical position forcing it to a precarious sharing of the Strait of Hormuz with Iran. Another distinguishing feature of the Sultanate, is that Arabism never had quite the pull here that it had elsewhere, the country having been largely locked away from the rest of the Arab world until 1970. All of these factors have helped determine the individual states' reactions to events.

THE GULF ARAB STATES AND IRAN DURING THE WAR

Although there were differences in the extent to which support for Iraq was expressed, the basic picture remained the same. That picture was also fundamentally unaffected, initially, by Iraq's changing fortunes. Although the Gulf states all hastened to express their official neutrality after the first Iraqi blitz failed to produce the expected quick win and Iran started threatening them for their co-operation with Iraq, they remained effectively on the latter's side. During this period of stalemate in the war, from November 1980 to late September 1981, very tangible support for Iraq was given by Saudi Arabia (with trans-shipment of military as well as civilian supplies, in addition to $6 billion by April 1981 and another $4 billion during the remainder of the year) and Kuwait (trans-shipment facilities and $4 billion by April). The UAE provided between $1–3 billion in financial assistance and Qatar probably some $1 billion.[5] It was also during this period that Saudi Arabia gave Iraq an agreement in principle for the construction of a crude pipeline to the Red Sea. In the Gulf conflict, therefore, the Kingdom was effectively allied to Iraq. Kuwait's vital support did not extend to giving in to Iraq's demand for a 99-year lease of Bubiyan island. This phase witnessed another important development, after Oman nearly clashed with the Iranian navy in late 1980 in a naval accident. This led Sultan Qaboos to work out a *modus vivendi* with Iran in Gulf waters. Although remaining politically part of the pro-Iraqi camp, Oman from then on became more and more 'actively neutral'.

For the Gulf six, since the Iraqi campaign had become bogged down, the whole pre-war configuration underlying their initial policies had changed. There was no longer any pressing need for the war as the aim of reducing Khomeini's appeal had been achieved. At the same time, they had never wanted a drawn-out conflict with its implications of economic drain and military spill-over. The need to avoid these dangers was more important than anything which could be gained from further bleeding the two combatants. The Gulf states' main concern therefore became to end the war, a point on which Iraq, particularly from the Spring of 1981, very much agreed. The second imperative was to prevent an Iranian victory; hence the active support given to Baghdad. However, the Gulf rulers' traditional suspicions of Iraq had not evaporated completely. In the security discussions leading to the creation of the GCC in May 1981, Iraq was never thought of as a potential partner and the council's creation confirmed the republic's status as an outsider.

During the period of the Iranian counter-offensive, from September 1981 to June 1982, the GCC began to profile itself, and adopted a neutral position in the war between Iraq and Iran. This masked an emerging divergence, however, between the individual Gulf states. Saudi Arabia and Kuwait were effectively supporting Iraq. Kuwait added another $2 billion to the aid it had already provided, after Iranian missiles struck oil installations on the emirate's territory. Saudi Arabia also gave further financial aid. Bahrain too stuck to the pro-Iraqi camp, and blamed the coup attempt in late 1981 on Iranian instigation (probably with justification). The UAE, Qatar and Oman kept very much a low profile. In the subsequent period of virtual stalemate, until the Spring of 1984 (during which time Iran carried the war into Iraq), this configuration remained similar: Saudi Arabia and Kuwait started giving Iraq the proceeds of the sale of some 330,000 b/d of 'war relief crude', but Bahrain now also adopted the low profile of the remaining three, even though all four were temporarily prodded into action by Iran's incursion into Iraq.[6]

The period from the Spring of 1984 to January 1986 may be called one of internationalized conflict and stalemate, pitting Iraq's siege of Kharg and Iranian oil outlets and tankers, against Iranian retaliation against Arab ships and tankers carrying Arab oil. Iran issued repeated threats against Saudi Arabia and Kuwait. The latter two states took the lead in bringing the GCC round to a stance of explicit condemnation of Iran, and the organization sponsored a UN resolution condemning Iranian attacks. The Iranian verbal assault on the Gulf states was stepped up in this period, heightening Gulf antagonism. However, the Iranian switch, in May 1985, to a policy of trying to mend fences with the six, resulted in a mellowing of the latter's attitudes. Prince Saud al-Faysal went to Tehran at the invitation of the Iranian leadership, although the Saudis never stopped their effective support of Iraq. The communiqué of the GCC's November 1985 summit was more even-handed towards Iran and Iraq than previously, but continued to insist on taking two UN Security Council resolutions as a basis for peace negotiations, although Iran had rejected them. Iran's Foreign Minister Velayati visited Riyadh in December but the talks did not produce any agreement on ways to end the Gulf War.

A Saudi official said in 1987 that secret negotiations had been conducted with Iran in West Germany in May 1984, followed by similar meetings in Tehran and Riyadh. According to the official, who took part in the negotiations, the Saudi side asked if the Iranians would accept negotiations in the war if Saddam Hussein were to disappear. The answer was 'let him disappear first, then we'll see', and when the question was repeated on later occasions a similarly evasive reply was obtained. The Saudi side was further irritated by Iran's insistence on 'observer rights' in Mecca and Medina – which was refused outright by King Fahd – and on a say in all Muslim states' actions, within a consensus that should include Iran.[7]

This indicates that, although probably not wedded to Saddam's leadership, the Saudis were by no means prepared to drop support for Iraq, and were constantly irritated by Tehran's intransigence and demands. Nevertheless, they were certainly prepared to accept an outstretched hand in bilateral relations.

Kuwait was similarly open to any improvement in bilateral relations and welcomed the Iranian change in attitude from May 1985. But the Emirate did not reduce its support for Iraq, and criticism and threats from Tehran soon resumed. Members of the ruling family, followed even more stridently by the press, made their support for Iraq explicit. After several efforts in previous years, the National Assembly in 1985 succeeded in getting the annual KD 100 million subsidy to Syria stopped on the grounds of the latter country's support for Iran, although it had to settle for a compromise with the government whereby the latter would get more funds, at its disposal to grant to friendly countries, at its own discretion.[8]

As for the southern Gulf states, by the end of this period they had come to accept, gently coached along by Iran, that neutrality was their best option and might even help to provide a better outlook for peaceful resolution of the conflict. Iraq had come to acquiesce in this reality. Collectively, however, in the framework of the GCC, they still tilted towards Iraq. Moreover, one can argue that the understanding stance adopted by the Iraqi regime helped avoid possible strain on the relationship between Iraq and these Gulf states.

1986: DEVELOPMENTS FOLLOWING IRAN'S FAO VICTORY

With the capture of the Fao by Iranian forces on 9 February 1986, the further escalation of the 'tanker war' and the plummeting of oil prices (putting Iraq under grave financial pressure), the shape of the Gulf War was transformed. Riyadh and Kuwait strongly and explicitly attacked Iran, and the GCC as a body issued a strong condemnation of Tehran's actions. Nevertheless, even Saudi Arabia still showed a willingness to opt for a diplomatic approach and conciliation, if possible. Kuwait stands out in that, from the start of this period, both government and press took an unequivocally pro-Iraqi stand.

Continuing Iranian pressure, combining the carrot and the stick, succeeded in gradually reducing the UAE, Qatar and Oman again to effective neutrality, although the GCC umbrella continued to provide cover for the expression of more pro-Iraqi sentiments. These, however, appeared by now to be little more than words, urged upon them by Saudi Arabia and Kuwait. Indeed, it is believed that when the latter two countries pressed their GCC partners to extend the AWACS patrols over the entire Gulf in August, Qatar, the UAE and Oman refused.[9] The Kingdom and Kuwait, on their part, are thought to have extended another $4 billion 'loan' to Iraq in the second half of 1986.[10] In addition, Saudi Arabia is reported to have allowed Iraqi planes to land and refuel after hitting Iranian oil facilities in the southern Gulf.[11] The general 'camps' within the GCC on relations with Iraq and Iran, which would endure until the end of the conflict, were now clearly crystallizing. They featured the neutral camp of Qatar, the UAE and Oman, working above all towards good bilateral relations with Iran while claiming this had nothing to do with their attitude towards 'sisterly Iraq'; and the basically pro-Iraqi camp of Kuwait and Saudi Arabia, cautiously supported by Bahrain. The latter's position may be explained by its experience of Iranian-inspired protest (most importantly the 1981 coup attempt), and the island economy's high degree of dependence on Saudi aid, oil supplies, and military protection.

This configuration did not imply rigidity, however. For instance, Saudi Arabia was by no means implacable towards Iran, still ready to respond to overtures and especially keen to co-operate with the Islamic Republic on oil issues – a stand which highlighted considerable friction with Iraq during late 1986 and early 1987. Although it should be stressed that there is no evidence that the Saudi authorities officially knew about, or approved of, the shipments of Saudi refined products to Iran since mid-1986, revelations about them must have inspired grave misgivings on the part of the Iraqis. Indeed, the latter half of 1986 and early 1987 saw considerable friction between the two, featuring Iraqi bullying for more support.[12]

A reported Saudi mediation effort in March, seeking a face-saving formula to end the war, did not bear fruit and the Saudi Foreign Minister was quoted the following month as saying that his country planned to ask the UN Security Council for sanctions against Iran.[13] By then, therefore, the 'wavering' intermezzo had come to an end, possibly as a result of exasperation with an Iranian inability to deliver as a consequence of internal divisions.

From then on, Saudi–Kuwaiti solidarity in supporting Iraq and confronting Iranian threats was again clearly established. Bombings in Kuwait during April, May and June 1987 only reinforced this position: Kuwait's government and press generally blamed the violence on Iran. They received severe threats from Tehran in return, and warnings that the emirate's plans to reflag its tanker fleet would not make it any less vulnerable to Iran's wrath. Iran subsequently seized several Kuwaiti speedboats and, in June, started deploying Silkworm missiles on the Fao peninsula, directly threatening Kuwait. It may be worth noting that in the days after an Iraqi aircraft struck the USS *Stark*, accidentally or not, there was no comment in the press. The Saudi position was possibly even more striking: a request from the AWACS personnel for Saudi aircraft to intercept the approaching Iraqi plane was not handled speedily enough by the Saudi authorities to stop the strike, nor was there any official comment on the event.

Bahrain's Foreign Minister expressed approval for the reflagging operation, which implied a larger presence of foreign naval military might, although he tried to argue rather implausibly that the mainly American military presence should not be seen as a direct challenge to Iran because 'we do not want confrontation with Iran'. He also tried to reassure Tehran that Bahraini military bases would not be used as a springboard for attacks against the Islamic Republic.[14]

The other states, however, and particularly the UAE and Oman, were making more of an effort to be on friendly terms with Iran, bringing guarded criticism from Baghdad. In May, Sheikh Zayed stated that the UAE did not need foreign protection for its vessels. The Iranian Deputy Minister of Foreign Affairs, Mr Besharati, visiting in the last week of May, said it was a pity that the 'wise attitude' of the UAE was not shared by other Gulf states. Iranian sources subsequently suggested that the UAE might not have been informed by Kuwait about the decision to invite the superpowers into the Gulf. The Iranians capitalized on this mood by sending Foreign Minister Velayati on a tour of the southern Gulf states in late May/early June, clearly trying to drive a wedge between Kuwait and the others, specifically over the reflagging issue with all its implications. It is probably indicative of Bahrain's continuing suspicion towards Tehran, that Velayati cancelled his visit there and sent an aide instead.[15] Such hesitations were no longer part of Oman's make-up. Qaboos sent his Foreign Minister to Tehran in the third week of May. Wide-ranging discussions resulted amongst other things in an agreement on economic co-operation and in follow-up visits, the most striking of which was Velayati's visit in mid-August. Nevertheless, although in its official statements the government agreed with Iran on the need to avoid superpower interference, the Sultanate did in fact stick to its view that Kuwait had a right to secure passage of its tankers in the Gulf.[16]

All six members subscribed to the communiqué of the GCC Foreign Ministers on 8 June, supporting peace moves but also stressing anew the principle that an attack on any member state would be considered an attack on all, condemning 'terrorist and sabotage acts' against Kuwait and supporting the latter's measures to secure its economic and commercial interests. Although some of this must be ascribed to heavy Saudi and Kuwaiti pressure, it would also seem to indicate that there were limits to the extent to which Iran could divide the Gulf six.

July 1987 marked the beginning of a new period in the war, as well as in Iraqi–Gulf–Iranian relations: at a press conference on 20 July, Kuwait's Crown Prince Sheikh Saad came out explicitly and strongly in support of Iraq. The following day the reflagging operation started. On 20 July also, the UN Security Council issued the famous Resolution 598, calling for a cease-fire in the war and a step-by-step resolution of the conflict. Only ten days later hundreds of pilgrims died in Mecca in the chaos and violence ensuing from political demonstrations by Iranians. This followed seven weeks' exchanges of Iranian threats and Saudi warnings over such demonstrations on the *Hajj*.[17]

Iran's continued attacks on Arab shipping, its rejection of Resolution 598 (which Iraq had accepted) and its perceived responsibility for the Mecca riots, all helped to change the atmosphere. Relations between Riyadh and Tehran consequently soured further (with a Saudi diplomat dying after an attack on the embassy in Tehran and Rafsanjani calling for the Al Saud to be uprooted from the area),[18] and would continue to decline until the break in diplomatic relations in April 1988. Velayati's explicit threats that Iran would no longer show restraint in retaliating against countries supporting Iraq (making specific reference to Kuwait) served to consolidate the latter's enmity.[19] The Emirate positioned itself squarely behind Saudi Arabia, and Bahrain too condemned Iran over the Mecca events.[20] Qatar remained virtually silent while the UAE and Oman, as before, tried to steer a neutral course. The UAE refused an Iranian offer to help clear mines after the British supply vessel *Anita* was sunk in mid-August, and the Omanis claimed in August (while receiving the Iranian Foreign Minister) that a powerful Iran was a source of pride for the Gulf, but supported Kuwait's right to reflag.[21] Baghdad's irritation with the two countries at this point flared up and the Ba'th Party mouthpiece published a piece criticizing those who were receiving 'enemies of the Arabs, . . . Islam . . . and humanity'.[22]

At the Tunis meeting of the Arab League's Foreign Ministers in the fourth week of August, Saud al-Faysal called the Iranians 'terrorists' and urged sanctions. In the event, the meeting stopped short of calling for a break in relations with Iran but issued a stern warning to Tehran that Resolution 598 should be accepted. Oman and the UAE were among those arguing most forcefully against a break.[23] The contrast with Saudi Arabia, where the press for the first time was now given carte blanche to attack Iran,[24] could not have been greater.

Following a missile attack from Fao on Kuwait in early September, the Emirate expelled five Iranian diplomats and Bahrain again openly condemned Iran, calling for international sanctions if Tehran failed to accept Resolution 598.[25] Further evidence of the firm support from Iraq's three Gulf allies may well be that Baghdad felt at liberty to resume the 'tanker war' in late August, and strikes on economic and oil targets in September. The Saudi stand was further illustrated by the signing, on 20 September, of the contract for the second phase of the IPSA-pipeline, which would, on completion, allow Iraq to export another 1.65 million b/d across the Kingdom.[26] Bahrain's attitude was recognized by Tehran for what it was and the Revolutionary Guards' commander stated in October that, as the island was 'US-occupied', it was fair game for attacks on the Americans.[27] Oman, meanwhile, was most explicit in stating its desire to see international evenhandedness towards Iran and Iraq. The Sultanate was clearly establishing itself as a go-between between the pro-Iraqi camp and the West on the one hand, and Iran on the other.[28]

After two tankers (one US-flagged) were hit in mid-October by Iranian missiles in Kuwaiti territorial waters, the US retaliated by striking and virtually destroying two Iranian oil platforms used by the Revolutionary Guards. The press in both Kuwait and Saudi Arabia justified the action. When the Iranians in turn hit a Kuwaiti oil terminal on 21 October, this not only kindled Bahraini protest; but generally provided a 'last straw' in the process of turning large sections of public opinion in the Gulf against Iran. One observer noted that 'for most citizens, the Iranian revolution ceased to mean anything more than war against the Arabs'. In Kuwait, 'big Shia families went so far as to put ads in local newspapers dissociating themselves from the [Iranian and Iranian-inspired] violence'.[29] Official policy in Qatar, the UAE and Oman stayed neutral, however. These countries, although subscribing to the strongly worded statement of the Arab summit in Amman in November, condemning Iran and coming out in clear support of Iraq, were not quite as anxious to blame Iran. Sultan Qaboos in fact stated in November that he wanted to maintain good relations with the Islamic Republic, these relations being 'dictated by history and geography', and that in the Gulf War *both* sides should observe the cease-fire order. Omani–Iranian economic co-operation, meanwhile, was developing further. It is worth noting that, prior to the GCC summit of late December, Saddam Hussein sent Tariq Aziz and Saadoun Shakir with messages to all the Gulf states except Oman. There was no doubt about the continued support of Kuwait and Saudi Arabia: the contract to supply war relief crude, which had in fact expired in January 1987 but had run on due to previous under-lifting, was renewed in November.[30] Nevertheless, pressure from mainly the UAE and Oman (and probably also Qatar) influenced decisions at the summit. The leaders noted with regret 'Iran's attempt to procrastinate on the implementation' of Resolution 598.[31] Still, a personal attack by King Fahd on Iran notwithstanding, the Kingdom and Kuwait acquiesced in the neutral partners' desire to try to keep channels to Iran open. Sheikh Zayed of the UAE was designated to lead the GCC dialogue with Tehran, in the hope that the leadership there might be persuaded to accept Resolution 598.[32] The regime in Baghdad was, as one commentator put it, 'enraged' about the suggested dialogue.

1988: TOWARDS A CEASE-FIRE

Whatever Baghdad's reservations, from the beginning of 1988 some movement in the GCC's position was discernible. In the course of January it became clear that in addition to the three 'neutrals', Bahrain was also, in principle, in favour of the dialogue with Iran, although remaining very wary. Manama rather played down a coup attempt it foiled in February and which was at least indirectly Iranian-inspired. The Syrian government indicated that it was playing a role in getting the dialogue on the road. Iraq was adamant that there should be no such exercise if Iraq was not a party to it or was not satisfied with it. In Kuwait, although newspapers derided the proposal, the official mood also became more pliant. Saddam had sent Izzat Ibrahim to Kuwait as well as Riyadh, in anticipation of the announcement of the agreement in principle on a dialogue. But the Kuwaiti Foreign Minister said on 25 January that contacts with Tehran had never ceased and that the Kuwaiti Embassy in the Iranian capital would be reopened.[33] Upon the return of Izzat Ibrahim to Baghdad, the regime let its anger be known through the state-controlled press, claiming that the GCC overtures to Iran were a flagrant violation of the Amman summit resolutions and seeing Syria's hand in it.[34] Kuwait and Saudi Arabia appeared to be excepted, but the subsequent statement by the Kuwaiti minister was a sign that in fact only the Kingdom was still holding out.

Following the flare-up of the 'war of the cities' from late February, during which Tehran and Qom were hit, the press in both Kuwait and Saudi Arabia supported Iraq.[35] The others were more circumspect, although the Bahraini leadership was privately expressing the wish that the US forces would give the Iranians a sound thrashing in the Gulf. Even Sheikh Zayed warned Iran not to pressure Kuwait into seeking defence aid from abroad.[36] This may have been an indirect result of the visit to the Emirates by Taha Yassin Ramadhan at the end of February, but was also probably a hint to Tehran that even its more sympathetic GCC interlocutors wanted it to show greater flexibility on the issue of negotiations. At the time of the GCC Foreign Ministers' meeting in Riyadh in mid-March, the organization's assistant Secretary-General, Sayf Hashid al-Maskari from the UAE, indicated that it was now up to Iran to show there was substance to its proclaimed principle of good-neighbourliness.[37] It should be noted that around this time Oman's assistance to US operations in the Gulf was openly acknowledged by Secretary of State Shultz. On the other hand, Sultan Qaboos opposed the idea of an arms embargo against Iran.[38]

The improvement of Iranian–Kuwaiti relations received a setback when a number of Iranian patrol boats attacked Bubiyan Island at the end of March. Interestingly a condemnation of Iran was forthcoming from the UAE and a further one with the hijacking of a Kuwaiti airliner to Mashad on 5 April. In both cases it is likely that at most a minority of the Iranian regime was involved and Kuwait initially hoped that these hitches could be overcome. Yet the outcome of the hijacking led both the Kuwaitis and the Saudis to accuse Tehran of complicity.[39] Bahrain reaffirmed its position in the pro-Iraqi camp in a different way when Sheikh Khalifa bin Salman went to Baghdad for top-level talks, described as 'supportive', on 12 April, Iran continued its own public relations offensive, sending envoys to Oman, Qatar and the UAE to present them with evidence of Iraq's use of chemical weapons against its Kurdish population in Halabja.[40]

This phase of the war effectively came to an end in mid-April 1988. The escalation of the US' military confrontation with Iran virtually coincided with a string of military successes on Iraq's part. In this last phase of the war Iran would see little other than reverses, culminating in Iraq's recapture of the Majnoon Islands on 26 June, and would ultimately accept Resolution 598, followed on 6 August by Iraq's agreement to a cease-fire.

Kuwait was accused by Iran of allowing Iraq the use of Bubiyan in the successful counter attack and retaking of Fao on 17–18 April. The Kuwaiti government denied this but Iraq's success was hailed in the Emirate by officialdom and press alike. The same fulsome praise was forthcoming from Saudi Arabia. Iran's hasty and probably mistaken bombing of the UAE's Mubarak oil field (jointly operated by Sharjah and Iran) on 20 April was immediately condemned officially by Saudi Arabia, Kuwait, and the UAE themselves.[41]

Only a week after the Iraqi recapture of Fao on 26 April, the Kingdom cut its diplomatic relations with Iraq's adversary, having failed to convince the Iranians to accept a quota of 45,000 for the 1988 *Hajj*, officially for reasons of construction work in the holy cities. Saudi fears about the numbers and activities of Iranian pilgrims at that year's *Hajj* and the complete Iranian intransigence on the subject, indeed appear to have been the most important reason behind the break although it did of course come after months of mutual recriminations. Taha Yassin Ramadhan could on 7 May describe Saudi and Iraqi viewpoints as 'identical' and King Fahd himself, in his *Id al-Fitr* message nine days later, abundantly lauded the Iraqi people, saying that they had been 'resisting various forms of obstinacy, oppression and tyranny over the past nine years, until, thanks to their wise leadership, God has enabled them to liberate their land'.[42]

The Kuwaiti press in the wake of the Saudi-Iranian break, argued strongly for following the Kingdom's example, urging the other GCC states to do the same,[43] although the government never appears to have considered doing so.

While Saudi Arabia and Kuwait were being accused by Iran of sabotaging an agreement with non-OPEC producers to cut production, preferring to support Iraq's line, Oman and the UAE received Iran's Oil Minister Aghazadeh in the fourth week of May. Earlier, Deputy Foreign Minister Besharati, on a visit to the UAE, had already stated that Iran still wanted good relations with the country, the Mubarak incident notwithstanding.[44]

At their meeting in the first week of June, the GCC Foreign Ministers congratulated Iraq on its military successes (Shalamcheh had been recaptured on 25 May and appealed yet again to Iran to accept Resolution 598. As usual, the wording was somewhat tempered by the 'neutrals', although that was not the case for Prince Saud al-Faysal's accompanying remarks. Bahrain's Minister of Defence, Sheikh Hamad bin Khalifa, somewhat surprisingly (yet in tune with the state's basic position) went so far as to visit the newly liberated areas of Fao and Shalamcheh on an official visit to Iraq on 20 June,[45] clearly undeterred now by Iran. In a further show of determination nine Bahraini members of the Tehran-based Islamic Front for the Liberation of Bahrain were jailed for dealings with Iran.[46]

Domestically, a key event foreshadowing subsequent momentous changes in Iran's attitude (which remains a, if not the, key determining factor for the GCC states' attitudes) was the appointment of Hashemi Rafsanjani, the Speaker of the Majlis, as acting commander-in-chief of the armed forces. He noted on that occasion that, 'one of the things we did in the revolutionary atmosphere, was constantly to make enemies . . . we pushed those who could be neutral into hostility, and did nothing to attract those who could become friends'.[47]

It is clear that a more pragmatic line of thinking was achieving prominence. The evolution towards acceptance of a cease-fire was hastened by the tragic shooting down, the following day, of an Iranian Airbus by an American warship. At the same time, the incident provided a cause for a gradual and tentative *rapprochement* with Kuwait and Saudi Arabia. The former expressed its 'deep regret and sorrow' and extended its condolences to those affected, while at the same time stressing the need to end the war. Iran sent its thanks in return. Saudi Arabia only reacted two days after the event, but then it too expressed its regret over the loss of innocent lives and called for an end to the war, although the Saudi press still showed little sympathy.[48]

When, on 18 July, Iran announced that it accepted Resolution 598, there was jubilation in Kuwait, expressed by government, press and public displays alike. The Saudis announced that they 'had been looking forward' to this development, but met it with less exuberance and more scepticism. In Bahrain the Iranian decision was welcomed and a cautious optimism prevailed. The UAE welcomed the decision as 'a turning point' and a message from Sheikh Zayed to the Iranian president spoke of Iran's courage in taking the decision; similar reactions were forthcoming from the Omani and Qatari governments and press.[49]

Nevertheless, when Iraq pushed on and into Iranian territory again, dragging its feet over the issue of a cease-fire, several newspapers in Kuwait and Saudi Arabia supported the Iraqi position. The Saudi-funded, London-based *Al-Sharq al-Awsat*, even went so far as to advocate the removal of the Iranian leadership.[50]

It is safe to assume, however, that all of the GCC states, including Saudi Arabia and Kuwait, were very eager indeed for Iraq to show some flexibility so as to put a cease-fire in place. A number of reports claimed that Riyadh was putting pressure on the Iraqi leadership to that effect. The official Saudi denial of this, on 2 August, joined with a reiteration of the Kingdom's 'trust in all views and measures taken by Iraq . . . and its plan which aims for a true and lasting peace', cannot quite be taken at face value.[51] Iraq did its best to convince its Gulf neighbours of its own views and sent Taha Yassin Ramadhan to Kuwait and Riyadh, and Saadoun Shakir to Qatar, the UAE and Oman on 1–2 August. In the latter three, the Iraqi envoy arrived on the heels of the Iranian Deputy Foreign Minister, whose message of peace and Iranian flexibility is likely to have received a more sympathetic hearing.[52]

On 4 August, King Fahd sent his Information Minister to Baghdad with a message which undoubtedly made the case for implementing 598 as it stood, implying the immediate acceptance of a cease-fire.[53] Having decided at least as far back as 1981 that the costs of a continuing situation of war outweighed the benefits, there was no longer any convincing reason for continuing to bankroll Iraqi military adventures once Iran had sued for peace. It must have been as clear to the leadership in Riyadh as to the realists in Iran that the Islamic Republic did not really have any alternative to peace. The subsequent Iraqi U-turn on 6 August, accepting a cease-fire, came after consultations the same day between Saddam Hussein and Saudi Arabia's Prince Saud al-Faysal among others. The Saudis (through their ambassador in the US, Prince Bandar) were closely involved in the UN negotiations before and after the Iraqi decision.[54]

AFTER THE CEASE-FIRE: THE PATTERN RESTORED?

On the whole a gradual strengthening can be observed in GCC–Iraqi links during the war, most emphatically so in the case of Saudi Arabia and Kuwait. This was largely due to the Iranian threat and the change in Iraq's own foreign policy and domestic character. Yet the picture is not at all straightforward: that much is clear from the foregoing account. Kuwait retained its apprehension of its overbearing neighbour and the latter's appetite for Kuwaiti islands. Oman, the UAE and Qatar risked irking Baghdad for staying on good terms with Iran when faced with Iranian carrots and sticks. All, including Kuwait and Saudi Arabia, remained intent on reducing tension with Iran when that was possible, but the former two were not prepared to reduce their support of Iraq to achieve that aim. Given Iran's attitude this led to sharp flare-ups in animosity, complicated by the Hajj issue in the case of Saudi Arabia. To a large extent it was the powerful antipathy against the Al Saud amongst Iranian radicals and on the part of Khomeini himself, which, translated via political condemnations and tangible acts, eventually pushed the Kingdom into its uncharacteristically tough anti-Iranian stance, reflected in a stridently pro-Iraqi position. A more long-term bone of contention remained the Kingdom's close ties with the United States. The Iranian leadership has continued to insist that the GCC states should take a genuinely neutral position between the superpowers as one way of avoiding international 'warmongering' in the region. While none of the six in fact want the protective American umbrella to be withdrawn (think in particular of the facilities enjoyed by the US in Oman and Bahrain), Saudi Arabia and the US presence and involvement there stand out by their size and by the Kingdom's reputation as a 'pillar' for US policy in the area. Nevertheless, the experience with, for instance, Omani–Iranian relations, indicates that even this area of disagreement could be subtly relegated to the background provided there is some Iranian flexibility and a Saudi change of *style*.

It is clear throughout, that the Gulf Arab states' attitudes depended on that of Iran towards (1) themselves and (2) a resolution of the war. On the second point, cause for animosity disappeared once Iran had accepted 598. On the first, the case of the 'neutrals' showed that Iran could be 'lived with', and the end of the war removed the main obstacle to this as far as Kuwait and Bahrain were concerned.

Iran's behaviour has remained a key factor in determining the GCC members' attitude towards their larger Gulf neighbours. As indicated at the outset, all essentially want a predictable, non-threatening environment and are therefore quite willing to ignore differing points of view if bilateral and regional stability can thereby be maintained or achieved. By definition therefore, given the end of the Iran–Iraq War, they were likely to accept eagerly Iran's outstretched hand if offered. This would not necessarily imply a conscious opting for cooler relations with Iraq, although it could of course, as has indeed been the case, be interpreted by the latter as somewhat of a slap in the face. In any case Gulf leaders have remained uneasy about an Iraq that felt victorious, not because it would again turn radical or subversive but because the regime in Baghdad might be tempted to try bullying again.

As was to be expected, the continuous Iranian charm offensive, aimed at all of the Gulf states except Saudi Arabia, resulted in a speedy improvement of their relationship with the Islamic Republic. Oman, already on good terms, sent its Foreign Minister to Tehran twice during August and September. The second visit appears to have come as a result of the GCC Foreign Ministers' meeting on 4–5 September, where a desire for 'friendship between all the peoples of the Islamic nation' was expressed. It is believed that the GCC decided to probe the possibilities of upgrading relations with Iran and to send envoys to both Iran and Iraq to try to break the deadlock in the Geneva peace talks. Iranian radio even quoted the Omani Minister as saying that the GCC 'saw no obstacles in the way of a GCC session being held, including Iran and Iraq, after the main differences between [them] are resolved'.[55]

Qatar stuck to its own very quiet pragmatism and has continued to do so, although an Iranian claim, in March 1989, to part of the gas field off Qatar threatened to throw up difficulties. As of June 1989, however, the Qataris had not responded officially. The same problem may surface between Iran and the UAE.[56] The latter have meanwhile continued to develop their economic relations with the Islamic Republic without any grand announcements and have, in some instances, indicated support for Iraqi rather than Iranian positions. An illustration of the latter was the issue of raising the Iraqi production quota in OPEC in September, when the UAE came out in favour of output parity.[57] Oman, however, continued its vigorous policy of expanding its Iranian links. Although ostensibly accepting Iraq's message that it no longer posed any threat, Sultan Qaboos in a mid-December interview implicitly took Iran's side when suggesting that 'forces' should withdraw behind their own borders in order to establish trust; once peace is established GCC states could establish closer relations with Iran, he said.[58] Oman's Minister of Commerce and Industry went to Tehran in late December, where a wide-ranging accord on economic co-operation was signed and a joint economic–industrial commission was established.[59]

Bahrain also responded, announcing on 10 October that agreement had been reached to upgrade relations with Iran to the level of Chargé d'Affaires, Sheikh Mohammed bin Mubarak, the Bahraini Foreign Minister, confirmed that they wanted to resume relations at ambassadorial level soon.[60]

The Iraqis were considerably irked by the GCC's haste to mend fences with Iran, especially so in the cases of Kuwait and, more tentatively, Saudi Arabia. In the former an official told the *Washington Post* on 28 September that his government was prepared to resume friendly relations with Iran, making the point that they did not need to consult Iran before doing so.[61] The Kuwaitis had in fact been preparing to reopen their embassy in Tehran for at least three months following the friendly exchanges after the shooting down of the Iranian passenger plane in early June. During the subsequent visit of Mr Besharati on 8 November, the highest-level visit since the cease-fire and part of a tour which took in all the GCC members except Saudi Arabia, a further upgrading of relations was agreed.[62]

The gap between Iran and Saudi Arabia appeared less easy to bridge given the legacy of the Mecca riots and Iranian intransigence on the issue of the *Hajj*, which had led to the rupture in diplomatic relations. This appeared in part to reflect Riyadh's alliance with Baghdad. Yet Saudi–Iraqi relations were not in fact quite as smooth as the leaderships wanted them to look, as will be illustrated below. For the Al-Saud the reasons for their animosity with the regime in Tehran had been: the threatening implications of the war; Iran's behaviour towards the Kingdom; and specifically the Iranian attitude on the *Hajj*, which would, if left unchecked, create a serious security risk, both directly and indirectly through eroding the regime's Islamic legitimacy. With the end of the hostilities the first point had disappeared. As to the second and third, since July a pragmatic, accommodationist foreign policy had become evident in Tehran and there was reason to believe that at least some elements in the Iranian leadership might be willing to come to an understanding on the *Hajj* issue.

An anti-Saudi outburst from Ayatollah Montazeri in early October notwithstanding, Prince Saud al-Faysal stated on 5 October that the Kingdom wanted 'normal ties' with Iran. When Iran nevertheless refused to attend the summit of the Islamic Conference Organization (ICO) in Jeddah the following week, King Fahd used conciliatory tones in expressing his regret, saying 'I am sorry, I would have wished the Iranian delegation to have been with us . . . Iran is an Islamic nation. I would have loved to see my Iranian brothers here today'.[63] Rafsanjani appeared to acknowledge the Saudi move, saying on 14 October: 'We feel there is no reason for us to quarrel with countries of the southern coast of the Persian Gulf – with *any* of them'. Both Kuwait, as indicated above, and the Kingdom in turn responded positively. On 19 October, King Fahd ordered the Saudi media to stop attacking Iran 'on anything at all', adding that 'the problems with Iran are limited . . . and will be replaced with harmony, agreement and friendship'.[64] In early November, Saud al-Faysal did 'not rule out at all the resumption of diplomatic relations with Iran'. Iran responded in kind and Deputy Foreign Minister Besharati, in Kuwait on 8 October as part of this Gulf tour (which left Saudi Arabia out) said explicitly that it was time to 'start a new chapter of better relations' with the Kingdom and that the resumption of diplomatic relations was being discussed. King Fahd's comment in Riyadh the same day that 'we want Iran to be a strength for Islam' appeared to indicate that the era of bitterness had indeed been left behind.[65] It must be stressed, however, that there were significant segments of public and official opinion in Iran opposed to the suggested warming to Riyadh. *Keyhan International* argued on 25 November against a resumption of diplomatic relations, pointing out that 'it must not be forgotten that the Saudi Kingdom . . . is mainly responsible for implementing Washington's direct dictates in the Gulf' and that 'the Saudis should pay a heavy price for their crimes'. This indicated that the supremacy of the pragmatist line in Tehran was by no means established. At the same time, Prince Sultan made the resumption of relations conditional on Iran's acceptance of the *Hajj* quota and a commitment to refrain from turning the pilgrimage into a political occasion.[66] The Saudi government denied in December that the Iranian and Saudi Foreign Ministers had met in Geneva, but it seems clear that negotiations of some kind were continuing, focusing on the *Hajj* issue. Rafsanjani expressed his belief, that month, that relations would be normalized 'in the not too distant future' and King Fahd called on the rich Arab states to help both Iran and Iraq in their reconstruction efforts.[67] Contacts between the two sides continued into 1989.

Throughout, one can assume, the GCC members and particularly Bahrain, Saudi Arabia and Kuwait, remained wary of Iran's unpredictability: relations could not become relaxed as long as Iran's internal divisions were not resolved. When Rushdie's *Satanic Verses* exploded onto the Islamic scene and Ayatollah Khomeini issued his 14 February *fatwa*, calling for the author to be killed, it soon became apparent that the voices of moderation were, at least temporarily, eclipsed. Even

Rafsanjani had to swing into line behind the renewed radicalization in Iran's foreign policy stance. Yet for the GCC states Iran appeared to pass the test at least to an extent. Whatever Tehran's renewed animosity with the West, it became clear that there was no change in its attitude towards the southern side of the Gulf. At the ICO meeting in Riyadh in March 1989, where the Rushdie case was to be discussed, Iran did not send a political heavyweight but it did participate in the person of the Deputy Head of the Islamic Propagation Organization at the Ministry of Islamic Guidance, to get other Muslim states' support for Khomeini's measure. In the event both Iran and the moderate countries, led by Saudi Arabia, came away without loss of face after what was in effect a compromise: Rushdie was condemned as an apostate, thus deserving punishment, but Saud al-Faysal could point out that the precise punishment had to be left to jurists, which the gathered dignitaries were not.[68] From both sides accommodation had again prevailed.

Whereas relations between the five smaller Gulf states and Iran, therefore, continued on a reasonably even keel (particularly so for Oman and the UAE) the *Hajj* question eventually soured the Saudi–Iranian relationship again. The Iranian side, driven by Khomeini's virulent hatred of the Al-Saud (as would become clear in his will), refused to budge on the issue. For the Saudi leadership the security implications were too important to give in from their side. Iranian statements on the question from April became more aggressive and critical of the Saudi regime, insisting on the right to send 150,000 pilgrims and accusing the Saudis anew of the 'massacre' in 1987.[69]

In subsequent mutual recriminations Saudi Arabia tried hard to sound reasonable, stressing it would still welcome the 45,000 quota of Iranian pilgrims which the ICO had adopted, provided that the *Hajj* was not disturbed. King Fahd maintained a pragmatic tone, leaving open the possibility of compromise, when he told the Kuwaiti News Agency on 3 May:

> We cannot change the geographic reality of Iran and Iran cannot change our geographic reality. . . . On our side, we do not ask Iran for anything more than mutual respect and good neighbourliness, which are the same things that Iran requests.[70]

Gradually, however, attacks on Iran became more prevalent in the Saudi press. The implacable enmity against the Saudi regime, which was revealed in Khomeini's will, and which, apart from expressing the feelings of at least part of the Iranian political elite, also forced the Iranian pragmatists to stay their hand for the time being, did not leave the Al-Saud much of an incentive to continue its active goodwill policy.

Not surprisingly, therefore, Riyadh maintained complete silence in reaction to the news of Khomeini's death on 3 June. The other GCC members sent bland messages of condolence to Tehran and some junior officials attended the funeral.[71] The leaders in all six Gulf Arab states were no doubt relieved at the post-Khomeini developments, with the new leadership tandem of the spiritual leader Khamenei and President Rafsanjani boding well for continuing pragmatism. But the continued presence within Iran of more radical factions, as well as the difficulty in shaking off at least the Khomeini legacy on Saudi Arabia, remain causes for concern. Oman can feel comfortable given its experience of the past seven years or so. Yet even here Iran's unpredictability has led government sources to say that they are 'not keen to give Iran everything at the same time. We give tit for tat. They must show that they are willing to pacify the area'.[72] Oman has, in any case, been very active during the latter half of 1989 in seeking further expansion of economic ties with the Islamic Republic. At the International Conference on the Persian Gulf, held in Tehran in the fourth week of November 1989 under the auspices of the Ministry of Foreign Affairs (the largest official foreign gathering since the revolution) a four-man Omani delegation including the ambassador and a cousin of Sultan Qaboos stood out both by their very presence and the priority treatment afforded them (some UAE participants were also, less prominently, present). The Omani leadership may well turn out to be the ideal mediator with Saudi Arabia.

Qatar and the UAE might have had equally few worries, had it not been for the Iranian claim to part of the offshore hydrocarbon fields so far exploited by the two countries. This came as somewhat of a shock, but at the same time of writing neither had reacted officially. Both Kuwait and Bahrain remain wary of the Islamic Republic, although relations have been restored to their previous level. Evidence of this is the crackdown on Shias in Kuwait in March,[73] and the withdrawal by the Bahraini authorities of two journalists' credentials, apparently for reporting the displays of grief which took place on the island after Khomeini's death.[74]

Against this background Iraq pursued its own diplomatic campaign. This proved not hugely successful. Oman, Qatar and the UAE have, in effect, stuck to their neutralist policy, accommodating both Iran and Iraq (the only qualification is that they made some allowance for Iraq's Arabness on occasions such as the US sanctions vote (over Iraq's use of chemical weapons), or in the framework of the GCC). A peculiar but far-reaching example of this attitude might be found in the Omani suggestion, reportedly made at the GCC summit in Bahrain in late December 1988 in response to Iraqi pressure to be allowed to join the GCC in some form, that both Iraq and Iran could be given observer status at further GCC summits.[75] This report was denied, however, by the Omani Ambassador in Tehran.

Bahrain's Sunni leadership, still suspicious of an unpredictable Iran and in tune with the Al-Saud, has maintained its position of support for Iraq while maintaining the 'medium' profile it had adopted earlier. It certainly did not want to jeopardize the rebuilding of relations with the Islamic Republic. Friction between Kuwait and Baghdad remained over the issues of the border, Warba and Bubiyan, the decrease in aid and also Kuwait's warming relations with Iran. No doubt hints were forthcoming from Baghdad that speedy rebuilding of relations with Iran would not be appreciated. Kuwait, of course, had its own imperatives on this matter and some irritation with Iraq was probably visible in the remark quoted earlier, by a Kuwaiti official in late September, that Kuwait did not need to consult Iraq before resuming friendly relations with Iran. Nevertheless, the economic/functional links between the two have been consolidated. The most spectacular instance of this was the agreement in mid-March 1989 for Iraq to supply Kuwait with 550 million gallons a day of fresh water for drinking and irrigation purposes via a 290-km pipeline to be financed by Kuwait, as well as linking the two countries' electricity grids.[76]

Friction between Baghdad and Riyadh also remained, particularly over the lower level of assistance which was forthcoming; for a while, over the Kingdom's tentative overture towards Iran; and over its insistence, at times, that Iraq adopt a somewhat more flexible line in the peace negotiations. Nevertheless, the bottom line in Riyadh remained support for Baghdad. Illustrations are the opening of the second stage of the IPSA pipeline in September 1989 and the Saudi–Iraqi non-intervention pact of March that year. This basic, though wary and often critical, leaning towards Iraq can largely be explained by the perception of, on the one hand, Iran as unreliable/unpredictable, and on the other, Iraq as having undergone a genuine change away from its erstwhile leftist radicalism.

CONCLUSION

In the wake of the cease-fire, for all of the GCC states except Saudi Arabia, the limitations on their foreign policy outlined at the beginning of this paper have clearly shown through again, restoring the 'normal' pattern. For Kuwait and Bahrain this happened after the guns fell silent; for Oman, Qatar and the UAE this process had begun much earlier. All have an intrinsic interest in good, peaceful, non-intrusive relations with everyone around, as long as no-one presents too great a threat. More specifically, they could be expected to be, and in fact are, more than willing to restore 'brotherly relations' with the Islamic Republic if the latter gives them half a chance. With the war out of the way, bridges could be rebuilt and crossed.

At the time of writing Saudi Arabia remains an exception. Yet the same logic applies for the Kingdom. Throughout, it has been Iranian actions and/or statements, combined and intertwined with the circumstances of the war, which have pushed the Al-Saud in a more pronounced anti-Iranian stance than they would have wished.

If the senior princes in Riyadh could, at some point, feel reasonably confident that a new wind was blowing in Tehran; and that the Iranian leadership believes, after all, that with the war over the only obstacle to re-establishing a working relationship are a series of misunderstandings rooted in the past; then the Al-Saud would, once again, revert to the foreign policy attitude that comes most naturally to it: one of accommodation, conciliation and compromise.

There is an obvious channel for mediation: the other members of the GCC. Spokesmen for the group have already expressed their willingness to work towards an overall normalization of relations with Iran, if they can be confident that there would be mutual respect and non-interference. Indeed, the leadership in Tehran appears to have recognized this. Foreign Minister Velayati was quoted in early September as saying that he would welcome moves by Arab states of the Gulf to improve relations between Tehran and Riyadh. A call for improved relations has also been made by the head of the Majlis' foreign relations committee, Said Rajai Khorasani, although radical voices criticized him for it.[77] The Iranian News Agency quoted Oman's Deputy Prime Minister, Qays al-Zawawi, on 5 September as offering his country's mediation.[78] At the Tehran conference in November 1989, mentioned earlier, the general tone from official and other Iranian speakers (including particularly President Rafsanjani) was one implying the strengthening of accommodationist policies towards the Gulf states, although in a few cases (but only a few) Saudi Arabia appeared to be excepted. Rafsanjani's address to the conference on 22 November made it clear that the main official obstacle, along with memories of the Hajj tragedy, remains the present shape of the Kingdom's close relationship with the United States. Equally clear, however, in the speeches of Velayati, Oil Minister Aghazadeh and others, was a recognition that Iran's reconstruction effort could be a great deal more effective when carried out in co-operation with the GCC states, and the suggestion that economic co-operation in this and other fields (oil, trade, industrialization, shipping, etc.) could form the way towards political co-operation. Clearly the significance of such economic co-operation would pale without the inclusion of Saudi Arabia. There is little doubt, moreover, that a realization exists among elements of the Iranian government that continuing enmity with the Kingdom would preclude the kind of closeness with the other five GCC states which Tehran is seeking. The pattern might, after all, move towards restoration sooner rather than later.

7 Iran–Iraq: the war and prospects for a lasting peace

Colonel Edgar O'Ballance

ASPECTS OF THE WAR

The Gulf War (1980–8) between Iran and Iraq has had profound and lasting effects on both countries. Its impact has been felt throughout the Gulf while it has exacerbated the on-going Arab–Israeli conflict and has brought to the surface differences between Iranian and Saudi Arabian religious leadership. An atmosphere of fear, prejudice and suspicion pervades the Gulf region today, with Iran, Iraq and Egypt striving to obtain the 'Triad Deterrent' of chemical warfare, ballistic missiles and nuclear weaponry which Israel already possesses. As the other Gulf states have busily stocked their armouries with the most modern weaponry that they can afford to buy, a frightening and escalating arms race has developed in the Middle East.

The causes and course of the Gulf War have been covered in detail elsewhere,[1] it is sufficient here briefly to identify and discuss certain of its more significant aspects. In doing so it will become clear that the war itself cannot be viewed in isolation but must be considered in the wider context of the Gulf Arab states, Egypt, Libya, Syria and Israel, all of which are strategically inter-related.

The first significant fact on which to focus is that both Iran and Iraq have emerged from the Gulf War intact. Both are confident, mature, independent nation states, bolstered by immense national pride and with a convincing degree of stability, none of which would be said of either prior to September 1980.

Iraq, which draws most of its territorial substance from the old Ottoman area of Mesopotamia, became an Arab kingdom just after the First World War. The monarchy was removed by the revolution of 1958 and the country swung away from the Western and into the Soviet sphere of influence.

In 1980 Iraq was a divided country with approximately six million Shias among its population of 14 million. For the most part they lived in the southern and eastern provinces and, having been neglected by successive

Ba'thist governments, they looked eastwards for religious guidance and were consequently viewed by Baghdad as being potentially (and for the government, threateningly) susceptible to Ayatollah Khomeini's subversive propaganda.

In the northern mountains some three million[2] Kurds lived in more open hostility to Baghdad's rule. Between 1961 and 1975 they had been in open revolt against the central government, but the support (arms and supplies) covertly supplied to them by the Shah of Iran had been halted under the terms of the 1975 Algiers Accords between Iran and Iraq, in which Iraq had forfeited much of its former control over the 72-mile Shatt al-Arab.

Saddam Hussein Takriti's Ba'thist regime was also at odds with several other political groupings including communists, anti-Ba'thists and the underground Hizb al-Dawa al-Islamiya (the Islamic Call), a Tehran-supported violent Islamic organization.

In July 1979, Saddam Hussein had quietly pushed aside President Ahmad Hassan Bakr to become President of Iraq and Chairman of both the ruling Revolutionary Command Council and the Regional (Iraqi) Ba'th Party. Having effectively been the 'power behind the throne' for some time (as Foreign Minister he had signed the 1975 Algiers Accords), he was quick to put down an alleged conspiracy, the so-called 'July Plot', led by Imam al-Sadr, leader of the Iraqi Shias. The ruthless suppression of this attempt to transform Iraq into a Shia theocracy established that President Saddam Hussein would not be prepared to suffer opposition gladly. The lid was to be firmly jammed onto the pot, with all its bubbling contents.

Iran, which had been governed since the Second World War by the British-installed Mohammed Reza Shah, was itself an empire of diverse peoples. While political weight resided in the Farsi majority, Azerbaijanis, Baluchis, Kurds and Turkomans formed a neglected periphery, some demanding autonomy, others independence, but all kept subservient to the Shah's iron grip.

The Islamic revolution of February 1979 ousted the Shah and installed the Islamic regime of Ayatollah Khomeini in his stead. In the wake of the revolution the Kurds rose up in rebellion and, as other ethnic groups also stirred uneasily, political militias and underground movements waged war on government troops on the streets of Tehran. The Khomeini regime replied with state terrorism, with wholesale arrests, detention without trial, torture and executions. Amid this turmoil, power-hungry personalities struggled and plotted to gain, or retain, political advantage. It might be argued that it was fortuitous for the Khomeini regime that Iraq launched its military invasion in September 1980, diverting attention away from domestic instabilities and refocusing it on the foreign enemy.

The war served to promote tremendous nationalism within both Iran and

Iraq, wartime suffering and hardship and combat experience stirring a great sense of national unity such that, throughout the period of the war and with the exception of the Kurdish minorities, neither regime was faced with significant ethnic unrest, nor did the Shia population in Iraq perceive its primary loyalties as being anywhere but with Baghdad. Thus with regard to the numerous political and ethnic groupings within both Iran and Iraq, the war has tended to unite, even if only papering over the cracks of, the potentially destabilizing vertical differentiations of those societies.

A second significant feature of the Gulf War was its 'containment'. Both the Western and Soviet strategists were convinced in 1980 that a war in so volatile a region as the Gulf would inevitably escalate and draw in its neighbours, if not the superpowers themselves, into the conflict. In previous Arab–Israeli conflicts, both the superpowers, despite some brinkmanship and posturing, had been eager to diffuse tensions and bring the belligerents towards cease-fires. The same was true of the Gulf War, although many did not believe its containment to be possible. Yet in the event the war was confined essentially to the (border) territories of its protagonists, with only a few Arab volunteers participating on behalf of Iraq.

Significantly the war also lasted for a far longer period of time than was initially anticipated by observers. The war could, and perhaps should, have ended in June 1982, by which time most of Iraq's troops had been pushed back onto Iraqi soil. Spurred by the Israeli march into southern Lebanon on 6 June, President Saddam Hussein announced a unilateral cease-fire on 9 and on 12 July the United Nations Security Council passed Resolution 514 calling for a cease-fire. The intransigence of the respective leaders of Iran and Iraq eventually dashed these initiatives and the war was resumed.

It might be added that certain other Gulf nations did not want an early end to the Gulf War, which would have left both combatants undefeated and their thirst for further foreign adventures unquenched. There seemed to be an unspoken determination by some selectively to fuel the war until both combatants should exhaust themselves and become too weak to pursue further military operations in the region.

The Gulf War itself produced a new and disturbing feature within the Iranian armed forces. Revolutionary distrust of the old Imperial Army meant that the latter was relegated to a secondary role in Iran's defences. Reduced in numbers to about 200,000, it provided the military framework, staff functions, planning and logistic branches, technical arms and services, armour, artillery and transportation. The infantry was provided by the *Pasdaran* (the Corps of Revolutionary Guards) or the *Sepah* (Corps) which had a standing strength of about 350,000 men and was completely separate from the Army with both its own Minister and Ministry. The *Pasdaran*, which represented a political counter-balance to the regular armed forces, was originally drawn from street gangs at the time of the Islamic revolution and was directly loyal to Ayatollah Khomeini.

There was also a local Home Guard directly responsible to and under the control of the *Pasdaran*. Totalling over 2 million men, the Home Guard could be called upon to supply 'volunteer' reinforcements whenever needed. In total, Iran maintained a standing field force of approximately 300,000, with a further 1,700,000 men under arms. These forces combined still represented a far lesser proportion of Iran's available manpower than those utilized by Iraq in its own forces.

While the *Pasdaran* had their own budget, the Home Guard volunteers were entirely recruited, mustered, fed, paid and clothed by local mullahs, each Mosque throughout the country being responsible for filling a continuing quota of troops to defend a particular few square kilometres of land near the battle front, providing a line of support for the front-line forces. It was intended that by this method the Iraqi armed forces would be continually fully extended. The Ministry of Defence only provided the Home Guard with arms and equipment. The local mullahs were responsible for raising funds locally to cover all the other expenses of the Guards. Every Friday, after prayers, convoys of trucks left local Mosques carrying volunteer reinforcements and provisions to their allotted forward areas, returning with those volunteers who had completed their active service commitment. This system of linking mullahs, Mosques and Home Guard volunteers removed an enormous economic burden from the central government and created local identification with national war aims.

Despite this support from the home front, the *Pasdaran* and their Home Guard volunteers were largely bereft of transport and integral support, such as armour or artillery. They thus resorted, with the aid of significant indoctrination, to mass 'human-wave' attacks against strongly defended Iraqi positions. Such attacks, launched mainly in the southern areas of the front where the terrain was more open and could accommodate huge numbers, rarely gained more than a few slivers of ground, usually at the cost of tens of thousands of casualties. In one such massed human-wave attack, (Operation Kheibar in February and March of 1984) launched across the Hawizeh Marshes, some 500,000 men were locked in battle in an area of 20 square kilometres. Wave after human wave of *Pasdaran* and Home Guard volunteers battered themselves to pieces against sophisticated Iraqi defences. Over 20,000 Iranians and 7,000 Iraqis died in Operation Kheiber.

Another aspect of this 'cannon-fodder' approach was the deployment of the youthful Baseej-e Mustazafin (Popular 'Mobilized' Army) in moving out ahead of the human-wave assaults, to walk through minefields to explode mines and booby traps and to cut through enemy barbed-wire.

Some of the Baseej were barely twelve years of age, the minimum age set by Khomeini, and their use in this manner, unique in military history, shocked and horrified the rest of the world. For armchair strategists, who had long debated over 'technology versus manpower', the conclusion emerged that technology was undoubtably the superior. Several Gulf Arab states with comparatively small populations reached the same conclusion, confidently bringing in much new 'high-technology' weaponry for their own defence.

Running concurrently with the land battle was the battle between Iran and Iraq to prevent each other's exports of oil, the vital resource which determined their abilities to continue their respective war efforts. This battle, which took place at sea, was exacerbated by the destruction, in the early stages of the war, of the Basra-Abadan-Khorramshahr oil and export complexes, the main exits for both. Moreover, the Shatt al-Arab was soon to be blocked with wrecked vessels, mines, underwater defences and the debris of war.

Iraq was able to maintain its export of its OPEC quota (averaging about 1.2 million b/d) mainly through land pipelines across Turkey, and later also across Saudi Arabia, but Iran was less fortunate, having few alternative oil exit routes. Iran's main oil outlet came to be off-shore Kharg Island, in the northern part of the Gulf, initially out of range of Iraqi aircraft, where foreign oil-tankers called to take oil on board. As Iraq received French Super Etendard aircraft and Exocet missiles, Kharg Island was continually attacked and adjacent waters became too dangerous for foreign oil-tankers. In March 1985, Iran began to operate its 'Sirri Shuttle', hiring small oil-tankers to load oil at Kharg Island and ferry it southwards in escorted convoys sailing close to land to Sirri Island in the Strait of Hormuz. There the oil was transferred to foreign vessels.

Iranian combat aircraft made occasional attacks on shipping visiting Gulf Arab ports while Iranian naval forces heavily mined Gulf waters, resulting in the appearance of American, British and French warships in the Gulf to protect ships of their own nationality. Other Western nations joined what eventually became a seventy-warship armada to 'ensure free international passage in the Gulf'. Kuwait, for example, 're-flagged' a number of its super-tankers to obtain American and Soviet naval protection. Latterly some foreign warships were attacked by the *Pasdaran* in small Boghammer craft from Abu Island base, firing rockets and missiles. In May 1987, the USS *Stark* was hit by an Iraqi missile, thirty-seven crew members being killed, and in July 1988, the USS *Vincennes* shot down an Iranian Airbus, with all on board perishing. Both were cases of mistaken identity. Despite dangers to shipping in the Gulf, a volume of Iranian oil continued to get through.

Still another important feature of the Gulf War was the use of chemical warfare, first by Iraq and later by Iran. Iran was eventually to admit that the use of chemical warfare (CW) was one of the major reasons why the cease-fire was accepted. Banned in the aftermath of the Great War by the 1925 Geneva Protocol, chemical warfare had long been known as President Saddam Hussein's 'secret weapon' and he made it clear from the earliest days of the war that he would not hesitate to deploy it should Iranian troops break through his own defensive line.

Iraq had actually begun to use CW in an experimental way probably in late 1981, releasing war gases in small quantities in various types of terrain and under varying conditions. The Iranian government complained to the United Nations that between 'May 1981 and March 1984' CW means had killed 1,200 and injured 5,000 Iranians. A United Nations Commission visiting both countries broadly confirmed the allegation. In the latter part of the Gulf War, the Iranians also began using CW, probably commencing sometime in 1987. Iraqi use of CW had caused Iranians to develop protective measures and detachments of the *Pasdaran* were often photographed on ceremonial parades wearing gas-masks and protective capes.

NO VICTOR – NO VANQUISHED

Usually wars in history end with a clear victor who dictates his terms to the vanquished, the latter having little option but to accept them. Arab–Israeli wars and the Gulf War have not terminated in this traditional manner and are in fact still continuing in 'Cold War' forms in which the guns merely fall silent while combatants prepare for the next round of hostilities. When at last Khomeini was persuaded to drink from his 'chalice of poison' and accept UN Resolution 598 for a cease-fire, it left several problems unsolved, there being no clear victor and neither party accepting its own defeat. These problems included sovereignty of the Shatt al-Arab and some tiny Gulf islands as well as minor border claims. President Saddam Hussein had abrogated the Algiers Accord on 17 September 1980. Khomeini still held fast to his three main demands; the removal of the Iraqi president from power, an admission of Iraqi guilt for starting the war and reparations (which had risen to $150 billion).

UN-organized negotiations between Iran and Iraq for a lasting peace settlement opened at Geneva but immediately proved sterile, an initial stumbling block being the clearing and dredging of the Shatt al-Arab for navigation (which Iraq wanted but Iran did not). Both sides had approached these negotiations in an arrogant and demanding manner, neither intending to modify its demands or concede the slightest point. Neither country showed any significant sign of demobilizing their huge armed forces, only of re-organizing them. Nor was there any talk of peace, arms reduction or reconciliation. Rather they both entered the Triad Deterrent race in conjunction with their respective and well-published 'reconstruction programmes'.

In Iraq the half-dozen Army Corps Commanders who had been instrumental in successfully fighting off Iranian attacks were retired or moved into low-profile appointments, to be replaced by less charismatic characters. Medium-grade 'war heroes', who had been lauded but who had critized the conduct of the war, were consigned to oblivion. The President was intent upon insuring against a military coup by discontented army officers. Indeed it seems that he may actually have pre-empted one in March 1989 when a number of officers were arrested and some reputedly executed. A wave of other arrests of critics of the regime followed (accompanied by a wave of suspicious deaths supposedly in helicopter 'accidents'). In May 1989 General Khairallah, the competent Defence Minister, died in one such helicopter crash.

President Saddam Hussein also turned on his dissident Kurds who had fought against him during the Gulf War with the support of the Tehran government. In March 1988, before the cease-fire, when it was feared that Iranian troops might break through into Iraqi Kurdish territory, he deployed chemical weapons against the Kurdish town of Halabja. A reputed 6,000 people died. This was followed by mass arrests and the resettlement of groups of Kurds southwards, causing many Kurds to flee across the border into Turkey. Military action against Kurds living in border regions continued during July and August when it was again alleged that chemical weapons were utilized against them. More resettlements brought the number of displaced Kurds in 1989 to over 100,000, while Kurdish refugees in Turkey exceeded 36,000.

Meanwhile morale in the Iranian armed forces was low. The *Pasdaran*, formerly regarded as heroes of the war to whom all credit was accorded, had fallen from favour, becoming scapegoats for losing the war and often accused of having sought safe jobs away from the Front. In June 1988, Speaker Rafsanjani was appointed Deputy Supreme Commander of the Armed Forces (Khomeini was the Supreme Commander) with a remit to merge the regular army with the *Pasdaran*. Although he personally was in favour of this move as it could only add to his personal power base, he delayed action temporarily knowing that such a move at that moment would provoke open hostilities between the two institutions. However, in March 1989 Khomeini re-assumed direct control of the *Pasdaran*, appointing Abdullah Nouri as his Personal Representative on that body, thus reversing his former merger plan. Mohsen Rafiqdust, *Pasdaran* Minister since 1982 and a friend of Rafsanjani, had been removed in September 1988 and replaced by Ali Shamkhani, Prime Minister Hossein Mussavi's nominee.

When the guns fell silent the struggle for the succession in Iran amongst top contenders became more intense. Ayatollah Montazeri, Khomeini's nominated successor, became an early casualty, while ministers and certain senior military commanders were re-shuffled or removed.

In October 1988 Iranian Defence Minister, Mohammed Hossein Jalali, stated that both the Army and the *Pasdaran* would be strengthened as he feared a resumption of hostilities with Iraq. On Army Day (17 April 1989) Khomeini urged all decision-makers not to neglect strengthening the Armed Forces and the same month President Khamenei, at a conference of senior military commanders in Tehran, announced that $5 billion annually would be allocated to increasing the Iranian defence capability. It is thought that $20 billion was ear-marked to rebuild the Iranian Ground Forces.[3]

GULF ARAB GROUPINGS

The outbreak of the Gulf War caused considerable consternation among the other Gulf Arab states, not all of whom were fully in accord with Iraq. Although fearful of Iran and yet equally eager to maintain existing trade links with Khomeini's regime, they nevertheless all backed Iraq, some openly and others covertly, at least in financial ways. Their mutual wariness of the war and its possible consequences spurred six of these states, Bahrain, Kuwait, Qatar, Saudi Arabia and the United Arab Emirates, to form the Gulf Co-operation Council (GCC) ostensibly for economic reasons but in reality for collective defence against Iran. Despite having traditionally Sunni governments, all of these states were wary of the potential impact of Tehran's aim to export Shia Islamic revolution upon their own sizeable Shia populations.

The Green Shield Force was established to provide for mutual defence, eventually reaching a strength of about 7,000 men. Based in King Khalid Military City at Hafi al-Batin, detachments were sent to Iraq in February 1986 when the Iranians invaded the Fao Peninsula. The first Green Shield exercise was held in 1983 and others have since been held annually in alternating states. However, military progress has been slow owing to the reluctance of independent states to co-operate fully with each other. Watching the progress of the Gulf War, GCC states opted to buy 'high-tech' weaponry to off-set the disadvantage of small populations.

Iran's relations with Saudi Arabia were particularly volatile during the war, primarily over differences of religious leadership. Khomeini made increasingly hostile postures and made critical and inflammatory remarks about the Saudi leadership, instigating Iranian pilgrims to disrupt the annual *Hajj*. The first incidents occurred in October 1981 when Iranian pilgrims chanted pro-Khomeini and anti-Saudi slogans. Year by year these demonstrations became more raucous and violent until, in a major incident in July 1987, 402 people were killed and 649 injured in clashes between Iranian pilgrims and the Saudi security forces. The Saudis imposed a quota on states sending pilgrims but further trouble in 1988 led to the breaking off of diplomatic relations between Saudi Arabia and Iran. Despite Saudi pressure this example was not followed by the other GCC states.

After the Gulf War broke out Saudi Arabia obtained four US AWACS on loan, manned by US personnel, to monitor the combat area. On 5 June 1984, with AWACS assistance, the Saudi pilots of two F-15s located and shot down two Iranian Phantom (F-4) aircraft. US Congress allowed Saudi Arabia to take delivery of five further US AWACS in 1985.

The Gulf War cease-fire brought new fears to some other Arab states as Iraq emerged strong, aggressive and in no mood to deal sympathetically with those Arab states which had only given her half-hearted support during the war. Moreover there was the danger that Iraq might elect to assert territorial claims including part of Kuwait and certain Gulf islands. Other Arab states perceived the emergence of a confident Iraq to be conducive to their own interests and, in February 1989, Egypt, Iraq, Jordan and North Yemen, having a combined population of just over sixty million people, formed the Arab Co-operation Council (ACC). Again ostensibly for economic reasons, this too was virtually a defence coalition, relying on the manpower reservoir, industrial base and skilled workforce of Egypt and the large, war-experienced Iraqi armed forces to make up for the smaller populations and lack of resources of Jordan and North Yemen. Differentiating themselves from the 'traditional' GCC states, the ACC states have become known, due to their systems of government, as the 'moderates'.

Also in February 1989, the Arab Magreb Union (AMU) of Algeria, Libya, Mauritania, Morocco and Tunisia was formed. With a total population of about 59 million, the union is somewhat out on an African limb, with only Libya deeply involved in the Gulf region. This left Syria isolated, perhaps too radical to fit easily into any Arab grouping, hostile to next-door Iraq over ideological Ba'th Party differences and to Egypt for making a peace treaty with Israel. Syria had supported Iran throughout the Gulf War and did not condemn that country until the Arab Summit in Amman of November 1987.

Finding itself now alienated from all Gulf Arab states, Iran began to work towards forming an Islamic grouping of Iran, Afghanistan and Pakistan as a barrier against both the Soviet Union and the Gulf Arab states coalitions.

ARMS: SUPPLY AND DEMAND

The vagaries of Western, Soviet and other arms suppliers to the Arab states since 1948, and to Iran and Iraq during the Gulf War, with their political blackmail, restrictive conditions, delayed deliveries, sudden cancellations and 'low-tech' availability have caused the Arab states, Israel and Iran to develop deep desires for weapons self-sufficiency. This requires a large, comprehensive military-industrial base to say the least, which only Egypt and Israel can now be said to possess.

Israel is almost self-sufficient in this respect, except that it still has to buy-in modern combat aircraft from the USA as well as certain materials to manufacture tanks, guns, rockets, missiles, radar, light aircraft, small naval craft and small submarines. Yet it is very advanced in early warning devices and avionics. Israel has managed to produce the Kfir light fighter aircraft, based on the old French Mirage model and, in theory, could produce its own modern combat aircraft (although not without American assistance). It almost did so with its multi-role Lavi, test flown in 1987, although 50 per cent of its components, including the engine, were American. Rising production costs together with the reprobation of two US aircraft manufacturing corporations which objected to Israel as an international competitor in this field caused the Lavi project to be aborted. Israel is reported to have about 100 Kfirs for sale[4] with some going to Chile and Colombia. Israeli military sales bring in about $400 million annually.

Egypt is not quite as advanced in weapons production as Israel, lacking the 'high-tech' capability which Israel has gained from the US and other sources. Yet Egypt is developing fast. In the 1960s and 1970s, Egypt became skilled in maintaining, copying and improving Soviet models and, with Soviet aid, fought Israel to a standstill in the 'electronic war' of 1968–70.[5] Since President Sadat expelled the Soviet advisers in 1972, Egypt has largely abandoned Soviet weaponry, obtaining advanced Western aircraft and 'high-tech' items, assembling them and then reproducing them under joint agreements. Examples are the Alphajet trainer aircraft, US M-1A1 Abrams tank, Gazelle helicopter, the Chinese F-6 (J-6) (copy of the Soviet MiG-19) and the F-7 (copy of the MiG-21).

Planned expansion lagged after Sadat's peace treaty with Israel in 1979 but was re-invigorated after his death in 1981. The late Iraqi Defence Minister, General Khairallah, stated that had it not been for Egyptian-produced ammunition for Iraqi-held Soviet weaponry, Iraq would have lost the Gulf War. Egypt, which produces its own armoured personnel carrier, the Walid, is almost self-sufficient in some weapons production, provided certain materials can be obtained. It still has to buy 'high-tech' items such as AWACS and modern combat aircraft. Once having seen itself as becoming the main, almost exclusive, arms supplier to Arab League states, Egypt now finds itself in competition with new arms-producing countries.

In general the military bases of both Iran and Iraq, and indeed most of the other Gulf states, have a very 'low-tech' capability and it will be some considerable time before they are even partly self-sufficient in weapons production.

Under the Shah, Iran had aimed at gradual attainment of weapons production self-sufficiency but had been dependent on foreign technicians to maintain and repair its 'high-tech' arms. The Islamic revolution's initial disinterest in the military machine led to neglect of Iran's fleets of aircraft, tanks, vehicles, weapons and equipment. The Iraqi invasion generated a frantic scramble to put these back into working order again, but spares had been mislaid and arms embargoes enforced, pushing the country into the international arms markets, 'vulturization' and improvization. The progress of the Gulf War was accompanied by substantial improvements in improvization techniques and domestic production. By January 1988 the Iranians were able to unveil the Shabavis helicopter, about to be put into production and which, they claim, is completely manufactured locally.

The Gulf and other Arab states had traditionally purchased their arms supplies from their respective 'sphere of influence' patrons. The Soviet Union supplied Iraq, Libya, Syria and (until 1972) Egypt, while the Western states, especially the US, Britain and France supplied Jordan, Kuwait and Saudi Arabia. The supplier states carefully controlled the amounts and types of weapons sold, minimizing their technical capacity and maintaining what was, in their view, a regional balance of power. The exception to the rule of course was Israel, which was provided with a substantial 'high-tech' advantage over its Arab neighbours by the US.

Jordan, however, obtained the US Hawk ground-to-air missile on strict conditions as to its positioning and Kuwait and Qatar were entirely excluded from purchasing the US Stinger shoulder-held ground-to-air missile. By the mid-1980s such political restrictions had become intolerable to the recipients. Already alternative sources were presenting themselves in the form of the international black arms market and the reaching to maturity of Third World arms production.

Saudi Arabia was perhaps the first to break the monopoly hold when, in 1985, US Congress refused to allow it to buy more F-15 combat aircraft and other 'high-tech' weapons. Britain smartly stepped in to clinch the two 'al-Yamamah' contracts, reputed to be worth more than $30 billion, selling to Saudi Arabia Tornado combat aircraft, naval crafts and other sophisticated items, all with the latest state of the art technology available. The Soviets, now in need of hard currency, abandoned their former policy of exporting only 'low-tech' models and, in the interests of commercialism, sent their latest 'high-tech' weapons and equipment such as the MiG-29 to Iraq, Libya and Syria. The Soviets have sent the Sukhoi-24s to Libya and Syria and is reported to be receiving them. Iran is hoping to obtain the MiG-29 and Su-22s. Arms supplying countries began to sell their wares to both sides in the Gulf War without shame or concealment. The arms race was on in the Gulf region; armaments had become big business to several nations and huge sums of money were involved. Former arms embargoes broke down and former political conditions were pushed aside as commercial considerations over-rode political principles. For the first time recipient states were able to pick and choose both their supplier and the weapons they required.

CHEMICAL WARFARE (CW)

While most Gulf states are busy stockpiling their armouries with whatever weapons they can obtain, at least three of them are concentrating upon achieving the Triad Deterrent to give them parity with Israel, the first leg of which is chemical weapons. The Arab states, among others, noted the devastating effects caused by chemical weapons in the Gulf War, seeing it as a cheap, easily obtainable deterrent which they could obtain for themselves. CW has come to be thought of as the 'poor nation's nuclear bomb'. Any country with a pesticide factory is able to manufacture crude war gases such as mustard and phosgene, which were used with deadly effect in the First World War. Additionally, if it has a reasonably developed industrial base and provided certain chemical compounds can be obtained, a state can also eventually manufacture 'nerve gases', usually categorized as Tabun, Sarin, Soman and VX.

Some Gulf states have already developed a CW capability and others may have this in mind. It must be accepted that both Iran and Iraq have stocks of such war gases. The CIA alleges, for example, that Iraq produces some 7,000 tons of mustard gases annually at its main Samarra plant and that in February 1988, Iran, at its chemical warfare centre at Semnan, test-fired a ballistic missile with a CW warhead . Libya is also visibly (although it is much denied) keen on attaining a domestic chemical weapons production capability and a great deal of controversy was raised by US allegations about a purpose-built plant at Rabta, fifty miles from Tripoli. 'Discovery' of the plant, which Libya claimed to be for innocent purposes, coincided with the arrival in Libya of Soviet Sukhoi-24 combat aircraft which, in theory, could make round trips to Israel carrying fuel-drop tanks.

It must still be said, though, that many allegations were revealed and made on the proliferation of CW at the United Nations Chemical Weapons Conference held in Paris in July 1989, which was intended by its organizers, the United Nations and France, to advocate prohibiting the spread of chemical weapons. Although the Conference ended with a weak, vaguely worded resolution supporting the 1925 Geneva Protocol against the use of CW, it became an international market place where certain nations openly touted to obtain this capacity.

Iraq admitted using CW in the Gulf War but not against its own Kurds at a later date. Iran was non-committal, alleging it had suffered 50,000 casualties from Iraqi CW. Israel openly alleged that Egypt, Syria and Libya all had large stocks of CW, denied by Egypt despite one report[6] which claimed that it had developed a plant at Abu Zaabali in 1985 with the help of a Swiss firm. The opinion of the CIA is that Syria is the most advanced Arab state in terms of CW production, Iraq the most experienced, with Iran a close second, while both Israel and Egypt are relative 'dark horses'. Israel has tacitly admitted that it possesses a CW capability and is known to have had occasional civil defence exercises covering this aspect.

The acquisition of CW means by the Gulf countries seems unstoppable. The UN Geneva-based Conference on Disarmament has produced a list of over fifty chemicals and compounds which it would like embargoed to prevent Third World countries from developing their own CW plants, but it is finding difficulty in formulating a workable implementation procedure. Some Western countries have already imposed their own embargoes on certain CW components but, often due to a government's indifference or covert policy, freelance firms blatantly avoid them for profit.

The CIA estimate that by the year 2000, at least twenty countries will possess a CW capability.

THE BALLISTIC MISSILE RACE

The second leg of the Triad Deterrent is possession of ballistic missiles which can cross national frontiers with impunity and so negate the demand for 'secure land frontiers'.

The value of ballistic missiles was truly realized during the Gulf War, especially in the spasmodic phases of the so-called 'War of the Cities' in which Iraq used Soviet FROG-7s (range up to 70km) and then SCUD-Bs (300km). Egypt improved the range of the SCUD-Bs and sent some to Iraq, but Iraq itself also worked on extending their range and in August 1987 unveiled its 'al-Hussayn' (500km). This was followed in April 1988 by the 'al-Abbas' (900km). Both of these brought Tehran within range. The Iraqis also invested in the Brazilian Astros-II short-range ballistic missile (up to 150km). Iraq and Egypt joined Argentina in its Condor project. The Condor-I is a short-range missile but is being superceded by the Condor-II (800km). The Argentine intention was to produce these missiles for overseas sales. It appears that US pressure has frozen this project for the moment.

The Iranians did not have any ballistic missiles until 1985 when fifty SCUD-Bs were received from Libya, to be followed by similar consignments from China and North Korea. Iran also produced two of its own versions, the Shahin-II and Nazeat (Iran-130), both short-range missiles. The Chinese also supplied Iran with the Oghab (70km) based on the FROG-7. During the main phase of the 'War of the Cities', which began on 29 February 1988, both Iran and Iraq were well stocked with ballistic missiles with which to bombard each others' cities. In a six-week period it was calculated that over 570 ballistic missiles were fired in all, and many more would have been but for the shortage of launchers. One source[7] estimated that Iraq was able to fire only ten missiles a day and Iran only three because of this restriction. Iraqi missile attacks on Tehran did much to sap Iranian morale and bring about acceptance of the cease-fire in August.

Anxious to gain influence in the Gulf region at the expense of the Soviet Union, China sold a number of Silkworm (HY-2) anti-ship missiles (50km) to Iran in March 1987, which were positioned near the Strait of Hormuz, the narrow entrance to the Gulf. The Silkworm is a copy of the Soviet SS-2-N Styx, which had made naval history in October 1967 by being the first missile to sink a warship, the Israeli destroyer *Eilat*.

The dominant missile power in the Gulf region until 1988 was Israel, which possessed twelve US Lance missiles (110km) and, with French help, produced their own Jericho-I missile (150km) and Jericho-II (1,400km). The latter was test-fired in May 1987 and would be able to reach Soviet territory.

The Soviets supplied Syria with both FROG-7s and SCUD-Bs as well as a few SS-12s (120km) but, lacking a sufficient industrial base, Syria has been unable to increase their ranges. Syrian requests for the Soviet SS-23 (500km) were refused. The Chinese are developing an 'M-series' of ballistic missiles with ranges of up to 500km for sale to foreign countries. Syria has reportedly ordered some M-9s (500km). Libya already had FROG-7s and SCUD-Bs but its requests for Soviet SS-21s and SS-23s were refused, as was one for Chinese M-9s. Libya is reputed to be financing the Brazilian Sonda-4 (600km) and hopes that one day it will have this ballistic missile to deliver its warheads.

Apart from Kuwait, which has a few FROG-7s, none of the other Gulf Arab states have any ballistic missiles, so it was a jolting surprise to the USA, USSR, Iran and Israel when in April 1988 it was revealed that Saudi Arabia had purchased seventy Chinese DF-3 missiles (2,200km), able to target both Iran and Israel. The reputed price[8] was $54 million each, the first being already in position at the Sulayyaul Oasis, 285 miles south of Riyadh. Although the Saudis explained that they were simply a deterrent against Iranian aggression, they caused Israeli anxiety and there was discussion in Israel as to whether or not to make a long-range pre-emptive strike to 'take them out'. The Saudis let it be known that if this happened any remaining DF-3s would be instantly launched against Israel. The Israelis shelved this for the time being. The Americans, who persuaded the Saudis to sign the Nuclear Non-Proliferation Treaty and to promise not to 'go nuclear', calmed the Israelis down. An American request to inspect the Saudi DF-3s was refused.

The ballistic missile race by Egypt, Iran, Iraq, Israel and Saudi Arabia is in full flow, with each seeking to buy and stockpile missiles with ever greater ranges, accuracy and warhead-carrying capabilities. Missile technology and components are often supplied openly by certain advanced countries or their 'freelance' firms. The process is accompanied by government hinderance, bribery and espionage. In June 1988, two Egyptian military personnel were arrested in the USA, accused of trying to smuggle '430lbs' of carbon-carbon heat-resistant material for the nose-cone of the Argentine Condor-II missile.

Alarmed at the sudden proliferation of ballistic missiles in the Gulf region and elsewhere, seven major industrial nations (USA, UK, France, Italy, Japan and West Germany), subsequently expanded to include the Benelux countries and Spain, formed the Missile Technology Control Regime (MTCR), which surfaced in April 1987 and was established to restrict the export of missile technology and components. So far the MTCR has failed to make any effective impact, especially since it has not drawn to its ranks other missile-producing states such as Argentina, Brazil, China or the Soviet Union.

Several nations have been trying to produce an effective Anti-Tactical Ballistic Missile (ATBM) system to counter ballistic missiles but so far none have been successful. Some have been able to add a 'partial-ATBM' capability to existing weapons systems such as the US Patriot and the Soviet SA-12. Some countries have on-going studies on ATBM projects and Iraq has (doubtfully) claimed its Fao-1 as a successful ATBM system. Israel began an ATBM project, the Arrow, some time ago, which lagged due to a lack of funds but which was revived when the USA took an interest (June 1988), providing $400 million annually for the project. It is possible that the Arrow is the only viable 'anti-missile missile' under development.

NUCLEAR BOMBS IN THE BASEMENT

We now come to the third leg of the Triad Deterrent, the possession of nuclear weapons, realization of which is far closer for certain Gulf states than is generally assumed. At the Paris Conference[9] Israel openly accused Egypt, Iran and Iraq of working to produce nuclear weapons while Arab states pointed their fingers at Israel. These states either flatly deny this allegation or refuse to discuss it. There is sufficient evidence, however, although mostly circumstantial, to support the claim.

The first myth to dissipate is that nuclear technology is in any way 'secret'. Its practitioners have carefully cocooned this industry in mystery to keep it remote and exclusive. Nuclear technology is an open book for those would-be nuclear powers who are able to obtain the ingredients and who are willing to brazen it out in the face of universal reprobation. Scientific nuclear literature is voluminous and easily obtainable and requires only the qualified scientist and the ingredients.

Basic source fuel comes from uranium dioxide (yellowcake) which has to be processed or 'enriched' in a reactor to become either U-235 or U-238, both suitable nuclear fuels. Reactor processing produces the by-product 'plutonium' which is required to make nuclear warheads. The Test Ban Treaty of 1963, signed by a majority of nations but by no means all, forbids the testing of nuclear weapons except underground. States developing a nuclear weapon capability are thus compelled to do so secretly and to leave it untested, a so-called 'bomb in the basement'. It is clear that nations using nuclear power for peaceful energy purposes are already half-way to a nuclear weapon capability.

Today Israel is rated as being the world's sixth largest nuclear military power, possessing, according to media reports, between 100 and 200 nuclear weapons of varying destructive power. Israel's nuclear military development programme began in the late 1950s in collaboration with France, using French extraction technology and a French reactor. Originally kept secret even from the USA, the Israeli nuclear research centre at Dimona in the Negev Desert was disguised as a textile factory to avoid detection by spy-satellites.

Covert means were employed to obtain uranium, sufficient it is generally estimated to produce ten warheads annually. The Israeli Atomic Energy Commission was established in 1952 and six years later the Israelis produced a hydrogen warhead. Israel's military nuclear capability was grossly under-estimated by foreign intelligence agencies until 1986 when Mordecai Vanunu, a Moroccan-born Israeli who worked at Dimona as a nuclear technician, was made redundant and defected. He told his story to a British newspaper[10] and produced sixty photographs which he had secretly taken at Dimona. Cross-examination by experts, who also studied these photographs, seemed to substantiate Vanunu's account of what included a fully operative U-238 extraction plant.

The Iranian Atomic Energy Commission was formed in 1974 to co-ordinate the Shah's $30 billion plan to build a dozen or so nuclear-powered stations to provide electricity. However, the Islamic regime, when it came to power, down-graded this programme until only the Tehran University nuclear reactor remained in operation. In 1987, four separate deposits of uranium were confirmed in Iran, which perhaps encouraged Ayatollah Khomeini (who had just suffered major military setbacks), to agree in December 1987 to re-activate the Iranian military nuclear industry. In the meantime, the Shah's policy of involvement with a number of foreign firms specializing in nuclear-technology and nuclear-resources (from Argentina, France and West Germany) had continued.

Five more Iranian nuclear military plants are planned and two are under construction, it being said that Argentine nuclear scientists have been working on the Bushehr plant since 1985. Iran's stake in a Namibian uranium mine entitles it to receive 1,000 tons of 'yellowcake' annually. To date it has collected over 8,000 tons, some of which has been brought into Iran, the remainder being either sold or used as barter.

In May 1987, a secret nuclear collaboration agreement was made between Iran and Argentina (with or without Khomeini's permission or knowledge) for Argentina to produce a 'reactor core' for the Tehran University reactor's 'other services' and the transfer of nuclear technology and apparatus to enable Iran to 'close the reactor fuel cycle', or in other words to enable it to become a military nuclear power. For some years Argentina had been secretly producing U-235 enriched fuel at a plant in Patagonia, the existence of which was only revealed in December 1983 when a civilian government came to power.

The Iranian government is now actively encouraging nuclear research at the Tehran University Isotopes Centre and the Isfahan Nuclear Technology Centre. In December 1988 Pakistan, which may soon have a 'nuclear bomb in its basement', agreed to co-operate in a project to exploit Iranian uranium resources. With such nuclear materials and technology available it can only be a matter of time before Iran also put its first nuclear bomb 'into the basement'.

The Iraqi Atomic Energy Commission was formed in 1956 to co-ordinate a programme for nuclear power for electricity. After the 1958 revolution some nuclear assistance was given by the Soviets and in 1974 the French agreed to supply and install two nuclear reactors, Tamuz-I and Tamuz-II (formerly named Osiris) at Tuwaitha, near Baghdad. Nuclear assistance was also obtained from Italy, Pakistan and Portugal. On 30 September 1980, two Iranian Phantom aircraft bombed Tuwaitha and there is still some dispute over exactly how much damage was done since the reactors were soon working again. In a long-distance aerial strike the Israelis bombed Tuwaitha on 28 June 1981, putting both reactors out of action completely, although '25lbs' of plutonium were reputedly salvaged.

At the moment Iraq is collaborating with Brazil, China and Italy in nuclear development. Italy has provided Iraq with four nuclear laboratories while it is believed that both Brazil and China, in separate secret deals, agreed to supply Iraq with enriched uranium and plutonium. Iraq also signed a number of agreements with West German 'freelance' firms dealing in nuclear technology. By May 1989 the French were again active at Tuwaitha. It was reported[11] that Iraq was secretly working on a crash programme, with some assistance from Pakistan, to build nuclear weapons, completion time being estimated to be five years ahead and the project being financed by Saudi Arabia.

Although the Egyptian Energy Authority Establishment was formed in 1955 the country's nuclear power programme has only made faltering progress due to a lack of money and resources, wars with Israel and a period of ostracization from the Arab League. Its first nuclear power station, to be at al-Debaa, has yet to be built. Israelis insist that Egypt has obtained quantities of plutonium, is producing a nuclear warhead, is training its nationals in nuclear technology establishments abroad and that an Egyptian nuclear research centre exists and is functioning. How far Egypt may have progressed in this respect can only be guessed at as its security has been good and little, if anything, is known for sure.

The conclusion must be that within a few short years there may be four nuclear powers in the Middle East region rather than the single one known at present.

A LASTING PEACE?

At the moment the Arab states, Iran and Israel are in the throes of a frantic free-for-all arms race in which commercialism predominates among the arms-producing nations. The latter seem to have abandoned the high moral ground as their sales teams tour the Gulf region. The parallel between the Cold War in Europe in the 1950s and 1960s and that which now exists in the Gulf region is striking. Just as NATO and Warsaw Pact countries sought then to stockpile weapons in a policy of Mutually Assured Destruction (MAD) so today certain of the Gulf states and their neighbours are striving to achieve military parity with, code words for superiority over, their potential enemies.

Having achieved weapons saturation, NATO strategy was modified to that of Flexible Response, a policy which basically remains but which has yet to be reached in the Gulf region. It is to be feared that suspicion, hostility and distrust which accompany the Gulf 'Cold War' will become, as was true of Europe, institutionalized and an accepted way of life. Brief conflagrations between hostile states cannot be ruled out and it is to be hoped that the superpowers could intervene to prevent them from escalating into nuclear catastrophes.

Meantime, it will take a new generation of leaders in the Gulf states, able to see through the mists of propaganda and prejudice and who realize that if Triad Deterrent buttons are pushed there can be no victor, as well as the development of education and communication among the peoples of those states, to wipe out the root causes of this new 'Cold War'.

Perhaps a similar course of discussions, arms reductions and detente can then be followed and the young people of the Gulf will be able to look forward to full, peaceful lives. Lasting peace may be slow to arrive in the Gulf region, but it should eventually come.

8 The political economy of Iran's foreign trade since the revolution: ideals and practice

Kamran Mofid

On 16 January 1979, the Shah's 37-year rule came to an end when he left Iran never to return. A price that it seems he had to pay for his misguided and unacceptable policies. On 1 February 1979, Ayatollah Khomeini returned to Iran and was greeted by millions. In April of the same year, Iran became an Islamic Republic.

According to the revolutionary leaders, as a result of the Shah's policies, Iran had become too dependent on oil revenues and had failed to diversify its exports. Moreover, it was argued that much of these revenues were being spent on imports of lavish consumer goods. It was also contended that Iran under the Shah had become too dependent on the West for its imports. Furthermore, it was also argued that the Shah's policies had resulted in the destruction of the agricultural sector, pushing Iran into a serious state of dependency on imported food.

The revolution, it was claimed, would expand the agricultural sector, make Iran self-sufficient in food, diversify and increase Iran's non-oil exports, reduce the consumer goods imports, and finally reduce Iran's reliance on the West.[1]

In this chapter, therefore, the focus of the analysis is to assess the post-revolution foreign trade performance, to note the changes in the country's foreign trade orientation, and to observe how far these changes comply with the revolution's goals and objectives.

To do this, it is useful to begin by looking at the trade targets as outlined in the First Five-Year Plan of the Islamic Republic. This is intended to provide an understanding of the regime's long-term intentions.

TRADE TARGETS OF THE FIRST FIVE-YEAR PLAN

In the First Islamic Plan the expansion of non-oil exports was strongly emphasized. Indeed, as noted in the plan document:

In view of the fact that elimination of the country's dependence on oil exports is an important aspect of reaching economic independence, the expansion of non-oil exports, including traditional, industrial and agricultural products, is especially important for development . . . . Oil reserves are finite and exhaustible. Iran cannot afford and the Islamic Republic does not want the country's continued dependence on oil exports. One of the main objectives and orientations of development is to gain economic independence and to do away with the country's dependence on oil exports.[2]

Tables 8.1 and 8.2 provide data on the projection of exports, imports, and their corresponding shares during the First Plan period (1983/84–1987/88). It was planned that the non-oil exports would increase at an average annual real growth rate of almost 44 per cent, from $0.63 billion in 1983/84 to $2.68 billion in 1987/88 (at constant 1982/83 prices). If this goal was achieved, the share of non-oil exports in total exports of the country would have risen from 3 per cent to 7.1 per cent respectively during the same period. The increasing share of the non-oil exports is correspondingly matched by a projected decline in the share of oil exports. It was planned that the share of oil exports will fall from 97 per cent in 1983/84 to 92.9 per cent in 1987/88.

Imports of goods and services during the First Plan was projected to grow from $19.5 billion in 1983/84 to $35 billion in 1987/88, representing an increase of 79.5 per cent. Capital and intermediate goods were to have the major share of total imports. Imports of intermediate goods were projected to grow at around 16.5 per cent per annum. Growth in import of capital goods was projected at 25 per cent per annum and that of consumer goods at 3.1 per cent per annum. The share of imports of immediate materials during the First Plan was projected to be around 51 per cent of the total. The share of capital goods imports on the other hand was planned to increase continuously from 19.1 per cent in 1983/84 to 26.3 per cent in 1987/88. It was envisaged that the consumer goods imports would have a decreasing share of total imports during the plan period, from 22.3 per cent in the first year of the plan to 14.2 per cent in the final year.

In view of the above points, the general orientation with respect to exports and imports is to decrease the country's dependency on oil revenues as the main supplier of the foreign exchange requirements, to limit consumer goods imports, and instead to allocate the currency resources to imports of intermediate and capital goods.

Table 8.1 Projection of imports and exports during the First Islamic Plan, 1983/84–1987/8 (billion dollars: at 1982/83 constant prices)

	1983/4	Growth %	1984/5	Growth %	1985/6	Growth %	1986/7	Growth %	1987/8
Exports	*20.91*	15.3	*24.12*	15.5	*27.86*	15.8	*32.27*	16.1	*37.48*
Oil	20.29	14.4	23.22	14.4	26.57	14.4	30.41	14.4	34.80
Non-oil products	0.63	43.8	0.90	43.8	1.29	43.8	1.86	43.8	2.68
Imports	*19.50*	15.3	*22.50*	15.6	*26.00*	15.9	*30.12*	16.2	*35.00*
Consumer products	4.40	3.1	4.53	3.1	4.67	3.1	4.82	3.1	4.97
Intermediary products	9.80	17.2	11.50	16.8	13.42	16.5	15.63	16.4	18.20
Capital products	3.77	25.0	4.71	25.0	5.86	25.0	7.36	25.0	9.20
Services (net)	1.54	14.4	1.76	14.4	2.02	14.4	2.31	14.4	2.64
Current account (net)	*1.41*	15.0	*1.63*	15.0	*1.87*	15.0	*2.15*	15.0	*2.47*

Source: First Five Year Economic, Social and Cultural Development Plan, 1983–1987, Plan and Budget Organization, Islamic Republic of Iran, August 1982
Note: ($1 = 84 Rials).

Table 8.2 Projected share of various products in imports and exports during the First Plan (%)

	1983/4	1984/5	1985/6	1986/7	1987/8
Exports	*100.0*	*100.0*	*100.0*	*100.0*	*100.0*
Oil	97.0	96.3	95.4	94.2	92.9
Non-oil products	3.0	3.7	4.6	5.8	7.1
Imports	*100.0*	*100.0*	*100.0*	*100.0*	*100.0*
Consumer products	22.3	20.1	17.9	16.0	14.2
Intermediary products	50.7	51.3	51.7	51.9	52.0
Capital products	19.1	20.3	22.6	24.4	26.3
Services (net)	7.9	7.8	7.8	7.7	7.5

*Source: First Five Year Economic Social and Cultural Development Plan, 1983–1987, Plan and Budget Organization, Islamic Republic of Iran, August 1982

THE STRUCTURE, COMPOSITION AND PERFORMANCE OF IRAN'S FOREIGN TRADE SINCE THE REVOLUTION

More than ten years have now passed since the revolution. Although this is a short period in Iran's history, none the less, it is long enough for changes to have been made in order to achieve some of the revolution's objectives. The figures that follow are mainly for the period before and since the First Five-Year Plan of the Islamic Republic. They can, however, be assessed in the light of the regime's long-term intentions as indicated by the plan.

At the outset, it should be emphasized that the revolution itself, and more importantly the war with Iraq have had a very destructive effect on Iran's economy which might have reduced the ability of the revolution to implement changes.

However, at the same time, it should be underlined that neither the revolution nor the war have stopped the flow of oil revenues, as happened, for example, after the nationalization of the oil industry in 1951. Moreover, revolutionary fervour and external threat, in my view, should have made it easier for the regime to carry out far-reaching and radical policies in order to achieve some of the revolution's objectives. Therefore, with this in mind, we shall analyse the post-revolution foreign trade of Iran.

The importance of oil in providing foreign exchange earnings during the period under study and the failure of the Islamic Republic to diversify Iran's foreign exchange earnings can best be seen in Table 8.3, where the value of Iran's total exports and its composition during the 1973 to 1986 period are given. As can be noted, in 1979 crude petroleum had provided 87.2 per cent of the total value of exports. By 1986, however, this share had increased to 94.0 per cent.

The share of non-energy merchandise exports has correspondingly fallen from the high level of 5.6 per cent in 1980 to 3.5 per cent in 1986. One reason for this is the jump in oil prices in the 1979 to 1980 period. The absolute decline of non-energy exports, however, indicates that the government's intentions are very far from being realized, even if price changes are allowed for. Furthermore, the failure to diversify the sources of foreign exchange earnings is also in contrast to the objectives of the First National Plan of the Islamic Republic.

If we compare and contrast the figures for the post- and pre-revolution periods, it can be noted that, indeed, since the revolution, Iran has become much more dependent on oil revenues. During the 1973 to 1988 period, such revenues, on average per year had provided 91.5 per cent of the total value of exports, while during 1982 to 1986, this has increased to 98.0 per cent per annum.

Table 8.3 Value of Iran's total exports 1973–86 (billion current rials)

	1973	1974	1975	1976	1977	1978	1979	1980	1981	1982	1983	1984	1985	1986
TX	426	1459	1367	1652	1713	1558	1408	994	981	1632	1685	1128	1219	840[e]
Petroleum	387	1414	1328	1610	1667	1528	1352	938	944	1608	1660	1103	1194	810
CPX	365	1336	1245	1539	1539	1470	1228	684	731	1508	1621	1066	1157	790
N-EX*	39	45	39	42	46	30	56	56	37	24	25	25	25	30[e]
Percentage share of petroleum in TX*	90.8	96.7	97.1	97.4	97.3	98.1	96.0	94.4	96.2	98.2	98.6	97.8	98.0	96.4
Percentage share of CPX in TX*	85.7	91.7	91.1	93.1	93.0	94.3	87.2	68.8	75.5	92.4	96.2	94.5	94.9	94.0
Percentage share of N-EX in TX*	9.1	3.1	2.8	2.5	2.7	1.9	4.0	5.6	3.7	1.5	1.5	2.2	2.0	3.5

Sources: International Financial Statistics, 1986, 1987 Yearbooks; Statistiques De L'Industrie Petrolière (Petrol), 1986 Yearbook

Notes: *author's calculation. (TX) Total exports, (CPX) Crude petroleum exports, (N-EX) Non-energy exports. The exchange rate for the period under observation: $1 = rials 68.9 (1973), 667. (1974), 67.6 (1975), 70.2 (1976), 70.6 (1977), 70.5 (1978), 70.6 (1979), 78.3 (1981), 83.6 (1982), 86.4 (1983), 90.0 (1984), 91.0 (1985), 79.0 (1986). (e) Author's estimation.

Table 8.4 shows the main recipients of Iran's oil exports. An important feature of this table is the fact that, in contrast to the many statements made by Iranian officials that 'the Islamic Republic of Iran would never sell oil to America',[3] Iran has been selling oil to that country. Although oil exports to the US have been reduced significantly since the revolution, in absolute terms, during 1982 to 1985, on average per year, the US has imported 4.5 per cent of Iran's total oil exports. By 1987, this share had increased to 6.6 per cent of the total, as in that year, the US had imported 4,872,000 and tonnes of oil from Iran.[4]

France's behaviour is also interesting. While France, as a major supplier of arms to Iraq, has indirectly been responsible for so much death and destruction in Iran, none the less, Iran has continued to sell oil to that country. In fact, during the 1979 to 1985 period, on average each year, France, similar to the US, has imported 4.5 per cent of Iran's total oil exports. By 1987, this share had increased to 6 per cent of the total, as in that year, France imported 4,401,000 tonnes of oil from Iran.[5]

In all, while in 1979, western Europe and Japan together had accounted for 50 per cent of Iran's total oil exports, by 1985, this share had changed to 58 per cent of the total, and rising to 71 per cent in 1987.[6] Moreover, if we compare these figures with those of the pre-revolution period (1973–8), it can be noted that, except for Italy, Spain and Turkey, the rest of the mentioned countries have reduced their overall imports of Iranian oil (in other words, they have reduced their overall dependency on Iran).

Another important feature of Table 8.4 is the emergence of Turkey as one of the main importers of crude oil from Iran. While in 1979, less than 1 per cent of Iran's total oil exports were destined for Turkey, by 1985 this share had increased substantially to 7 per cent of the total oil exports. In 1987, Turkey imported 6,284,000 tonnes of oil from Iran, representing 8.2 per cent of Iran's total oil exports in that year.[7]

Table 8.5 provides data on the value of total non-military imports from 1973 to 1985. It can be seen that the value of imports during the period under study has been the subject of much fluctuation. This is due to the fact that the value of imports is closely related to the value of foreign exchange earnings (i.e. the amount of oil exports and oil prices). Thus, an imbalance in oil revenues has also caused an imbalance in the value of imports.

As can be noted, total non-defence imports were $9,695 million in 1979, and rising to $11,630 million in 1982. However, by 1982 to 1983, foreign exchange earnings had improved significantly (see Table 8.3). Given the close relationship between this, and the imports, by 1983 the value of imports had increased also significantly to $18,227 million.

However, since 1983, as a result of sustained Iraqi attacks on Iran's oil facilities, as well as a decline in oil prices in general, there has been a rapid

Table 8.4 Oil production and major recipients of Iran's oil exports, 1973–85 (thousand tonnes)

	1973	1974	1975	1976	1977	1978	1979	1980	1981	1982	1983	1984	1985	Percentage share of total exports*					
Oil production	293,908	299,949	266,676	293,951	282,224	262,436	159,496	74,077	66,252	120,396	122,150	101,400	110,100						
Oil export	263,443																		
Destination:																			
USA	12,496	21,655	13,693	28,230	39,790	43,061	27,733	1,077	3,388	2,608	5,028	2,896	3,412	4.9	16.4	19.5	22.8	6.2	4.4
Canada	5,172	6,209	9,300	7,861	6,056	5,137	2,274	65	–	465	2,189	417	533	1.9	2.5	2.3	1.8	2.7	0.7
West Germany	3,500	4,785	14,190	19,290	15,770	17,289	11,540	5,735	1,504	2,311	2,067	2,423	2,666	1.3	6.5	7.8	9.5	2.5	3.4
UK	48,512	46,831	20,423	22,713	14,193	11,895	5,069	1,249	1,284	2,578	749	2,773	623	18.4	5.8	5.3	4.1	0.9	0.8
Italy	12,691	6,509	12,860	14,530	14,410	14,335	2,224	952	2,800	13,116	11,854	9,496	7,292	4.8	5.9	6.5	1.8	14.6	9.4
France	10,514	11,005	13,290	14,550	9,385	10,904	6,130	1,228	1,520	3,761	4,248	3,395	4,077	3.9	3.9	4.9	5.0	5.2	5.3
Netherlands	19,925	32,839	17,415	17,690	13,525	20,559	5,284	644	473	7,220	6,855	7,653	4,381	7.5	5.6	9.3	4.3	8.4	5.6
Belgium	7,221	4,685	5,358	5,338	7,296	7,478	2,685	1,066	1,494	1,198	950	808	1,413	2.7	3.0	3.3	2.2	1.2	1.8
Spain	5,384	3,275	4,506	11,854	11,043	8,600	4,379	3,152	5,085	6,339	7,449	5,883	4,246	2.0	4.5	3.9	3.6	9.9	5.5
Japan	84,580	66,752	55,677	46,168	40,570	38,860	23,659	13,443	6,820	11,595	19,587	12,805	12,894	32.1	16.7	17.6	19.5	24.1	16.6
Australia	500	300	1,033	854	901	359	134	50	–	493	–	–	54	0.1	0.4	0.1	0.1	–	0.1
Turkey	374	867	113	1,674	1,740	4,970	1,100	2,771	1,485	3,168	5,376	7,453	5,448	0.1	0.7	2.2	0.9	6.6	7.0
Others (inc. Eastern bloc)*	52,116	62,495	65,446	69,938	68,212	36,989	26,966	8,121	15,266	26,114	14,748	16,598	30,418	17.9	26.2	14.7	22.2	18.2	39.3

Sources: K. Mofid, *Development Planning and Modernisation in Iran: From Monarchy to Islamic Republic*, Wisbech, MENAS Press, 1987, table 4.3, pp. 150–1; *Statistics De L'Industrie Petrolière (Petrol)*, 1979 to 1985 Yearbooks; *World Energy Statistics*, 1979 to 1981 Yearbooks; *Oil and Gas Statistics*, 1984 Yearbook and 1986/no. 1; BP *Statistical Review of World Energy*, June 1986

Notes: * Author's calculation: all the percentages have been rounded up and, therefore, totals may not add up to 100.

Table 8.5 Value and distribution of Iran's imports by main countries: 1973–85 (million current dollars)*

Country	1973	1974	1975	1976	1977	1978	1979	1980	1981	1982	1983	1984	1985
USA	477	1,313	2,316	1,974	2,347	1,508	1,181	25	330	134	209	178	81
Canada	23	56	84	103	121	57	21	30	21	161	182	120	53
West Germany	717	1,178	2,033	2,273	2,789	2,142	1,413	1,657	1,766	1,536	3,310	2,518	1,812
UK	342	508	989	890	1,028	843	542	1,006	811	635	1,047	1,030	745
Italy	137	197	418	735	810	596	455	632	829	796	994	1,039	672
France	176	241	519	715	661	508	468	793	735	367	408	201	176
Netherlands	88	152	332	443	489	215	261	386	430	298	470	417	298
Belgium	112	172	291	279	348	257	175	297	281	160	270	253	195
Switzerland	71	115	188	227	271	275	245	304	260	211	336	311	219
Sweden	52	79	151	140	192	145	75	207	215	226	464	522	210
Spain	28	35	126	109	140	259	121	327	337	328	452	327	312
Japan	537	993	1,853	2,200	2,321	1,757	1,013	1,697	1,629	1,033	3,102	1,862	1,496
Australia	51	67	191	172	228	151	146	311	220	219	258	411	235
Turkey	15	38	55	41	40	23	21	93	257	811	978	969	661
India	54	113	435	315	193	94	118	144	158	150	129	132	110
Brazil	52	24	59	66	69	68	79	263	214	231	385	328	234
Others (inc. USSR and Eastern Europe)	727	1,262	1,546	1,824	2,400	1,474	3,482	2,235	4,844	4,662	5,233	4,132	4,149
Total imports	3,659	6,543	11,586	12,506	14,447	10,372	9,695	10,080	13,000	11,630	18,227	14,750	11,658

Sources: Central Bank of Iran, Annual Report and Balance Sheet, 1356, 1358; Direction of Trade Statistics, 1981, 1985, 1986 Yearbooks; International Financial Statistics, August 1985, December 1985 and November 1986; K. Mofid, Development Planning and Modernisation in Iran: From Monarchy to Islamic Republic, Wisbech, MENAS Press, 1987, table 4.5, pp. 154, 155
Note: * Excluding military-related imports.

decline in foreign exchange earnings and thus, the value of imports has fallen sharply. In 1984, total imports fell to $14,750 million and still further to $11,658 million in 1985. By 1986 total imports had fallen to $9,527 million, and fell further to only $8,981 million in 1987.[8]

In all, total non-military imports have indeed declined by 0.1 per cent on average each year between 1979 and 1987. However, if we compare the 1987 imports with those of the 1983 period (the highest level since the revolution and the war), it can be noted that the total imports during this period, fell on average by 16.2 per cent each year.

Such a decline in imports, and the fact that Iran's industrialization has been based on 'dependent capitalism' and the import-substitution strategy of development with its massive import requirements, must have created many problems and setbacks in the economy. It should be emphasized that, since the revolution, the import dependency of the economy has increased. For example, while in 1977, each 100 rials of non-oil gross domestic product (GDP) produced, required 33 per cent of imported primary and intermediate inputs; by 1983, the corresponding figure had increased to 37 per cent (all figures based in constant rials, 1974 = 100).[9]

The serious state of import dependency of the 'large' (with ten or more workers) manufacturing establishments can further be seen, when, according to the Statistical Centre of Iran, imported primary products accounted for 54 per cent of total imports of these establishments in 1983. For chemicals and basic metal industries, these shares were 69.7 per cent and 71.5 per cent respectively in the same year.[10]

Given such a high dependency on imports, it would not be too difficult to note the effect of such imbalance and fluctuation in total imports on the performance of the industrial sector in Iran, since the revolution and the war.

At this point, if the values of the pre- and post-war non-defence imports are compared, it can be noted that for example, during the 1973–7 period, they had increased by 41 per cent on average each year, while the corresponding figures for the 1979–87 and 1983–7 periods show a decline of 0.1 per cent and 16.2 per cent respectively.

Table 8.6 provides figures for the share of non-military imports in GDP; that is, the measurement of import-penetration during the 1973–86 period. As can be noted, the share of total non-military imports in GDP (including oil) on average per year during 1979 to 1986 is 10.1 per cent. The corresponding figure for the period 1979–83, to take account of the drastic fall in imports during 1984–6 is 11.9 per cent.

The composition of Iran's non-defence imports (percentage share in total) during the 1973–86 period is given in Table 8.7. The import substitution (I-S) strategy of development and the goal of 'self-sufficiency'

Table 8.6 Iran's share of non-military imports in GDP* (oil incl. and oil excl.) 1973–86 (billion current rials)

	Total non-military imports	GDP (incl. oil)	Import/ GDP ratio*	GDP (excl. oil)	Import/ GDP ratio*
1973	248	1,784	14	1,196	21
1974	442	3,072	14.4	1,630	27
1975	782	3,479	22.5	2,103	37
1976	875	4,480	19.5	2,802	31
1977	1,022	5,207	19.6	3,545	29
1978	721	4,917	14.7	3,692	20
1979	685	6,053	11.3	4,377	15.7
1980	863	6,759	12.8	5,778	14.9
1981	985	8,218	12.0	7,288	13.5
1982	1,185	10,621	11.6	8,852	13.4
1983	1,528	13,471	11.7	11,662	13.6
1984	1,328	15,030	8.8	12,926e	10.3
1985	1,061	15,306	6.9	13,163e	8.1
1986	772	15,509	5.0	13,183e	6.0

Sources: Central Bank of Iran, *Annual Report and Balance Sheet*, 1351, 1356, 1357–82; *International Financial Statistics*, 1980, 1987 Yearbooks
Notes: * author's calculation. (e) author's estimation.

since the revolution, has meant that a large portion of imports have been intermediate and capital goods imports. Indeed, during the 1979–86 period, on average each year, 56.9 per cent and 19.1 per cent of total imports were intermediate and capital goods imports.

At this point, if the figures of the pre- and post-revolution war periods are compared, it can be observed that the share of intermediate goods imports has remained more or less unchanged; while the imports of capital goods on the other hand have declined significantly.

The most significant change, given the revolution's goals and objectives, in particular to 'prevent consumerism', has been a substantial rise in imports of consumer goods. As shown in Table 8.7, the import share of consumer goods which during the period 1973–8 was 17.5 per cent of the total on average each year, has rapidly increased to 24.0 per cent on average per annum in 1979–86 period.

In our analysis so far, we have used the current values of imports. We now analyse constant price figures. The data on the value of total imports at 1974 constant prices has been calculated by using the index of industrial countries' export values, whose figures are given in Table 8.8. As can be seen, the total non-military imports at 1974 constant prices was 434 billion rials in 1979, rising continuously and significantly to 983 billion rials in 1983.

Since 1983, however, given the rapid decline in oil revenues and consequently the fall in imports at current prices, there has also been a decline in imports at constant prices. They fell significantly to only 462 billion rials in 1986.

In all, during 1979 to 1986, the imports at 1974 constant prices have increased by 0.9 per cent on average each year. The corresponding figure for the 1979–83 period, to take account of the drastic fall in imports during the 1984–6 period, is the rise of 22.7 per cent on average each year, while the figure for the 1983–6 period is the decline of 22.2 per cent on average each year. Total imports at 1974 constant prices during the pre-war period of 1973–8 had increased by 5.6 per cent on average each year.

What all these figures tell us, is, of the existence of very chaotic and disorganized economic conditions in Iran, which in turn, have created a 'nightmare' for planners and planning in general. One cannot plan the economy on a long-term basis, when there are yearly fluctuations of these magnitudes in imports, given, the 'dependent' capitalist nature of the economy.

At this point, the origins of Iran's imports since the revolution/war, whose data was provided in Table 8.5, are the subject of analysis. At the outset, it should be emphasized that, since the revolution, the motivation of foreign trade policy has been partly political, because for example, there exists a ban on trade with the US, and there has been a declared preference for trading with the Third World, as well as attempts to reduce the volume of trade with the West.[11]

However, as it will be demonstrated shortly, the war and the desire to satisfy the immediate needs of the population, have made the achievement of the objectives of the revolution much more difficult, if not impossible.

By looking at the table, it can be noted that the major pre-war suppliers, namely, West Germany and Japan, are still the main exporters to Iran. In 1979, they had accounted for 14.5 per cent and 10.4 per cent of Iran's total imports. The corresponding figures for 1985 are 15.5 per cent and 12.8 per cent.

In all, while in 1980, industrial countries had provided 66 per cent of the total imports, by 1987, they had increased their share to 79 per cent of the total.[12] However, the European countries' share of the total, during the same period, had increased from 7 per cent to 14 per cent. The share of African countries has remained unchanged, accounting for about 0.3 per cent of the total during the same period.[13]

If we now compare the above figures with those of the pre-war period, it can be seen that the share of the industrialized countries in that year was 71 per cent of the total. Therefore, in comparison to 1987, since the revolution, there has been a modest decline (1 per cent) in Iran's total imports from these groups of countries. However, on the other hand, there has been a massive increase in the share of European countries, as their share in 1979 was only 3.4 per cent of the total; at the same time, the African countries' share has also declined from 3.4 per cent of the total to only 0.3 per cent.[14]

In conclusion, it can be said that, because of the fall in total Iranian oil exports, it is also true that Western European countries as well as Japan have substantially reduced their oil imports from Iran since the revolution. But, as was noted, Iran has not decreased its imports from these countries. Overall, although there has been some diversification of trading partners in post-revolution Iran, the changes have not been significant enough to reduce Iran's dependency on countries like West Germany and Japan, although, at the same time these countries have reduced their dependency on Iranian oil.

As noted already, the revolutionary leaders had argued that the Shah's modernization policies had resulted in the destruction of the agricultural sector, as evidence, for example, in massive increases in food imports. Again, as noted, the revolution, it was claimed, would make agriculture the 'axis of development', leading to the expansion of the agricultural sector and make Iran self-sufficient in food. In what follows an attempt is made to

Table 8.7 Commodity composition of Iran's imports (non-military) classified by their use, 1973–86 (%)*

	1973	1974	1975	1976	1977	1978	1979	1980	1981	1982	1983	1984[†]	1985[†]	1986[†]
Intermediate goods (a)	60.3	65.2	53.2	52.5	53.9	51.5	54.6	57.2	60.0	57.9	59.5	55.5	54.0	52.0
Capital goods (b)	24.8	20.3	29.8	9.8	26.5	28.0	18.9	16.0	15.8	19.5	23.9	20.1	19.5	20.0
Consumer goods (c)	14.9	15.5	17.0	17.7	19.6	20.5	26.2	26.3	23.8	22.6	16.6	24.4	26.5	28.0
Total	100.0	100.0	100.0	100.0	100.0	100.0	100.0	100.0	100.0	100.0	100.0	100.0	100.0	100.0

Average share/year (a) 1979–86*   56.9
Average share/year (b) 1979–86*   19.1
Average share/year (c) 1979–86*   24.0

Average share/year (a)* 1973–8   56.1
Average share/year (b)* 1973–8   26.5
Average share/year (c)* 1973–8   17.6

Sources: Central Bank of Iran, *Annual Report and Balance Sheet*, 1356, 1358, 1361, 1362; K. Mofid, *Development Planning and Modernisation in Iran: From Monarchy to Islamic Republic*, Wisbech, MENAS Press, 1987, table 4.10, p. 164
Notes: * Author's calculation. † Author's estimation. All figures rounded up, totals may not add up to 100.

Table 8.8 Estimation of Iran's non-military imports at 1974 constant prices*, 1973–86 (billion constant rials)

	1973	1974	1975	1976	1977	1978	1979	1980	1981	1982	1983	1984	1985	1986
Total non-military imports (current prices)	248	442	782	875	1022	721	686	863	985	1185	1583	1328	1061	772
Index of industrial countries' export values 1974 = 1	0.62	1.0	1.1	1.3	1.4	1.3	1.6	1.8	1.7	1.7	1.6	1.5	1.5	1.7
Total non-military imports at 1974 constant prices	400	442	711	673	730	555	434	482	573	714	983	862	689	462

Average annual growth of imports at 1974 constant prices (%)*

1973–8	5.6
1979–86	0.9
1983–6	−22.2

Sources: Central Bank of Iran, Annual Report and Balance Sheet, 1356, 1359; International Financial Statistics, 1980, 1985, 1987 Yearbooks
Notes: * Author's calculations.

assess the outcome of the revolutionary policies with regard to the achievements of the said objectives.

Nowhere is the failure of the revolution to achieve its agricultural objectives and goals better seen than by looking at the figures given in Table 8.9, where the annual average growth rates of total and per capita agricultural and food production for selected years since 1961 are noted.

It can be seen that, while in the 1970–80 period, total and per capita food production had increased by 4.7 per cent and 1.5 per cent, by the 1980–5 period they have fallen to 2.7 per cent and 0.2 per cent respectively.

Such a shortfall in food production and the inability of the Islamic Republic to feed its people has resulted in a massive increase in agricultural imports. Table 8.10 provides information on imports of principal agricultural products and main livestock items during the period 1973–85. As can be seen, on average each year, the imports of many items have increased significantly both before and since the revolution. But, it should not be forgotten that the revolution had promised self-sufficiency in food, and had declared agriculture as the 'axis of development'. All the planning and policy instruments, it seems, at least at the beginning were directed towards the achievement of this objective.

Therefore, the failure to reverse past policies and at least reduce Iran's dependency on the outside world for food supplies, although all the intentions were there to do so, must be seen as one of the major failures of the Islamic Republic.

SOME OF THE ECONOMIC REASONS FOR THE FAILURE OF THE ATTEMPTS AT EXPORT-DIVERSIFICATION AND SELF-SUFFICIENCY

This chapter has attempted to provide a 'balance sheet' of the political economy of Iran's foreign trade since the revolution. It has tried to demonstrate that the goals of the Islamic Republic in its foreign trade policy have not been achieved so far.

We now turn our attention to the reasons for not attaining these objectives. We shall find that these are varied and complex: they are economic as well as socio-political; cultural as well as historical, and; internal as well as external. It is my intention to concentrate on some of the economic arguments, but a more detailed treatment is available elsewhere.[15]

Both before, and since the revolution, Iran's industrialization has been based on an import-substitution (I-S) strategy of development; with the emphasis on large-scale and capital-intensive industrial projects.

The adoption of this type of strategy of development has been wrong, because Iran has continuously relied on oil revenues to provide the necessary massive amounts of imports that are required for such a development policy. Industries created have not been forced to pay for their own import needs through their own exports. Therefore, inefficiencies have been allowed to remain unchecked, and become more problematic.

The technology transferred has been inconsistent with Iran's indigenous endowments. The imports of inappropriate technology, which has been financed through oil revenues, has led to an acute state of 'dependent capitalism', with its harmful consequences.

In order to encourage the import of capital and intermediate goods and assist the rapid expansion of the manufacturing sector, the exchange rate has 'artificially' been kept overvalued. The unfavourable exchange rate policies towards 'exports' as well as high inflation, have led to a rapid decline in Iran's index of competitiveness.[16]

This means that while imports are being subsidized, to export from Iran has become much more difficult, resulting in a serious imbalance in foreign trade, as more and more people are finding it to be more profitable to participate in commerce at the expense of production.

In order to bring about change, the government should limit the implementation of capital-intensive industrial projects to those already begun, and put added emphasis on low capital intensity as a criterion for evaluating future projects. The government then should make the existing manufacturers more accountable, and thus, force them to pay for at least some of their import needs through their export earnings. No export should mean no more imports. The strategy of development then, should be based on small-scale industry and the usage of intermediate technology.

The government should also adopt a more realistic exchange rate policy, in order to facilitate the non-oil exports. Finally, the planners should encourage the establishment of regional small-scale industrial boards, to be supplemented by the creation of cottage industries and handicrafts boards.

These boards should act as information and technical centres, providing the means by which the projects could get started, and assist the producers to market their products, both domestically and internationally.[17]

The result of such a strategy of development will be the emancipation of local talents, regional know-how and the creation of future 'Captains of industry'. In all, it would result in the *real* 'take-off' and the *real* 'big-push' towards development and stability.

Table 8.9 Annual average growth rates of total and per capita agricultural and food production, Iran

	1961–70	1970–80	1980–5	1983–4	1984–5	1985–6
Total agricultural production	4.3	4.2	2.8	-0.7	2.5	2.7
Per capita agricultural production	0.8	1.1	-0.1	-2.2	-0.4	0.0
Total food production	4.3	4.2	2.7	0.1	3.0	2.6
Per capita food production	0.9	1.5	-0.2	-2.7	0.0	-0.2

Source: UN Conference on Trade and Development, *Handbook of International Trade and Development Statistics*, (1987)

Table 8.10 Iran's import of principal agricultural products, 1973–85 (thousand metric tonnes)

Item	1973	1974	1975	1976	1977	1978	1979	1980	1981	1982	1983	1984	1985
Wheat and flour (wheat equivalent)	785	1,456	1,472	844	1,159	1,354	750	1,341	1,620	1,770	2,688	3,919	2,819
Rice	12	191	286	250	590	500	500	402	586	432	622	710	400
Barley	107	178	203	230	334	464	200	388	472	420	471	581	450
Corn	131	223	78	215	344	450	500	647	869	652	979	640	810
Sugar (total raw equivalent)	299	228	633	313	488	876	746	412	652	866	310	643	598
Sugar (refined)	161	98	424	220	449	732	686	379	600	674	285	592	550
Fresh/frozen bovine meat	4	5	15	22	40	28	42	60	46	53	119	85	50
Fresh/frozen sheep meat	12	19	38	58	60	50	59	110	124	162	114	145	130
Fresh/frozen poultry	3	2	17	22	18	21	28	64	65	40	43	42	10
Dry/fresh milk	7	11	14	11	19	28	29	21	47	41	53	25	20
Butter	16	21	27	26	28	26	45	38	66	43	67	59	52
Cheese	2	7	11	22	41	40	46	62	78	67	92	138	100

Sources: (FAO) *Trade Yearbook*, 1975, 1977, 1979, 1982, 1983, 1985 Yearbooks
Note: * Figures are rounded to the nearest thousand tonnes.

9   Salman Rushdie, the Ayatollah and the limits of toleration

Iain Hampsher-Monk

The Ayatollah has explicitly denounced liberalism as the enemy of Islam, both within and without his state. And he could hardly have chosen an issue, or addressed it in a way more calculated to disturb the slumbering assumptions on which liberalism and the modern liberal state rests. Khomeini's claims of jurisdiction, spectacularly if fantastically, as well as the claims of British Muslims, moderately if more insidiously, threaten to unravel a set of painfully arrived at historical compromises in which are embodied, precariously – as it now seems – the principles of a half-way tolerant and free society.

But reaction to the Rushdie affair has highlighted two very different kinds of liberalism. Whilst there is no liberal support for Khomeini's 'sentence' there is considerable support amongst some liberals – not all of whom are motivated by electoral considerations – for indigenous Muslims' more limited aim of suppressing Rushdie's book. Such a position springs at one level from a decent cultural sensitivity to Muslim values, but it is backed up by a very thorough-going cultural relativism which pervades recent work in political philosophy. Admirable, indeed necessary, as is sensitivity in the practical matter of dealing with conflicting ethnic demands, there is a danger that this sensitivity will spill over into assertions that the very principles of a liberal toleration are simply, like fundamentalism, another cultural form, between which there is no choosing. The well-meaning liberal relativist here endorses a kind of moral agnosticism which can, and has, led to the triumph of ideologies which he or she would find anathema.

This liberal relativism is no froth on our cultural sea but derives from deep currents the movements of which can be seen in the implications of a wide range of philosophical positions associated with the later Wittgenstein, the modish extension of Thomas Kuhn's scientific paradigm into the social sciences, and Alasdair MacIntyre's case that virtues must be rooted in practical communities. Each of these tends towards, if they do not all entail, the view that different sets of moral, and similarly political principles are to be construed as constitutive practices which, like the rules of a game or a language, make sense within their own boundaries but not outside them. To adopt Kuhn's notion, a 'paradigm' is an all-embracing cognitive perspective which determines all relevant epistemological as well as judgemental criteria that may be applied within it. On this view the possibility of comparing paradigms, and hence making rational judgements between them, simply does not exist, for all the ideas needed to conduct such comparisons would have themselves to be drawn from within one or other of the world-views being compared. There simply is no privileged transparadigmatic stance, no archimedian point from which to exert normal leverage. The moral relativism to which the adoption of the 'paradigm' consigns us is as utter as the physical relativism of Einstein.[1]

For Wittgenstein too, substantive debate about moral values seems to be one of those areas which, as philosophers, we must 'pass over in silence'. The most philosophers can do is to understand the moral world as constituted in the use and force of particular key terms and patterns of discourse in a given community.[2] One of the most famous and influential essays in this tradition denies even that we can confute belief in such practices as 'witchcraft' since we can only do so by importing Western standards of evidence and rationality, and the status of these is exactly the same, within our own cultural environment, as the status of witchcraft belief within a witchcraft culture.[3]

Both these approaches tend to sociologize principles, in that they implicitly or explicitly view a structure of argument, the capacity to make judgements etc., as derived from the practice of scientific or social community; and they focus on this sociality – the necessarily shared nature of meaning – rather than on the particular logical properties of the principles derived. MacIntyre, who by no means joyfully embraces relativism, has approached this from the other, negative end, arguing that the very incapacity of modern moral philosophy to make sense of its subject matter – in particular to give content to the notion of virtue – derives largely from the collapse of the stable community from which such meaning could be derived.[4]

I want to argue against this slide from the recognition of moral diversity into political relativism and authoritarianism (for they are but aspects of the same condition). It seems that – short of discovering objective moral certainty – we can avoid this only by adopting, at the political level, the principles of secularism and toleration. These principles are however, largely procedural, and do not elicit the kind of fervour in their support which attaches to beliefs that characterize cultural or ethnic diversity. They are not the 'Western equivalent' of such beliefs, nor do they perform the same role in people's lives. Rather they are meta-principles of a different order, standing above them and indeed allowing different substantive beliefs to co-exist. The Rushdie controversy – that is the range of responses on both sides – evokes and requires clear-sighted discussion of the difference between a well-meant but ultimately bankrupt cultural relativism and certain principles underpinning the liberal secular state, in which resides the logical possibility of the peaceful co-existence of diverse cultures within a single state.

In the modern world, the idea of a state which is multi-ethnic and does not coerce over matters of belief or expression of opinion, has emerged from Western European experience, and is, in that sense the product of a particular culture: but the parochiality of the principle's historical origins must not be allowed to undermine consideration of its logical properties. All ideas have an origin in historical time, and therefore within a particular culture, but this does not forever relegate their relevance to the circumstances which gave birth to them. Despite our current strong sense of the historicity of ideas and political principles it would be disastrous to lose sight of the fact that certain ordering principles and their entailed consequences provide unique solutions to certain political problems and have potentially general application. The cultural origin of a principle of toleration is irrelevant to the fact that it is, in a logical sense, *the* principle that allows ethnically and religiously diverse groups to co-habit within a single state.

Khomeini broached two major, if interrelated issues: the relationship between clerical and secular authority, and the issue of freedom of religious and artistic expression. Let us consider first the issue which he raised – eventually one suspects, for clerical Iran, as well as for the West – of the conflict between religious and secular jurisdictions. This holds out not only the spectre of political conflict between religious hierarchies and the state, but the parallel plight of the individual caught between competing jurisdictions. One major advantage – and one that was quickly recognized – of the constitutional secular state, is the provision of a unified secular law: under it individuals know precisely what they must do to avoid punishment.[5] Where other groups or leaders – secular as well as religious – claim overlaying and potentially contradictory jurisdictions, individuals are put in the situation where they cannot avoid contravening one set of laws – or even worse, arbitrary and unpredictable edicts. The medieval and early modern Papacy, the IRA and the Ayatollah – perhaps an unlikely trio – exemplify attempts to do this.

Moreover the difficulties of reconciling secular and religious authority are exacerbated when the religious authority lies outside the state. Khomeini may have picked up the idea of trying to ban books in other people's countries from Margaret Thatcher, but she did, so far as we know, limited herself to using the judicial processes of the target country. Khomeini, by extending his domestic Iranian dominion over a foreign country's citizens – not only Rushdie, but those of his British followers whom he would have carry out his sentence of death – recalls the fear seventeenth-century Englishmen had of Catholics. They could not be trusted with civic office, or indeed much else, for they owed allegiance to a foreign ruler – the Pope. And the Pope had declared that they might with impunity lie to Protestants and kill their rulers. We are still seeing the fruit of such mistrust in Northern Ireland. Khomeini, surely wittingly, by associating his call for execution with domestic Muslims' calls for censorship, threatens, quite unjustly, to render ambivalent the perceived loyalty of British Muslims, and establish a new running historical sore in a potentially liberal state.

For church (or indeed any secondary association) and state to exist in harmony, there must be a clear demarcation between not only their areas of competence, but the means of enforcement available to them. The classic English language statement of this is John Locke's famous *Letter on Toleration*. Religious law, he says, should be allowed only those sanctions which are 'suitable to the nature of such things . . . exhortations, admonitions, and advices' or failing that, ex-communication.[6] Churches or Mosques, any more than trade unions or trade associations should not be allowed to exercise civil, economic or physical sanctions against recalcitrant members. For this to be denied them churches must be perceived as voluntary associations, membership of, or resignation from which is entirely optional and a matter for the individual. Perceptive as ever, the Ayatollah denied this too, claiming that it was not merely Rushdie's blasphemy, but his very renunciation of Islam that justified his being killed.

The limitations Locke wanted to place on the powers available to religious organizations was not based on any confidence he had in the truth of his own religious belief. On the contrary it was quite explicitly based in his scepticism about the degree of certainty that human understanding was capable of achieving in these matters.[7] Both in England and in France religious toleration had a sceptical basis which derived from an environment of religious conflict and uncertainty which presages remarkably the moral uncertainties of our own time.[8] But although a benign scepticism is the political answer to such a situation, its emergence is by no means guaranteed by the fact of diversity and conflict. Fundamentalist belief is well armed to sustain bloody opposition through parables of trial, salvation through suffering, and personal election. These devices make fundamental religious belief incompatible with tolerant politics. Fundamentalists – of whatever religion – threaten the order of the secular state because their conviction that they possess the truth is such that no secular consequences can dissuade them from whatever actions are required by it. The belief in martyrdom is an extreme form of this. The secular state works because, and if, its citizens are motivated by secular desires and constrained in the end by secular threats, to take their life, liberty or property away from them.[9] Martyrs and saints are unattached to these things. A state of saints would be as ineffectual as it would be unnecessary, but a state attempting to rule those who *believe* themselves to be saints is in trouble.

The vital point is to stress the logic, and not just the particular cultural environment in which emerged the principle that secondary associations – which include churches – should not require of their members actions prohibited by the state, nor exercise sanctions other than expulsion or ex-communication.

Having said this the political acceptability, or practical viability of a principle of tolerance undoubtedly rests on aspects of the prevailing patterns of opinion and belief, and is to that extent culturally dependent. To say this is not to concur in relativizing the principle, it is simply to recognize that recognition of, or support for it will depend on the prevalence of certain attitudes and beliefs. Two in particular are crucial, neither of which seem to be making much headway in the fundamentalist camp.

The first is the recognition that the mere strength of opinion, belief, or outrage at what you have said or written cannot (logically) be a moral justification for imposing my views on you, or prohibiting the expression of yours, as long as you regard your rightness, or strength of feeling as grounds for similarly imposing on me: at least, not without recourse to violence or an imposed solution. This may now appear simple logic: it nevertheless required extensive historical demonstration. Modern European toleration was a product of a century and more of religious warfare. Quakers excepted, no Christian denomination voluntarily adopted the ideal of toleration, until experience had thoroughly convinced them of their inability to impose their views on others. The historical record will not bear the claim, nor am I making it, that toleration is the product of an 'enlightened' European culture into which Muslims must be inducted. On the contrary, toleration was the outcome of the exhaustion of European religious bigotry, and the violence and persecution from which it sprang can only be repeated if this experience is forgotten.

The second attitude is indeed one that looks much more culturally specific: the notion that religion is, by and large, a matter of individual internal belief rather than outward action, and that the sacred lies in the spirit rather than resting in objects, ceremonies or specific words. Once this is accepted the *occasion* for religious conflict diminishes, for it is a property of actions and objects that they occupy space uniquely and so exhibit difference and offer opportunities for conflict. Thought by contrast is supple, ambiguous, and, in the last resort, secret.[10]

Within English Reformation thought, major controversies existed about where to position the altar, the formal structure of services (quite apart from doctrinal issues which the content of them might have raised), and the wearing of vestments. A first step to peace was to establish that all of these were, in theological terms, 'indifferent matters'. Yet even this did not establish grounds for practical toleration. Anglicans argued that being matters indifferent, there could be no objection to the national church establishing regulations governing them. The underlying assumption here was that the community was the unit which was responsible for orderly worship of its god, and so, also responsible, and culpable for allowing disorder.[11] The same attitude is found in that most tolerant of regimes, the later Roman empire. Allowing freedom of worship to all its many cultures, it required only that, to avoid outraging them, all paid religious respects to the indigenous gods of Rome. It was only the refusals of Jews and Christians to acquiesce that brought about their intermittent proscription and Rome's quite undeserved reputation for religious persecution.[12] Toleration of religious difference thus seems to require religion to be seen as an individual and not a community responsibility.

Once it is accepted that religion is not only a matter of individual belief, but also that belief cannot be achieved by external compulsion – an acceptance that Europeans once again took some time to achieve, coercion for religious reasons, or reasons to do with other kinds of belief, becomes pointless. No doubt it seems to some that in attempting to demarcate the principles of a workable secularism from what is culturally specific to Western secular politics, I have built too much of the latter into the former. This may be so, but if the debate once centres around where the line is to be drawn rather than being premised – as absolute relativism requires – on the absence of one, the central point will have been secured.

Discussion of the distinction between religious and secular authority has already raised the second major topic, the question of the toleration of religious and other expression. Although to different degrees, all fundamentalist objections to 'blasphemous' or 'obscene' literature invoke the same issues. Thus they are only more luridly illustrated by Khomeini's claims. Democracy itself provides no guarantees of freedom here. Recent decisions regarding the application of the common law of public decency to works of art would seem to imply the right of juries to exercise censorship on the basis of their own feelings, without judicial direction. The principle of the freedom of religious, political, sexual, or other expression is hardly a principle over which the United Kingdom can currently claim any monopoly of virtue. The principle which is worth defending is not, at present, one embodied in our legal practice. That principle is the tolerationist principle of the right to the unlimited freedom of worship and written expression of opinions – a principle from which religious minorities in Britain benefit in a way signally denied to religious minorities in Iran.

But this principle, as we have recently seen, is insufficient as stated. Rights to religious and to other expression are intimately related. Any principle of freedom of religion must include the toleration of non-religious writings. For firstly they could only be excluded by presuming to judge what is and what is not religious – a notorious point of contention in the Rushdie case.[13] But second, once more than one religion is protected, there is no reason to rule out, and every reason to presume, that someone's religious beliefs, writings or practices will appear irreligious to others. It is a paradox, but true, that freedom of religious expression logically entails the freedom of *irreligious* expression. To take one simple example. The Koran asserts that Jesus did not die on the cross.[14] It would not be difficult to imagine fundamentalist Christians who might find such a denial of a central tenet of their faith quite as offensive as anything in *The Satanic Verses*. How could a demand, on these grounds, that the Koran be banned, be logically distinguished from a demand that *The Satanic Verses* be banned?

The principle of religious freedom of expression has been bounded in another way too. Once again as Locke pointed out, anything permitted as a secular act should be permitted as an act of worship. But acts which in a secular context would be disallowed cannot be allowed on the grounds that they are acts of worship. Religious acts which offer physical violence to another, are, or perhaps should be ruled out, because such unrestrained liberty – whether claimed on religious grounds or not – is always potentially the suffering of another. The physical harming of another cannot be allowed as a matter of religious belief, any more than it can be as matter of religious authority. Suppose a religious practice required child-sacrifice? Or merely child mutilation? Female – or come to that male – circumcision? These are clearly delicate issues, and it may be far better to let existing and customary practice be, than to raise the issue of principle. However, this is not always a possible tactic, since in culturally diverse states raising the issue of principle is a favoured tactic of disadvantaged groups to advance their own practices under the principle's protection.

The idea of a secular state logically implies recognition of *a* boundary of non-interference between politics and religion but logic cannot tell us where it should be drawn. The difficulty is that although the physical integrity of the person seems a clearer place than most to draw a line, it is unclear that there is anything absolute or rationally inviolable about this particular boundary. Depending on our conception of the person we may want to draw the boundary further away than that. If we accept the notion that the state has a responsibility to see its members equipped for citizenship (as opposed to heaven) this would imply an extension of intervention beyond mere prevention of physical harm. It may be that some British Muslims have more to lose than to gain by opening up the issue of the scope of state intervention in religion. Attitudes to the education, or non-education of women, – so central to Rushdie's own work – may prove to be precisely the issue where radical-chic NW1 enthusiasm for relativist multi-ethnicity parts company with the aspirations of some minority community practices.

Questions of education, the transmission of culture and the formation of personality threaten to deepen the level of discourse to a point which, according to some, undermines the relatively simplistic distinctions on which the defence of a tolerant secularism has so far rested. For it is a recurrent and valid criticism of much, especially vulgar liberalism, that it fails to concern itself with either the formation or identity of human personality; that in assuming the autonomy of personal preferences it ignores the whole process by which personality – and therefore belief and desire – is shaped and ordered in society. Both economists' assertions about the autonomous character of consumers' preferences – an assumption belied by the massive expenditure devoted to manipulating them – and the problematic character of attempts by philosophers such as John Rawls to construct an, as it were, 'contentless' personality, to choose impartially the principles of justice, demonstrate this belief. Liberals, it is held, operate with a very thin theory of the self. They are thus vulnerable to one of two charges. For either the liberal model of the 'self' is so devoid of that culturally acquired particularity which alone makes us recognizable as persons, as to be a totally inadequate conception of what it is to be human. Or, and here is the nearest I can come to sympathy with the Ayatollah, liberalism in action actually succeeds in creating a kind of cultural void, eroding the 'thickness' of personality and substituting empty, vapid, culturally deracinated individuals; suitable fodder for the media campaigns of advertising magnates and politicians.

Such a view finds considerable support in recent philosophical literature critical of liberalism in general and Rawls in particular. In a powerful and movingly written book Michael Sandel concludes that the kind of self required by Rawls (and many another liberal project) is invariably characterized in terms of possession, advantage, rights, freedoms, etc. In other words, in terms external or extrinsic to any notion of the self as we experience selfhood – that is as a member of a particular community with particular beliefs, loyalties and attachments:

> To imagine a person incapable of constitutive attachments such as these is not to conceive an ideally free and rational agent, but to imagine a person wholly without character, without moral depth. For to have character is to know that I move in a history that I neither summon nor command, which carries consequences none the less for my choices and conduct. It draws me closer to some and more distant from others; it makes some aims more appropriate, others less so. . . . Where the self is unencumbered and essentially dispossessed, no person is left for *self*-reflection to reflect upon.[15]

Or again consider Michael Ignatieff, no less moving and eloquent on the same theme:

> It is common in the language of rights to define essential requirements – 'basic goods' as John Rawls calls them – as preconditions for personal freedom. The advantage of this way of thinking is that it seeks to reconcile a theory of the good with the freedom of each individual to live his life as he chooses. The disadvantage is that many of the essential requirements of a decent life – love, respect, solidarity with others – cannot be sensibly justified as necessary for personal freedom. I don't need to be loved in order to be free; I need to be loved to be at peace with myself and to be able to love in turn. A theory of the human good cannot, I think, be premised on the absolute priority of liberty.[16]

I have tremendous sympathy with these views. But, and this is also a part of what Ignatieff is saying, there is a limit to what we can expect of politics, more especially of politics in a state comprising groups with determinedly different views of what the human good consists in. Such a state cannot – if indeed a state or politics ever can – concern itself with the realization of that good. It cannot itself provide although it can enable the pursuit of, religious community, a sense of identity, moral and social attachment. It must do so not because these things limit our freedom, like the resistant air that Kant's dove nevertheless needed for its flight these things too may paradoxically not limit our freedom but be conditions for the exercise of it. It must do so because to be dragged into that arena, when no agreement on the content of the human good can be found is to make peaceful politics impossible. In situations of cultural diversity only 'thin' politics can be practised, not because what the different groups wish to provide for their members is not good, nor because (though this may be true) there are some things that politics cannot in principle supply, but because the state cannot be the vehicle of their provision or protection where that impinges on the equal expectations of another group.

But where exactly are the limits of politics to be found in any given circumstance? Since I have suggested, that both UK practice with regard to toleration of expression and religious offence is limited, and the boundaries of toleration are logically flexible, why not limit toleration further? As the British Muslim community has rightly pointed out, there are blasphemy laws protecting Christianity, why not in fairness extend them to protect Islam too?[17] The observation is totally reasonable, and the situation is inequable. But extension of such laws is the wrong direction to go in. Equity can also be restored by abolishing those laws which are in existence. I believe there are compelling reasons for choosing that direction.

Firstly because abolishing laws increases freedom of expression rather than limits it. Freedom of expression is, if not an absolute principle, one which is believed to be both good in itself, and for well-canvassed reasons, productive of good consequences. Moreover, it is a principle which British Muslims should support on both logical and purely prudential grounds, for freedom of expression is the more general principle under which they and other minorities enjoy their religious worship.

But the second reason for favouring abolition rather than extension of blasphemy laws is more unequivocally logical, it is because legal guarantees of protection are only possible where the resulting rights can be guaranteed without conflict. Increasing the rights of religious groups to be protected against religious offence – especially where that offence is subjectively assessed by the group in question – increases and not decreases the likelihood of religious conflict. This is not merely a tautological point akin to the one that more laws create more crimes. Increasing legal guarantees against offence will quickly heighten both expectations and legal rights to the point at which they couldn't, logically, all be fulfilled. The Koranic denial of Christ's divinity is a case in point.

Extending the law of blasphemy, or of offensiveness, would necessitate, at the very least, minute negotiations with all the religions (and their sects) embraced by British citizens, to decide what the limits of mutual offensiveness are – always supposing there are any to be found. Moreover the prospect of legal protection in this sphere would undoubtedly increase, rather than decrease such groups' sensitivity in this area.

The toleration of views made possible by a secular approach to these problems is undoubtedly linked to a number of principles which are, or may well be culturally specific to parts (and parts only) of the Western European liberal tradition. Amongst these are the notion that the use of words – even words which some deem sacred – must be allowed a freedom rightly denied to actions; that the strength of religious or any other conviction carries with it no guarantee of its truth; and that religious and epistemological scepticism can be foundational rather than the destructive.[18] But if these principles, whatever their cultural origins, are denied logical superiority over more fundamentalist claims – Christian or Muslim – we shall in the end be reduced from arguments about the principles of possible co-existence to a brutal and ugly clash of cultures, and that will mean the coercion of the weak by the strong. Unless we acknowledge the higher claims of a principle of toleration, cultural relativism will be powerless before authoritarianism.

Notes

INTRODUCTION IRAN AND THE WORLD: REASSERTION AND ITS COSTS

1 On the foreign policy of the Islamic Republic see also: my chapter 'Iranian foreign policy since 1979: Internationalism and nationalism in the Islamic Republic', in N. Keddie and J. Cole (eds) *Shi'ism and Social Protest*, New Haven, Yale University Press, 1986; N. Keddie and M. Gasiorowski (eds), *Neither East Nor West: Iran, the Soviet Union, and the United States*, New Haven, Yale University Press, 1990; R.K. Ramazani, *Revolutionary Iran*, Johns Hopkins University Press, 2nd edition 1988.
2 BBC, *Summary of World Broadcasts*, Part 4, 6 June 1990.
3 Iran's claim that it was bound by religious law to uphold the sentence on Rushdie was invalidated by Khomeini's own doctrine of *maslahat*, or interest, under which state interest could override Islamic principle.

2 THE UNITED STATES AND IRAN, 1981-9

1 I have analysed Reagan administration policy toward Iran within the context of these three broad policy objectives elsewhere. See Eric Hooglund, 'The policy of the Reagan administration toward Iran', in N. Keddie and M. Gasiorowski (eds) *Neither East nor West: Iran, the Soviet Union, and the United States*, New Haven, Yale University Press, 1990, pp. 269–93.
2 *New York Times*, 23 January 1980.
3 John Campbell, 'The Middle East: a house of containment built on sand', in *Foreign Affairs*, vol. 60, no. 3, 1981, pp. 598–9; and David Newsom, 'America Engulfed', in *Foreign Policy*, no. 43, Summer 1981, p. 17.
4 R.K. Ramazani, 'Iran: burying the hatchet', in *Foreign Policy*, no. 60, Fall 1985, pp. 66–7.
5 For a typical example of an analysis of Iran's 'moderates' and 'radicals', see Shireen Hunter, 'After the Ayatollah', in *Foreign Policy*, no. 66, Spring 1987, pp. 80–2.
6 Gary Sick, 'Trial by error: reflections on the Iran–Iraq war', *Middle East Journal*, vol. 43, no. 2, Spring 1989, p. 239.
7 *New York Times*, 7 and 8 April 1981.
8 See Alexander Haig, *Caveat: Realism, Reagan, and Foreign Policy*, New York,

Macmillan, 1984, p. 6; and Jeanne Kirkpatrick, 'Dictatorships and double standards', in *Commentary*, November 1979, pp. 40–1.

9 For details about the alleged plot in Bahrain, see Robin Wright, *Sacred Rage: the Wrath of Militant Islam*, New York, Simon and Schuster, 1985, pp. 114–19.

10 Michael Sterner, 'The Iran–Iraq war', in *Foreign Affairs*, vol. 63, no. 1, Fall 1984, p. 135.

11 For an analysis of the US military role in Lebanon, see Fred Lawson, 'The Reagan Administration in the Middle East', in *MERIP Reports*, no. 128, November–December 1984, pp. 31–2.

12 Robin Wright, *In the Name of God: the Khomeini Decade*, New York: Simon & Schuster, 1989, pp. 119–21.

13 See John Tower, Edmund Muskie, and Brent Scowcroft, *The Tower Commission Report*, New York, Bantam Books, 1987, 112–21.

14 James Bill, *The Eagle and the Lion: The Tragedy of American–Iranian Relations*, New Haven, Yale University Press, 1988, p. 312.

15 For details about Iran's role in securing the release of the TWA plane and its hostages, see Ramazani, op. cit., p. 68.

16 Ramazani, op. cit., p. 67.

17 Elizabeth Gamlen, *US Military Intervention in the Iran–Iraq War 1987–8*, Peace Research Report no. 21, University of Bradford: School of Peace Studies, March, 1989, pp. 10–11.

18 ibid., pp. 12–13; and Barry Rubin, 'Drowning in the Gulf', *Foreign Policy*, no. 69, Winter 1987–8, p. 125.

19 Nikki Keddie, 'Iranian imbroglios: who's irrational?', in *World Policy Journal*, Winter 1987–8, 44.

20 Sick, op. cit., p. 240.

3 THE SOVIET UNION AND IRAN, 1979–89

1 *Iran–USSR*, no. 25, 'International boundary study', US Dept of State, 28 February 1978.

2 *PRAVDA*, 19 November 1978.

3 S. Chubin, 'Soviet policy towards Iran and the Gulf', IISS Adelphi Papers, Spring 1980, p. 33. Quote from a TASS broadcast of 18 November 1978.

4 Martin Sicker, *The Bear and the Lion: Soviet Imperialism and Iran*, London, Praeger, 1988, p. 111.

5 Stelianon Scarlis, 'Two examples of Soviet reporting', Radio Liberty, RK251179, August 1979.

6 *Soviet World Outlook*, 15 February 1979, p. 2.

7 Shireen Hunter, 'Soviet–Iranian relations in the post-revolution period', in R.K. Ramazani (ed.) *Iran's Revolution, The Search for Consenus*, Indiana, Indiana University Press, 1990, p. 87.

8 Foreign Broadcasts Information Service, South Asia, 6 November 1979.

9 Muriel Atkins, 'The Islamic Republic and the Soviet Union', *The Iranian Revolution*, Conference Proceedings, Washington DC, Middle East Institute, 1982.

10 Sepehr Zabih, *Iran Since the Revolution*, New Jersey, Princeton University Press, 1982, p. 82.

11 Radio Tehran, 12 June 1979; BBC 14 June 1979.

12 Radio Tehran, 7 June 1979.
13 One of the leaders of the followers of the Imam's Line, Mosavo Khoieniha, studied in Patris Lumumba University in Moscow.
14 *Etala'at* 7 November 1979.
15 Quoted from *Le Monde* 1814/80 in Adam Davison, 'An investigation of Soviet foreign policy formulation based on the case study of the Iran–Iraq war', unpublished MA dissertation, Exeter University, 1986.
16 Foreign Broadcasts Information Service, South Asia, 10 July 1980, p. 15.
17 TASS, 30 September 1980.
18 Z. Khalilzad, 'Soviet dilemmas in Khomeini's Iran', *Australia Journal of International Affairs*, April 1984, p. 5.
19 Martin Sicker, *The Bear and the Lion*, New York, Praeger, 1988, p. 118.
20 A.Y. Yodfat, in Adam Davison op. cit., quote from Foreign Broadcasts Information Service, South Asia, 27 October 1980, pp. 117–18.
21 Keesings Contemporary Archives, 21 March 1980, p. 30177.
22 Elaine Giolino, 'Iran's durable revolution', *Foreign Affairs*, Spring 1983, p. 912; Martin Sicker op. cit; and Foreign Broadcasts Information Service, South Asia, 7 February 1983, p. 13.
23 N. Kianoori, 'Problemi Mirai Socialisma', Moscow, 10 February 1983.
24 *Etehada Mardom*, nos 97–120, (Tudeh Party Publication).
25 Foreign Broadcasts Information Service, South Asia, 15 September 1983, p. 15; and 14 October 1983, pp. 12–13.
26 *The Times*, 7 June 1984.
27 *Financial Times*, 25 June 1984.
28 Foreign Broadcasts Information Service, South Asia, 9 July 1985, pp. 14–15.
29 Foreign Broadcasts Information Service, South Asia, 18 July 1985, p. 16.
30 Sharam Chubin, op. cit., p. 6.
31 For further information see, Bob Woodward, *Veil: The Secret Wars of the CIA 1981–1987*, New York, Pocket Book, 1987; and Jonathan Marshall, Peter Dale Scott, Jane Hunter, *The Iran Contra Connection*, Boston, South End Press, 1987.
32 Country report, no. 3, 1987, EIU.
33 Joseph L. Nogee, Robert H. Donaldson, *Soviet Foreign Policy Since World War Two*, Oxford, Pergamon Press, 1988, p. 350.
34 John Bulloch and Harvey Morris, *The Gulf War*, London, Methuen, 1989, p. 211.
35 Alvin Z. Rubinstein, *Moscow's Third World Strategy*, Princeton, Princeton University Press, 1988, p. 165.
36 *Iran Times*, 9 December 1988.
37 *Iran Times*, 16 December 1988.
38 *Iran Times*, 6 January 1989.
39 Oliver Roy, 'Iran–Soviet relations since the Persian Gulf War cease-fire', *The Echo of Iran*, London, June 1990, p. 22.
40 *Jane's Defence Weekly*, 20 November 1985.
41 *Middle East International*, 23 June 1989.
42 In this part I would like to thank Nazenin Ansari for information and assistance.

4 IRAN AND THE EUROPEAN COMMUNITY

1 K. Nassoori, 'Iran and the West', Middle East Journal, no. 155, 31 July 1981, p. 13.
2 ibid.
3 A. Ehteshami, 'The Islamic Republic of Iran model: a new alternative to socialism in the Third World?', paper presented at the European Consortium for Political Research Joint Sessions Conference, Bochum (FRG), 2–7 April 1990.
4 ibid.
5 The information for this section has been derived from A. Ehteshami, op. cit., pp. 26–9.
6 OECD, *Statistics of Foreign Trade, Series A*, Paris, OECD Secretariat, various years.
7 IMF, *Direction of Trade Statistics Yearbook, 1989*, Washington, IMF, 1989.
8 ibid.

5 IRAN, THE SOUTHERN MEDITERRANEAN AND EUROPE: TERRORISM AND HOSTAGES

1 J. Chipman, 'Europe and the Iran–Iraq war', in E. Karsh (ed.) *The Iran–Iraq War, Impact and Implications*, London, Macmillan, 1989, p. 215.
2 M. Nishihara, 'Japan: vulnerabilities and responses', in H.W. Maull and O. Pick (eds) *The Gulf War: Regional and International Dimensions*, London, Pinter, 1990, p. 171; E.G.H. Joffe and K.S. McLachlan, *Iran and Iraq: Building on the Stalemate*, London, EIU-BI, 1988, p. 33; EIU, *Country Report: Iran*, no. 4, London, EIU-BI, 1989, p. 19.
3 Dilip Hiro, *The Longest War, the Iran–Iraq Military Conflict*, London, Grafton, 1989, p. 124.
4 *Le Monde*, 6 May 1988.
5 *Financial Times*, 5 May 1987.
6 *Financial Times*, 5 May 1989.
7 H.V. Hodson (ed.) *The Annual Register: A Record of World Events, 1987*, Harlow, Longman, 1988, p. 60.
8 Dilip Hiro, op. cit., p. 127.
9 The first Western hostage was taken on 19 July 1982, just after the Israeli invasion of Lebanon. He was David Lodge, the acting president AUB, who was released a year later. (R. Wright, *Sacred Rage: The Wrath of Militant Islam*, London, Deutsch, 1986, p. 80.) The major spate of the hostage-taking began in February 1984, weeks after the 18 January 1984 assassination – by Hizbullah – of Dr Malcolm Kerr, who had replaced David Lodge at the AUB. European hostages, however, were not taken until 22 March 1985, when two French diplomats, Marcel Carton and Marcel Fontaine, were kidnapped by Islamic Jihad (*Le Monde*, 6 May 1988).
10 S. Chubin and C. Tripp, *Iran and Iraq At War*, London, Tauris, 1988, p. 207.
11 J. Chipman, op. cit., p. 224.
12 S. Zabih, *Iran Since the Revolution*, London, Croom Helm, 1982, pp. 192–3.
13 A. Taheri, *Holy Terror: The Inside Story of Islamic Terrorism*, London, Hutchinson, 1987, p. 99.
14 See W. Montgomery Watt, *Islamic Fundamentalism and Modernity*, London, Routledge, 1988, pp. 136–9.

15 S. Zabih, op. cit., pp. 46–61.
16 F. Ajami, *The Arab Predicament*, Cambridge, Cambridge University Press, 1981, p. 52.
17 O.J. Voll, 'Islamic fundamentalism and regional dynamics', in H.W. Maul and O. Pick (eds) *The Gulf War, Regional and International Dimensions*, London, Pinter, 1990, pp. 34–6.
18 R. Wright, 'The War and the Spread of Islamic Fundamentalism', in E. Karsh (ed.) The Iran–Iraq War, Impact and Implications, London, Macmillan, 1989, p. 112.
19 A. Taheri, op. cit., pp. 89–91.
20 S. Chubin and C. Tripp, op. cit., pp. 181–2.
21 F. Ajami, *The Vanished Imam*, New Haven, Cornell, 1986.
22 R. Wright, *Sacred Rage: The Wrath of Militant Islam*, London, Deutsch, 1986, p. 110.
23 *Financial Times*, 5 May 1988.
24 *Le Monde*, 5 May 1988
25 J. Chipman, op. cit., p. 222. Alfred Cordes, a West German hostage was released in November 1988 as a result, West German Foreign Minister Hans Genscher claimed, of West Germany's quiet diplomacy with Iran through the Gulf War.
26 A. Taheri, op. cit., p. 149.
27 H.V. Hodson, *Annual Register 1987*, London, Longman, p. 137.
28 A. Taheri, op. cit., pp. 104–5.
29 H.V. Hodson, op. cit., p. 139.
30 *Le Monde*, 6 January 1988. Some North Africans also became involved in secular protest, such as the bombing of a Marks & Spencer store in 1985 by Habib Ma'amar who claimed pro-Palestinian sympathies. *Le Monde*, 15 December 1989.
31 H. Munson Jr, 'Islamic revivalism in Morocco and Tunisia', *The Muslim World* 76, 1986, p. 203.
32 R. Leveau, 'Islam officiel et renouveau Islamique au Maroc', in C. Souriau (ed.) *Le Maghreb Musulman en 1979*, Paris, CNRS, 1984.
33 H. Munson Jr, op. cit., p. 210.
34 EIU, *EIU Annual Regional Review 1985*, London, Economist Publications, 1985.
35 A. Taheri, op. cit., p. 184.
36 J. Benomar, 'Monarch, Islamic movement and religious discourse in Morocco', *Third World Quarterly* 10, 2 April 1988, p. 553.
37 M. Harbi, *Le FLN, Mirage et Réalité*, Paris, Editions Jeune Afrique, 1980.
38 H. Roberts, 'Radical Islam and dilemma of Algerian nationalism', *Third World Quarterly* 10, 2 April 1988, p. 578.
39 H. Munson Jr, op. cit., p. 211.
40 EIU, EIU Annual Regional Review 1984, London, Economist Publications, 1984.
41 M. Boulby, 'The Islamic challenge in Tunisia since independence', *Third World Quarterly* 10, 2 April 1988, p. 611.

6   THE GCC AND THE ISLAMIC REPUBLIC: TOWARDS A RESTORATION OF THE PATTERN

1 This chapter is based in part on earlier research on regional relations in the Gulf. Some sections were published previously in A. Ehteshami and G. Nonneman, *War and Peace in the Gulf*, London, Ithaca Press, 1990.
2 See W. Quandt, *Saudi Arabia in the 1980s*, Washington, The Brookings Institution, 1981.
3 A. Cordesman, *The Gulf and the West*, Boulder, Westview, 1988, p. 158.
4 I have argued this more extensively in G. Nonneman, *Iraq, the Gulf States and the War*, London, Ithaca Press, 1986, chapters 1 and 2.
5 ibid., pp. 39, 96.
6 ibid., chapters 4, 5.
7 *Le Monde*, 20 August 1987.
8 *The Arab Gulf Journal*, November 1985, pp. 89–90.
9 A. Cordesman, *The Iran–Iraq War and Western Security*, London, Jane's, 1987, p. 109.
10 *MEED*, 13 September 1986.
11 F. Axelgard, *A New Iraq? The Gulf War and its Implications for US Policy*, New York, Praeger, 1988, p. 75.
12 *MEED*, 29 November 1986, 21 March 1987; *Guardian*, 18 December 1986; *Financial Times*, 12 March 1987; Cordesman, op. cit., p. 125.
13 *The Times*, 14 April 1987; *De Standaard* (Belgium), 21 April 1987.
14 *MidEast Mirror*, 20 July 1987.
15 ibid., 11 May 1987; 1 June 1987; *MEES*, 25 May 1987.
16 ibid., 18 May 1987; Economist Intelligence Unit, *Country Report: Bahrain, Qatar, Oman and the Yemens* (henceforth: *Country Report: Bahrain . . .*) no. 3, 1987, p. 20.
17 See *MidEast Mirror*, 3 August 1987.
18 *Financial Times*, 3 August 1987. For a report on Prince Nayif's press conference in the last week of August – the first such since 1979 – see *Financial Times*, 28 August 1987; and *Sunday Times*, 30 August 1987.
19 *MidEast Mirror*, 29 July 1987.
20 ibid., 21 August 1987.
21 IRNA and KUNA dispatches, 10 August 1987.
22 *Al-Thawra* (Baghdad), 19 August 1987.
23 *MidEast Mirror*, 24 August 1987, 25 August 1987; *Financial Times*, 26 August 1987; EIU, *Country Report: Bahrain . . .*, no. 4, 1987, p. 19.
24 *Financial Times*, 28 August 1987.
25 *MidEast Mirror*, 7 September 1987; EIU, *Country Report: Bahrain . . .*, no. 4, 1987, p. 11.
26 *MEES*, 28 September 1987.
27 *MidEast Mirror*, 15 October 1987.
28 *Kuwait Times*, 3 October 1987; EIU, *Country Report: Bahrain . . .*, no. 4, 1987, p. 19.
29 *Middle East Report*, January 1989, p. 24.
30 *MEES*, 21 December 1987.
31 EIU, *Country Report: Bahrain . . .*, no. 1, 1988, p. 18.
32 *MidEast Mirror*, 20 December 1987. See also, EIU, *Country Report: Bahrain*

..., no. 1, 1988, p. 12; and G. Joffe and K. McLachlan, *Iran and Iraq. Building on the Stalemate*, London, EIU Special Report no. 1164, 1988, p. 15.

33 *MidEast Mirror*, 7 January 1988, 15 January 1988, 18 January 1988; and EIU, *Country Report: Bahrain...*, no. 2, 1988, p. 10.

34 *Al-Jumhuriya* (Baghdad), 19 January 1988; *Baghdad Observer*, 29 January 1988.

35 See *MidEast Mirror*, 3 March 1988; and *Al-Sharq al-Awsat*, 8 March 1988.

36 *Al-Musawwar* (Cairo), 10 March 1988.

37 *MidEast Mirror*, 16 March 1988.

38 EIU, *Country Report: Bahrain...*, no. 2, 1988, p. 18.

39 *MidEast Mirror*, 11 April 1988; *Riyadh Daily*, 13 April 1988.

40 *MidEast Mirror*, 13 April 1988.

41 ibid., 18 April 1988, 19 April 1988, 20 April 1988.

42 SPA dispatches and the Saudi press on 16 May 1988.

43 *MidEast Mirror*, 29 April 1988.

44 ibid., 3 May 1988, 23 May 1988; *Khaleej Times* (UAE), 23 May 1988.

45 EIU, *Country Report: Bahrain...*, no. 3, 1988, p. 10; *MidEast Mirror*, 21 June 1988.

46 *MidEast Mirror*, 24 June 1988.

47 *Financial Times*, 22 December 1988.

48 *MidEast Mirror*, 5 July 1988; *al-Sharq al-Awsat*, 5 July 1988, 6 July 1988.

49 See *MidEast Mirror*, 19 July 1988, 20 July 1988.

50 *Al-Qabas* (Kuwait), 26 July 1988; *Al-Ra'y al-'Am*, 26 July 1988; *Kuwait Times*, 26 July 1988; *Al-Sharq al-Awsat*, 27 July 1988.

51 *MidEast Mirror*, 2 August 1988.

52 ibid., 1 August 1988, 2 August 1988, 3 August 1988.

53 ibid., 4 August 1988.

54 *Washington Post*, 7 August 1988.

55 EIU, *Country Report: Bahrain...*, no. 4, 1988, pp. 23–4; *SWB* ME/0250, 7 September 1988.

56 *Financial Times*, 17 March 1989.

57 *MidEast Mirror*, 21 September 1988.

58 *Al-Siyasa*, 17 December 1988.

59 EIU, *Country Report: Bahrain...*, no. 1, 1989, p. 22.

60 ibid., no. 4, 1988, p. 11.

61 Quoted in *Iran Focus*, November 1988, p. 3.

62 *Kuwait Times*, 9 November 1988.

63 See *MidEast Mirror*, 5 October 1988; and *Arab News*, 12 October 1988.

64 *MidEast Mirror*, 17 October 1988, 20 October 1988.

65 ibid., 3 November 1988, 9 November 1988; *Kuwait Times*, 9 November 1988.

66 *Al-Siyasa*, 15 November 1988; *Kayhan International*, 25 November 1988.

67 *Iran Focus*, January 1989; *SWB* ME/0341, 22 December 1988; *FBIS*-NES-88-251, 30 December 1988.

68 *The Middle East*, May 1989, p. 22; *Independent*, 18 March 1989; *Sunday Times*, 19 March 1989.

69 *SWB* ME/0428, 7 April 1989.

70 *FBIS*-NES-89-085, 4 May 1989; see also 89-087, 8 May 1989.

71 *Financial Times*, 14 June 1989.

72 *The Middle East*, May 1989, p. 23.

73 *International Herald Tribune*, 21 March 1989.
74 *Financial Times*, 14 June 1989.
75 *Al-Azmina al-'Arabiya*, no. 206, 2 February 1989.
76 *MidEast Mirror*, 23 October 1987; *MEES*, 21 November 1988; Nonneman, op. cit., p. 109; *MEES*, 20 March 1989; *MidEast Mirror*, 1 March 1989; *SWB* ME/W0096 21 March 1989.
77 *Arab Times*, 5 September 1989.
78 *SWB* ME/0554 i, 6 September 1989.

7 IRAN–IRAQ: THE WAR AND PROSPECTS FOR A LASTING PEACE

1 For detailed account, see Edgar O'Ballance, *The Gulf War*, London, Brassey's, 1989.
2 *The Kurds*, London, Minority Rights Group Report no. 23.
3 *Gulf Report*, London, Gulf Centre for Strategic Studies, February 1989.
4 *Gulf Report*, London, Gulf Centre for Strategic Studies, October 1988.
5 Edgar O'Ballance, *The Electronic War in the Middle East: 1968-70*, London, Faber and Faber, 1974.
6 *Middle East*, May 1989.
7 IISS, *Strategic Survey: 1988-89*, London, Brassey's 1989.
8 IISS, *Strategic Survey: 1988-89*, London, Brassey's 1989.
9 United Nations Chemical Weapons Conference, Paris, January 1989.
10 *Sunday Express*, 5 October 1986.
11 *Washington Post*, 31 March 1989.

8 THE POLITICAL ECONOMY OF IRAN'S FOREIGN TRADE SINCE THE REVOLUTION

1 For further reading on these issues see K. Mofid, *Development Planning in Iran: From Monarchy to Islamic Republic*, Cambridgeshire, MENAS Press, 1987.
2 See Islamic Republic of Iran, Plan and Budget Organization, *The First 5-Year Economic, Social and Cultural Macro Development Plan of the Islamic Republic of Iran*, 1983/4–1987/8, Tehran, 31 August 1982, p. 12.
3 See *Statistics de l'Industrie Petrolière*, Paris, 1987.
4 ibid.
5 ibid.
6 ibid.
7 ibid.
8 See *Direction of Trade Statistics*, 1987.
9 For evidence on these figures see Sohrab Behdad, 'Foreign exchange gap, structural constraints and the political economy of exchange rate determination in Iran', *International Journal of Middle East Studies*, vol. 20, no. 1, 1988, Table 4, p. 10.
10 See Statistical Centre of Iran, *Large Manufacturing Establishments' Statistics: Results of the 1984 Survey*, Tehran, February/March 1985.

11 K. Mofid, op. cit.
12 See *Direction of Trade Statistics*, 1987.
13 ibid.
14 ibid.
15 K. Mofid, op. cit.
16 See further K. Mofid, op. cit., Table 4.15, p. 174.
17 For further reading on these issues see K. Mofid, op. cit., and also K. Mofid, 'Economic consequences of the Gulf War: assignment of a dollar value', in Royal United Services Institute as Brassey in *Defence Yearbook 1990*, and *The Economic Consequences of the Gulf War*, London, Routledge, 1990.

9 SALMAN RUSHDIE, THE AYATOLLAH AND THE LIMITS OF TOLERATION

1 Thomas Kuhn, *The Structure of Scientific Revolutions*, Chicago, Chicago University Press, 1962, passim. See also 'Reflections on my critics', in I. Lakatos and A. Musgrave (eds) *Criticism and the Growth of Knowledge*, Cambridge, Cambridge University Press, 1970, for the most succinct expression: 'The point-by-point comparison of two successive theories demands a language into which at least the empirical consequences of both can be translated without loss or change. That such a language lies ready to hand has been widely assumed since at the least the seventeenth century . . . Philosophers have now abandoned hope of achieving any such idea . . . Feyerband and I have argued at length that no such vocabulary is available . . . Successive theories are thus, we should say, incommensurable'. pp. 266–7.
2 'Philosophy may in no way interfere with the actual use of language; it can in the end only describe it. It cannot give it any foundation either. It leaves everything as it is'. Ludwig Wittgenstein, G.E.M. Anscombe (tr.), *Philosophical Investigations* I, Oxford, Oxford University Press, 1963, para. 124.
3 Peter Winch, 'Understanding primitive society', *American Philosophical Quarterly* I, 1964: reprinted in Bryan R. Wilson (ed.) *Rationality*, Oxford, Oxford University Press, 1977.
4 A. MacIntyre, *After Virtue*, Oxford, Oxford University Press, 1981, passim, e.g. '. . . any specific account of the virtues presupposes an equally specific account of the narrative structure and unity of a human life and *vice versa*', and 'Moral philosophy, as it is dominantly understood, reflects the debates and disagreements of the culture so faithfully that its controversies turn out to be unsettlable in just the way that political and moral debates themselves are'. pp. 226, 235.
5 The point is commonly made. See especially Hobbes' *Leviathan*, part 3, passim, esp. chs 36, 39; Rousseau, *The Social Contract*, London, Everyman, 1968, p. 108, since the establishment of Christian states 'men have never succeeded in finding out whether they were bound to obey the master or the priest'.
6 John Locke, *A Letter Concerning Toleration*, Indianapolis, Bobbs-Merrill, 1955, p. 23.
7 John Locke, *An Essay Concerning Human Understanding*, esp. book IV, ch. xviii, para. 11, Indianapolis, Bobbs-Merrill. 'If the boundaries be not set between Faith and Reason, no Enthusiasm, or extravagancy in Religion can be contradicted'.

8 Michel de L'Hôpital, was the first of a group of French writers known as the *Politiques* to assert both Royal absolutism and toleration on grounds of civil peace. 'No Calvinistic Hugenot could have accepted such a declaration; and few convinced Catholics could easily have persuaded themselves that this could be true. But after the long experience of those evils of which L'Hôpital had forewarned his countrymen, France as a whole was to come round substantially to his opinion'. (J.W. Allen, *A History of Political Thought in the Sixteenth Century*, Methuen, 1928, repr. 1977, p. 296.)

9 A point which is as old as St Augustine, see *The City of God*.

10 Hobbes' trump card in establishing the sovereignty of secular authority was to exploit the 'Christian liberty' from external forms claimed by Reformation thinkers. A Christian subject could obey even a sovereign who commands him to deny Christ for, he claims 'profession with a tongue is but an external thing'. W.G. Pogson-Smith, (ed.) *Leviathan*, para. 3, chapt. 42, p. 387, 1909.

11 See most recently, Peter Lake, *Anglicans and Puritans*, London, Unwin Hyman, 1988, esp. p. 197: 'Hooker started where previous conformists had started – with the concept of things indifferent . . . His point was that structures of law and authority produced by the autonomous action of human reason . . . were perfectly competent to direct and order those things upon which scripture had not pronounced, but over which public control was essential if the life of the church, and indeed society in general, were to continue in peace. To hold otherwise would be "injurious . . . unto God the author and giver of human capacity, judgement and wit" '.

12 G. de St Croix, 'Why were the early Christians persecuted?', *Past and Present* 26, 1963, reprinted in M.I. Finlay (ed.) *Studies in Ancient Society*, London and Boston, Routledge & Kegan Paul, 1974.

13 But why stop at *The Satanic Verses?* As Anthony Burgess pointed out, once we open up the issue there are other candidates for suppression, Medieval Guild Plays, Fitzgerald's *Rubaiyat* and so on. The *Independent*, 16 February 1989.

14 *Koran*, 157, 4; cited by Keith Ward, Professor of History and Philosophy of Religion, Kings College, London, The *Independent*, 18 February 1989.

15 Michael J. Sandal, *Liberalism and the Limits of Justice*, Cambridge, Cambridge University Press, 1982, pp. 179–80.

16 M. Ignatieff, *The Needs of Strangers*, London, Chatto, 1984, p. 15.

17 As demanded by Sher Azam, President of the Bradford Council for Mosques, The *Observer*, 19 February 1989, p. 15.

18 Locke, Kant and Mill, perhaps the three most prominent thinkers in the liberal canon, all ground their defence of liberty of expression, and liberal politics in scepticism. In the excitement of fashionable post-modernism we seem to have forgotten our existing culture already owes to an intelligently applied scepticism.

Index